STRUGGLE FOR ETHNIC IDENTITY

CRITICAL PERSPECTIVES ON ASIAN PACIFIC AMERICANS SERIES

Volumes in *Critical Perspectives on Asian Pacific Americans* take on a spectrum of current issues facing Asian American communities by critically examining key social, economic, psychological, cultural, and political experiences. They are theoretically engaging, comparative, and multidisciplinary, reflecting the complexity of contemporary concerns that are of importance to the understanding and empowerment of Asian Pacific Americans.

BOOKS IN THE SERIES

Volume 1: Diana Ting Liu Wu, *Asian Pacific Americans in the Workplace* (1997)

Volume 2: Juanita Tamayo Lott, *Asian Americans: From Racial Category to Multiple Identities* (1998)

Volume 3: Jun Xing, *Asian America Through the Lens: History, Representations, and Identity* (1998)

Volume 4: Pyong Gap Min and Rose Kim, *Struggle for Ethnic Identity: Narratives by Asian American Professionals* (1999)

SUBMISSION GUIDELINES

Prospective authors of single or co-authored books and editors of anthologies should submit a letter of introduction, the manuscript or a four-to-ten-page proposal, a book outline, and a curriculum vitae. Please address proposals or questions to:

Critical Perspectives on Asian Pacific Americans Series
AltaMira Press
1630 North Main Street, Suite 367
Walnut Creek, CA 94596
(925) 938-7243

Struggle for Ethnic Identity

NARRATIVES BY
ASIAN AMERICAN PROFESSIONALS

EDITED BY

Pyong Gap Min

AND

Rose Kim

ALTAMIRA
PRESS

A Division of Sage Publications, Inc.
Walnut Creek • London • New Delhi

For information address:

AltaMira Press
A Division of Sage Publications, Inc.
1630 North Main Street, Suite 367
Walnut Creek, CA 94596
explore@altamira.sagepub.com
http://www.altamirapress.com

SAGE Publications Ltd.
6 Bonhill Street
London EC2A 4PU
United Kingdom

SAGE Publications India Pvt. Ltd.
M-32 Market
Greater Kailash 1
New Delhi 110 048
India

PRINTED IN THE UNITED STATES OF AMERICA

Library of Congress Cataloging-in-Publication Data

Struggle for ethnic identity : narratives by Asian American professionals / edited by Pyong
    Gap Min and Rose Kim.
    p. cm. — (Critical perspectives on Asian Pacific Americans series; v. 4)
    Includes bibliographical references.
    ISBN 0-7619-9066-6 (cloth: acid-free paper)
    ISBN 0-7619-9067-4 (pbk.: acid-free paper)
    1. Asian Americans -- Ethnic identity. 2. Asian Americans -- Biography. 3. Professional
employees -- United States. 4. United States -- Ethnic Relations. I. Min, Pyong Gap, 1942–
II. Kim, Rose.

E184.06S76   1999
920'.009296073—ddc21   98-040171
                                                            CIP

00 01 02 03 04 05 06 07 08 09 7 6 5 4 3 2 1

Interior Design and Production by Rachel Fudge
Editorial Management by Josh Calder
Cover Design by Josh Calder and Joanna Ebenstein

Table of Contents

Acknowledgments

We would like to thank the fourteen contributors who agreed to participate in this book. Without their willingness to share their personal stories or take time from their hectic schedules to write and revise their essays as we needed, the publication of this book on schedule would have been impossible. We also wish to thank several anonymous reviewers for providing helpful comments and suggestions. We owe a great deal to Mitch Allen and Jennifer Collier, our editors at AltaMira Press, who supported our book idea from the beginning and helped shape the manuscript into its final form. Finally, our gratitude goes to Josh Calder and Rachel Fudge, who copyedited the final draft in such a timely, meticulous manner.

Pyong Gap Min

I would like to acknowledge a 1995 grant from the PSC-CUNY Research Award Program that helped fund the costs of a part-time editorial assistant for this project. I also commend Rose Kim, my coeditor, for doing a superb job editing the essays. I originally asked her just to write an essay for this book, but her writing skills were so impressive that I invited her to serve as coeditor. She also suggested several contributors, all of whom submitted stimulating essays. I wish to thank Mehdi Bozorgmehr and Steve Gold for identifying contributors in Los Angeles, Manju Sheth for asking her son Shay to write an essay for the book, and Dean Savage for providing me with moral support and technical assistance throughout this project.

Rose Kim

This book has been one of the most challenging and gratifying projects I have ever undertaken. I am indebted to several people who supported me throughout. I wish to thank Pyong Gap Min for giving me the opportunity to be a part of this book. I am also grateful to David Palinsky for his loving support and for his careful readings of the manuscript. Curt Simmons, Casey Maddren, and Renee McHarris also generously gave their time to review sections of the manuscript on short notice. Finally, I wish to recognize others whose lifelong support has always given me sustenance. I thank K. W. Lee and my sister, Sophia, for encouraging my love of writing. I cherish my parents for working so hard to establish me and my siblings in a new country that I feel lucky and proud to call home. I'm grateful for friends, such as Renee and Casey, who have had such unwavering faith in me; and for my cat, Feral, who kept me company during many long, cold nights working on this book.

Part One

Introduction

This introductory part includes two chapters. The first chapter, entitled "About the Book," and written by the two coeditors, serves as the introduction to the book. It clarifies why this collection of autobiographical essays by fifteen Asian American professionals is important, how the essayists were selected, and on what aspects of their lives they were asked to focus.

The second chapter, by Pyong Gap Min, provides a comprehensive review of theoretical and empirical research conducted on the phenomenon of ethnicity since the early 1970s. It succinctly summarizes the major theories of ethnicity from the primordial and mobilizationist perspectives. It also includes sections on subethnicity and panethnicity, two concepts that have received a great deal of scholarly attention during recent years. Finally, this chapter discusses revival of ethnicity during recent years, and the interrelationships among ethnicity, assimiliation, and social mobility. The latter topic is theoretically important, particularly in connection with segmented assimilation theory.

INTRODUCTION / **Pyong Gap Min and Rose Kim**

About the Book

A GENERATION HAS passed since the contemporary mass migration of Asians began, and the children of those immigrants have come of age. Many have completed a college education and entered the job market. No longer confined to science and business roles by language and cultural barriers, Asian immigrants are represented in a wide variety of professions—such as politics, journalism, and the fine arts.

Research on Asian Americans, however, has tended to focus on the adjustment of first-generation immigrants. Over the last twenty-five years, hundreds of articles and dozens of books have documented the lives of post-1965 Asian immigrants. In contrast, only a few monographs covering children of Asian immigrants have been published since the late 1980s.[1] Researchers as a whole have neglected the children of not only Asian immigrants, but those of other post-1965 immigrants. Only recently have researchers begun examining the "new second generation"[2] of immigrants. Most of these studies are based on the children of Latino, Caribbean, and Indochinese immigrants. Until this book, no major empirical study has focused on the children of Asian immigrant groups—such as Chinese and Koreans—who traditionally come from a higher socioeconomic background than most Indochinese refugees.

Several empirical studies have examined the ethnic attachments and identity of the new second generation.[3] These studies are based on two types of data sources: questionnaire surveys and personal interviews with selected samples. Although survey data are useful in understanding group differences in patterns of ethnicity and their causes and consequences, they cannot capture the dynamism and fluidity of an individual's construction and experience of ethnicity and identity. In addition, previous studies—mostly based on samples of high school students—have failed to include information about the social relations of the second generation, such as the ethnic composition of their dating partners, their views about intermarriage, and their affiliations with ethnic clubs. While ethnographic studies based on in-depth personal interviews are effective for understanding the processes

11

of ethnic formation, they are often limited by being restricted to a particular point in time, and thus they fail to capture the changes in ethnic identity and other aspects of life experiences that occur throughout an individual's life.

Through fifteen autobiographical essays (or narratives, as we've titled them), this book examines ethnic attachment and ethnic identity among 1.5- and second-generation Asian Americans—in other words, those who emigrated at a young age and those born in this country. Depending on their socioeconomic class, members of the same ethnic group can have significant differences in identity and life experiences.[4] For example, one ethnographic study of high school–aged children of black Caribbean immigrants in New York City indicated that middle-class respondents had a strong national identity, whereas lower-class respondents identified more with blacks.[5] Despite their successful image, Asian Americans are far from homogenous in socioeconomic status. Although native-born Asian Americans are more likely than white Americans to obtain a college education, the majority of them do not complete four years of college.[6] Second-generation Asian Americans who are college graduates are likely to have different life experiences from their non-college-educated counterparts. Furthermore, Asian Americans who have graduated from prestigious universities, such as Harvard and Yale, differ in their life experiences from those who have graduated from less competitive colleges and universities.

Because we cannot examine class differences with only fifteen contributors, we decided to focus on younger-generation Asian American professionals who have achieved a moderate degree of professional success. We felt they were at an interesting juncture in their lives, having completed college and being in the early stages of their professional careers. We thought their perspectives would be particularly relevant and interesting to college students, for whom this book is intended as a textbook for a variety of Asian American courses.

As mentioned earlier, the model-minority thesis leads us to believe that most native-born Asian Americans excel academically and achieve high levels of professional success. While it is true that many Asian Americans graduate from prestigious universities and eventually enter professional occupations, we do not know what barriers they have encountered in the workplace. Furthermore, researchers have failed to examine whether "successful" Asian Americans have been incorporated into the white middle class, thereby losing much of their cultural tradition and ethnic identity, as the "segmented assimilation" theory suggests.[7] The essays in this volume aim to shed light on these important questions.

We asked our contributors to write about their lives and the issues they have faced growing up as Asian Americans. Although we edited the essays and asked the contributors to revise certain paragraphs or to add more information, as much as possible we have tried to maintain the individual voice, character, and style of each contributor. Such a collection of personal essays written in a variety of styles should appeal to college students and lay readers alike.

Growing Up Asian American: Stories of Childhood, Adolescence and Coming of Age in America from the 1880s to the 1990s, edited by Maria Hong (1993), also includes autobiographical essays by American-born Asians. The thirty-two essays in Hong's book were written by eminent Asian American writers such as Maxine Hong Kingston, Toshio Mori, and Amy Tan. Because her contributors are professional writers who are familiar with Asian American issues, Hong's book has stylistic and scholarly advantages. However, we believe our book, containing essays by younger Asian Americans from a variety of occupational backgrounds, will appeal to young people who may be contemplating careers represented by our contributors.

Three of the essayists are immigrants who completed high school in their native countries. The remaining dozen are 1.5- and second-generation Asian Americans. The contributors were selected for a number of reasons. First of all, they were willing participants; second, they satisfied our various criteria of balancing ethnic groups, gender, and occupations. They represent seven different ethnic groups: Chinese, Japanese, Korean, Filipino, Vietnamese, Indian, and Bangladesh. The contributors range in age from twenty-six to forty-nine, but the vast majority are in their early or mid-thirties. They represent a variety of professions: comptroller of a small, private college; social worker; assistant district attorney; medical doctor; political aide; and actor. We tried to maintain a gender balance in selecting contributors. However, as often occurs with an edited volume, not all of the contributors came through. Three men dropped out of the project at the last minute and, as a result, ten of the fifteen contributors are women.

Although each essay is intended to serve as an autobiography, we knew it would be impossible to cover one's life within fifteen or so pages. We thus asked the writers to focus on one or more of the following sociologically important issues: 1) experiences with prejudice and discrimination; 2) the retention of ethnic subculture; 3) ethnic vs. nonethnic friendship networks and dating patterns; and 4) ethnic and racial identities. We asked them to discuss the issues in connection with their own experiences growing up at home, school, or in the workplace. We gave the contributors detailed guidelines as to which particular questions they needed to answer to cover each topic. With regard to family lives, we asked the contributors to touch on their parents' immigration backgrounds and the struggles they faced in the early stages of immigration.

Recently, feminist scholars have emphasized race, class, and gender as dialectically interacting in creating the disadvantages and powerlessness experienced by women of color.[8] Research has indicated that younger-generation Asian American women have qualitatively different experiences from their male counterparts, particularly at home.[9] We expected our female contributors to be very critical of their parents' marital relations and of the more conservative gender-socialization practices based on the patriarchal ideology inherited from their home countries. We asked the respondents to comment on their parents' marital relations and gender socialization. We also asked the married contributors to address their own marital relations, including the gender division of work, assuming that they would maintain more egalitarian marriages than their parents.

When they are very young, many native-born Asian Americans consider themselves Americans, but, as they grow older, they increasingly adopt the ethnic identity of their parents. We asked the contributors to discuss these kinds of changes in their own experiences. Some contributors considered ethnic and pan-Asian identities a far more important issue than experiences of discrimination, whereas others had much to say about their family lives. Not all of the contributors devoted equal space to the same topics. We encouraged each contributor to introduce any other topic that was personally important to his or her life experience as an Asian American.

Pyong Gap Min, a coeditor of this book, is a first-generation Korean American scholar specializing in Asian Americans. The other coeditor, Rose Kim, is a second-generation Korean American freelance writer who is in a sociology doctoral program. This book has benefited from our collaboration across generations and professional fields. Although we worked together in all stages of publication of this book, we also divided major tasks based on each editor's professional strengths. As a professional writer, Kim specialized in editing the chapters, making each essay as interesting and clear as possible. As a sociologist specializing in Asian Americans, Min made sure each essay addressed the four issues outlined in the guideline. He was more involved in organizing and writing the introduction and comments, and is also the sole author of the first part of the book, entitled "Ethnicity: Concepts, Theories, and Trends."

ENDNOTES

1. Margaret Gibson, *Accommodation without Assimilation: Sikh Immigrants in an American High School* (Ithaca, NY: Cornell University Press, 1988); Stacy Lee, *Unravelling the Model Minority Stereotype: Listening to Asian American Youth* (New York: Teachers College Press, 1996); Betty Lee Sung, *The Adjustment Experience of Chinese Immigrant Children in New York City* (Staten Island, NY: Center for Migration Studies, 1988); Min Zhou and Carl Bangston III, *Growing Up American: How Vietnamese Children Adapt to Life in the United States* (New York: Russell Sage Foundation, 1998).

2. Alejandro Portes, *The New Second Generation* (New York: Russell Sage Foundation, 1996); Ruben Rumbaut and Wayne Cornelius, *California's Immigrant Children: Theory, Research, and Implications for Educational Policy* (San Diego: University of California at San Diego, 1995); Min Zhou, "Growing Up American: The Challenge Confronting Immigrant Children and Children of Immigrants," *Annual Review of Sociology,* vol. 23 (1997), pp. 63–95.

3. Yen Espiritu, "The Intersection of Race, Ethnicity and Class: The Multiple Identities of Second-Generation Filipinos," *Identities,* vol. 1 (1994), pp. 234–251; Nazli Kibria, "The Construction of 'Asian American': Reflections on Intermarriage and Ethnic Identity

Among Second-Generation Chinese and Korean Americans," *Ethnic and Racial Studies,* vol. 20 (1997), pp. 523–544; Pyong Gap Min and Youna Choi, "Ethnic Attachment among Korean-American High School Students," *Korea Journal of Population and Development,* vol. 22 (1993), pp. 167–179; Alejandro Portes and Dag MacLeod, "What Shall I Call Myself? Hispanic Identity Formation in the Second Generation," *Ethnic and Racial Studies,* vol. 19 (1996), pp. 523–546; Ruben Rumbaut, "The Crucible Within: Ethnic Identity, Self-Esteem, and Segmented Assimilation among Children of Immigrants," *International Migration Review,* vol. 28 (1994), pp. 748–794; Mary Waters, "Ethnic and Racial Identities of Second-Generation Black Immigrants in New York," *International Migration Review,* vol. 28 (1994), pp. 795–820.

4. Milton Gordon, *Assimilation in American Life: The Role of Race, Religion, and National Origin* (New York: Oxford University Press, 1964), pp. 52–54; Alejandro Portes and Ruben Rumbaut, *Immigrant America: A Portrait* (Berkeley: University of California Press, 1990), pp. 212–215.

5. Waters, 1994.

6. According to the 1990 census, 36 percent of U.S.-born Asian Americans twenty-five years old and over completed four years of college education in comparison with 22 percent of white Americans. See U.S. Bureau of the Census, *1990 Census of Population, Asian and Pacific Islanders* (Washington, D.C.: U.S. Government Printing Office, 1993), p. 75.

7. For a discussion of segmented assimilation theory, see the section titled "Ethnicity, Assimilation, and Social Mobility" of the next chapter ("Ethnicity: Concepts, Theories, and Trends").

8. Esther Ngau-Ling Chow, Doris Wilkinson, and Maxine Bach Zinn (eds.), *Race, Class, and Gender: Common Bonds, Different Voices* (Newbury Park, CA: Sage Publications, 1997); Patricia Hill Collins, *Black Feminist Thought: Knowledge, Consciousness, and the Politics of Empowerment* (New York: Routledge, Chapman, & Hall, 1990); Karen Rosenblum, *The Meaning of Difference: American Constructions of Race, Sex and Gender, Social Class, and Sexual Orientation* (New York: McGraw-Hill Companies, Inc., 1996).

9. Yen Espiritu, *Asian American Women and Men: Labor, Laws, and Love* (Newbury Park, CA: Sage Publications, 1997); Keyyoung Park, "Women of the 1.5 Generation: Alternative Manifestation of Korean American Identities," Paper Presented at the 1998 Annual Meeting of the Association for Asian American Studies, Hawaii; Diane Wolfe, "Family Secrets: Transnational Struggles among Children of Filipino Immigrants," *Sociological Perspectives,* vol. 40 (1997), pp. 457–482.

Ethnicity: *Concepts, Theories, and Trends*

RESEARCHERS HAVE USED interchangeably the terms ethnicity, ethnic identity, ethnic attachment, ethnic cohesion, ethnic solidarity, and ethnic mobilization to indicate two interrelated but separate social phenomena. The first is the degree to which members are culturally, socially, and psychologically attached to the ethnic group. The term *ethnic attachment* seems best to capture this meaning.[1] The second phenomenon is the degree to which members use ethnic collective actions to protect their common interests. *Ethnic solidarity* seems the most appropriate term here, although many researchers use ethnic solidarity to indicate ethnic attachment as well.[2]

Unless one identifies as a member of a particular ethnic group, one will not be culturally or socially attached to that group. Without some level of ethnic identity—particularly political identity—one will not participate in ethnic collective actions such as boycotts and demonstrations. Accordingly, ethnic identity is key to both ethnic attachment and ethnic solidarity. For this reason, some researchers have examined ethnic identity as the central element of ethnicity.[3]

Until the 1960s, the dominant paradigm in the study of ethnic relations in the U.S. was the assimilation model.[4] Assuming all immigrant groups would achieve acculturation, social integration, and socioeconomic mobility in due time, researchers in the assimilationist tradition tried to measure levels of assimilation over generations. However, since the 1970s, the pendulum has gradually swung from assimilation to cultural pluralism and ethnicity. As a result, many scholars have conducted research—both theoretical and empirical—on the causes and consequences of ethnicity over the last quarter century, leading to conceptual clarifications and theoretical refinements. This chapter will review the literature on the causes and consequences of ethnicity and point to their implications for understanding Asian Americans' ethnicity.

Many theories of ethnicity can be classified into two contrasting perspectives: the primordial approach and the mobilizationist approach.[5] The primordial perspective emphasizes premigrant, primordial group ties associated with a physical affinity, a common language, a common religion, and other cultural and historical commonalities as the basis of ethnicity.[6] According to this perspective, an ethnic or minority group whose members share many commonalities in physical characteristics, culture, religion, and historical origin is likely to maintain a higher level of ethnicity than other groups with fewer commonalities. In contrast, the mobilizationist perspective rejects the assumption that ethnicity is determined largely by commonalities in physical and cultural characteristics and historical experiences shared by members of a group prior to migration. Rather, it accepts the concept of "emergent ethnicity,"[7] the view that ethnicity is created and re-created in the context of adjustment in the host society. Thus it emphasizes residential segregation, occupational concentration, and other structural factors in the host society—including economic competition and the level of discrimination against the group—as the sources of ethnicity.[8]

In the beginning of this chapter, I made a distinction between ethnic *attachment* as the cultural, social, and psychological attachment to one's ethnic group, and ethnic *solidarity* as the use of ethnic collective actions to protect common interests. The primordial perspective is more useful in understanding the level of ethnic attachment, while the mobilizationist perspective is more effective in explaining the development of ethnic solidarity. However, no researcher would deny that each of these two perspectives is helpful in explaining both types of ethnic phenomena. To phrase it alternately, both primordial group ties prior to migration and postmigration adjustment patterns in the host society affect cultural preservation, ethnic identity maintenance, and ethnic mobilization.

PREMIGRANT PRIMORDIAL TIES

The primordial school considers ethnicity an extension of a premodern social bond, such as kin and tribal ties, based on commonalities in physical and cultural characteristics and common historical experiences associated with the place of origin, often called "homeland." In this view, ethnicity is "primarily a sense of belonging to a particular ancestry and origin and of sharing a specific religion or language."[9] People have a natural inclination to seek out others who share ancestry, physical affinity, language, and/or religion—what one anthropologist calls the "building blocks of ethnicity."[10] From the primordial perspective, this primal bond, which "is more emotional than rational, even 'irrational' in certain respects,"[11] is the central element of ethnicity. Members of an ethnic group often participate in collective actions to protect their economic and political interests. However, ethnic collective actions differ from class-based actions in that the former "combine an interest with an affective tie,"[12] while the latter are entirely based on the "rational" calculation of interest. Two or more different ethnic groups may make a coalition to protect their practical interests. But, unless they have an emotional bond based on their physical or cultural affinity or their place of origin, their coalition will not last long after they achieve their intended goal.

In the primordial perspective, homeland, or territoriality, is an important basis for ethnicity. If an indigenous population is conquered by an alien population, as was the case with Native American tribes, the original territory will remain central to the conquered group's ethnic identity. The indigenous people will try to achieve political independence and to restore their lost territory. For most other ethnic groups in the U.S., homeland is the country of origin, though some immigrants, such as Italian immigrants at the turn of the century, were so provincial that it took them a long time to identify with national origin.[13] For other groups, the country of origin is not their homeland. For example, Jews who originally settled in today's Palestine in the Middle East lost their homeland in the first century and were subsequently dispersed throughout the world. The vast majority of today's Jewish Americans are descendants of immigrants, or are emigrants from European countries who migrated here well before Israel was established in 1948. Even before the modern state of Israel was established, their imagined homeland in the Middle East was, along with Judaism, the symbol of Jewish Americans' ethnic identity. Since 1948, Israel as a Jewish state has provided an important vehicle for Jewish identification in the lives of both individual Jews and the organized Jewish community.[14]

Ethnicity differs from race, class, and gender in that it is characterized mainly by cultural distinctions—language, dress, food, holidays, customs, values, and beliefs. As Richard Alba points out, "ethnic groups generally define their uniqueness in regard to other ethnic groups largely through the medium of culture."[15] Language is the central component of culture, and as such it has the strongest effect on integrating members into a particular ethnic group.[16] Research shows that there is a high correlation between the use of a mother tongue and other components of ethnicity. Yet language is also the first element of the immigrant culture to disappear over generations.[17] In Alba's survey study conducted in the late 1980s, only 16 percent of his native-born white respondents said that "they actively use a mother tongue, either as a language for conversation or as an ethnic garnish when speaking English."[18] A recent study by David Lopez based on 1990 census data indicates that rapid intergenerational language shift is also occurring among Asian Americans, although it is less rapid among Latinos. He found that 53 percent of second-generation Latinos aged twenty-four to forty speak both their mother tongue at home and English very well, in comparison with only 19 percent of second-generation Asian Americans.[19] Latino ethnic groups have advantages over Asian and white ethnic groups in maintaining their mother tongue because they share a common language.

Ethnic foods and ethnic holidays are much easier to maintain over generations than language. Research shows that even intermarriage does not do much to hinder the preservation of ethnic cuisines.[20] Herbert Gans coined the term *symbolic ethnicity* to indicate the tendency of third- and fourth-generation white ethnic groups to maintain ethnicity without practicing ethnic culture or participating in ethnic networks.[21] According to Gans, by the 1970s, most third- and fourth-generation Jewish and Catholic white ethnics achieved high levels of acculturation and social assimilation, losing much of their ancestral cultures and moving into nonethnic primary groups. They continued to perceive themselves as ethnics, however, and maintained their ethnic identity through major symbols such as ethnic foods and festivals—symbols that required little effort, and rarely interfered with other aspects of their lives.

Religion has stronger effects on ethnic attachment than the home-country culture. Non-Protestant religious groups—largely Catholic, Jewish, and Eastern Orthodox Christian—make up the vast majority of white ethnic groups in the U.S. today. The white ethnic groups that have achieved the greatest success in preserving their ethnic traditions and rejecting assimilation are the Amish and the Mormon—the two most fundamentalist ethnoreligious groups.[22] The close connection between religion and ethnic solidarity is also supported by the persistence of ethnoreligious conflicts and movements all over the world.[23]

Religion sustains ethnicity in part by helping members of ethnic and minority groups maintain their native cultural traditions. European immigrant groups in the U.S. at the turn of the century turned to their ethnic churches to preserve their cultural traditions when threatened with their loss. The Italian Catholic parishes "functioned to maintain the personality by organizing the group around the familiar religious and cultural symbols and behavioral symbols of the fatherland."[24] Starting with the Sephardic Jews in the seventeenth century, the synagogue has been the center of Jewish cultural activities for different waves of Jewish immigrants in the U.S.[25] It is important to note that immigrants usually establish ethnic language schools within ethnic churches to transmit their language and culture to the second generation. Religion also sustains ethnic attachment partly by helping to maintain social interactions with co-ethnic members. Many people become affiliated with ethnic churches to meet their needs for primary social interactions with co-ethnics. As one of the Hebrew words for synagogue, *Beth Haknesseth* (the place of gathering), denotes, the Jewish synagogue has probably played the most important role in providing communal ties for Jews settled in the U.S., as well as in other parts of the world.

Members of an ethnic group have emotional ties, not only because they share commonalities in physical and cultural characteristics, but also because they have lived through the same historical experiences. I like to make a distinction between the premigrant historical experiences in the home country—or in a third country in the case of "twice minorities" (minority groups that remigrated from a another country)—and the historical experiences in the host society. Most ethnic groups have a history of one or more premigrant tribulations suffered by their ancestors: the occupation of the territory by a foreign power, the loss of the homeland, subjection to violence and hostility in an alien land, colonization, and/or even genocide. The collective memory of a major historical event provides members of an ethnic group with an important source of ethnic identity. More than one hundred thousand Armenians were killed by the Turkish army before and during World War I, and this Turkish massacre heightened the ethnic identity of Armenians in the U.S.[26] Jews have been subject to violence and hostility more than any other group in the world. Georges Friedman[27] views anti-Semitism as the major force in the development of Jewish identity and solidarity. In particular, the Nazi extermination of six million Jews during World War II strengthened the group identity of American Jews more than anything else.[28] Twice-minority immigrants (or *twice migrants*), such as Jewish immigrants from Russia and Chinese immigrants from Vietnam, arrive in the U.S. with already-established moderate levels of ethnic identity and solidarity.[29] Twice-minority groups have already experienced discrimination as minority groups prior to migration (in contrast with other immigrant groups, who have yet to change their status from majority to minority groups).

I would like to make three important generalizations regarding the present and future of ethnicity for Asian groups from the primordial perspective. First, contemporary Asian immigrant groups have brought with them distinctive cultural and religious traditions—probably more distinctive from Anglo American culture and Christian religions than are European and Latino traditions. For example, Chinese, Korean, Japanese, and Vietnamese immigrants brought with them Confucianism and Buddhism. Indian and other South Asian immigrants transplanted three other non-Christian religions—Hinduism, Sikhism, and Islam. Because of the distinctiveness of their cultures and religions, contemporary Asian immigrants generally maintain a strong ethnic identity and a cultural boundary of ethnicity. However, exactly because of their distinctiveness, the second and later generations may have difficulty maintaining their ethnic cultures and religions— probably greater difficulty than the descendants of turn-of-the-century white immigrants. It is interesting to see to what extent second-generation Asian Americans will maintain their ancestral cultures.

Second, Asian immigrant groups have differing levels of cultural homogeneity. Korean immigrants have the highest level of homogeneity while Indian and Filipino groups are characterized by significant subgroup differences in culture and religion. This means that Korean immigrants have advantages for maintaining ethnic solidarity over Filipino and Indian immigrants.

Third, since some Asian ethnic groups share more physical and cultural similarities than others, they can form a panethnic coalition more effectively than all Asian groups together. I will discuss these points in more detail in connection with subethnicity and panethnicity in the third and fourth sections of this chapter.

ADJUSTMENTS TO THE HOST SOCIETY
AND ETHNIC MOBILIZATION

Until the early 1970s, both assimilationists and pluralists emphasized premigrant primordial ties as the basis for ethnicity. However, since the late 1970s, social scientists in general and sociologists in particular have put more emphasis on structural factors related to adjustments to the host society as the major source of ethnicity than on the transplanted cultural heritage. The first significant piece of work that formulated structural explanations of ethnicity was an article by William Yancy, Eugene Ericksen, and Richard Juliani, which was published in *American Sociological Review* in 1976. Rejecting the traditional primordial approach, the authors argued that the development and persistence of ethnicity is dependent upon structural conditions characterizing American cities and the position of groups in American social structure. In particular, they emphasized the ecology of occupations and residence as largely determining the development and persistence of ethnicity. In their view, the industrial and urban structures at the turn of the century made non-Protestant white immigrant groups more concentrated occupationally and residentially than the previous Protestant immigrant groups. They argued that these non-Protestant (Jewish and Catholic) ethnic groups were able to develop higher levels of ethnicity not because of their cultural distinctiveness, but as a result of their occupational and residential concentration.

Since the publication of *The Urban Villagers* more than thirty-five years ago,[30] researchers interested in ethnic groups have paid special attention to ethnic ghettos or ethnic enclaves, such as Chinatown, the Barrio, and Little Havana.[31] Recently arrived working-class immigrants and even some second-generation working-class ethnics reside in ethnic enclaves, where they maintain strong primary-group social interactions among kin and co-ethnic members and preserve the old world culture. Yancy and his associates and other structurally oriented social scientists have argued that industrial and urban structures, along with discrimination against new immigrants and minority members, largely determine the formation of immigrant/ethnic enclaves. When we examine closely the formation processes of ethnic enclaves, we find this argument to have an element of truth. For example, protection of Chinese immigrants from the discrimination and racism of the larger society was the main impetus for the formation of Chinatowns in many American cities in the latter part of the nineteenth century.[32]

However, the formation of contemporary immigrant enclaves, which is more voluntary than that of earlier ethnic enclaves, is determined more by the group characteristics than by structural factors in American society. Among major Asian immigrant groups, Chinese, Korean, and Vietnamese immigrants have established their own territorial communities called Chinatown, Koreatown, or Little Saigon,[33] while Indian and Filipino immigrants are widely dispersed in suburban areas without establishing their own ghettos. On the one hand, due to their linguistic-regional subgroup differences and lack of national identity, Indian and Filipino immigrants have disadvantages—compared with Chinese, Korean, and Vietnamese immigrants—for organizing their territorial community.[34] On the other hand, Indian and Filipino immigrants, who represent higher socioeconomic status and who are more fluent in English than other Asian immigrant groups, may not need an immigrant ghetto, historically a residential area for lower-class immigrants. The absence of a territorial community on the part of Indian and Filipino immigrants, which is partly determined by their lack of group homogeneity, gives them further disadvantages for preserving their native cultures and developing a national identity.

It is not difficult to understand how occupational concentration enhances ethnicity. Members of an ethnic or minority group, when concentrated in a few occupations, frequently interact socially with co-ethnics. They also feel a strong sense of group solidarity because of the overlap of their class and ethnic interests.[35] In contrast, Michael Hechter and his associates have focused on the "ethnic division of labor" rather than on occupational concentration in general to illustrate the so-called *reactive-ethnicity* or *internal colonialism* model.[36] According to Hechter, ethnic solidarity is a reaction of a culturally distinctive minority group against economic exploitation by the dominant group. Reactive solidarity occurs when there is such a cultural division of labor that members of a culturally distinctive group are assigned to low-level occupations. Members of the minority group who are being economically exploited will use their ethnic collective actions to change the ethnic stratification system. The greater the economic inequalities between groups in a given society, the greater the likelihood of ethnic solidarity. The relative salience of ethnic solidarity to class solidarity in a given society is dependent upon the degree of the ethnic division of labor relative to the class division.[37]

Another theory emphasizing the positive effects of a minority group's economic position on its solidarity is *middleman minority theory*. Historically, middleman minorities concentrated in small businesses, often distributing products made by the ruling group to minority customers.[38] Jews in Medieval Europe, Chinese in Southeast Asia, and Indians in Africa are prominent examples of middleman minorities. Located in a vulnerable position between producers and consumers, middleman minorities encountered intergroup conflicts with and host hostility from both groups. Middleman merchants' business-related intergroup conflicts and experiences with host hostility, in turn, have enhanced their solidarity. Contemporary Korean immigrants in the U.S. play a role similar to traditional middleman minorities, connecting white corporations and low-income African American and Latino customers. Elsewhere, I have shown how Korean immigrants' business-related intergroup conflicts solidified the Korean communities in New York and Los Angeles.[39] In particular, I indicated that the victimization of many Korean merchants during the 1992 Los Angeles riots heightened Korean Americans' political consciousness and second-generation Koreans' ethnic identity.

The reactive-ethnicity model outlined above assumes that levels of ethnic solidarity have risen in modern industrial societies because industrialization has increased, rather than diffused, ethnic inequality. The proponents of the *competition model* also claim that there have been ethnic resurgences in modern industrial societies. But their argument for the ethnic resurgence is based on the opposite assumption: that industrialization has *reduced* ethnic inequality and thereby increased ethnic competition.[40] In this view, modernization and industrialization have increased levels of contact with and competition among various ethnic populations for jobs, housing, and other scarce resources, which, in turn, has increased levels of ethnic mobilization. Contrary to the reactive-ethnicity model, the competition model hypothesizes that ethnic groups with higher levels of assimilation are likely to show greater levels of ethnic awareness and mobilization than other less-assimilated groups, and that more-assimilated members of an ethnic group also appear more likely to support ethnic movements.[41] This hypothesis gained support from a longitudinal survey study of Cuban refugees in Miami by Alejandro Portes.[42] According to the study, as a result of Cuban refugees' increased interethnic competition, the responses to the 1979 survey showed Cuban respondents' greater ethnic awareness than the responses to the 1976 and 1973 surveys.

The *political construction of ethnicity* should be considered as another mobilizationist theory. In this view, when the government recognizes ethnicity as the basis for political organization and claimsmakings, ethnic identity and ethnic mobilization are likely to increase.[43] There are many examples in which governmental policies and measures toward ethnic and minority groups have strengthened ethnic identity and facilitated ethnic mobilization. When in recent years the Chinese Communist government adopted a minority policy that emphasized ethnic equality and ethnic autonomy, hundreds of Korean families in China who had lost their nationality over the course of many generations applied for a change of nationality from Han to Korean.[44] As a result of linguistic social movements, India currently consists of fourteen semi-independent multilingual states. Linguistic ethnic movements in India were originally facilitated by British colonial administrative practices. Jyotirindra Das Gupta indicates that "[t]he creation of these language communities was sometimes facilitated by the system of the administrative division of India into provinces as carved by the colonial rulers."[45]

In the first half of the twentieth century when Asian immigrants were not eligible for U.S. citizenship, Indian leaders organized the "citizenship movement" to get Indian immigrants considered Caucasian and thus eligible for citizenship. However, when the U.S. Census Bureau classified Indians as white in 1970, Indian community leaders lobbied the U.S. government to reclassify them as Asian Indians.[46] They wanted Indians to be classified separately as a minority group partly because minority groups were entitled to a number of benefits in the post–civil rights era. Responding favorably, the U.S. Census Bureau has classified Asian Indians as one of the Asian and Pacific Islander groups since 1980.

Although Indians and other South Asians culturally and physically differ from other Asian groups, the governmental classification of Indians and other South Asians into the Asian and Pacific Islander category has influenced their ethnic and panethnic identities.[47]

African Americans have lost much of their African cultural identity through slavery and have maintained little connection with their places of origin in Africa. Nevertheless, they have maintained strong racial and ethnic identities both as blacks and as African Americans. Their ethnic and racial identities have been generated almost entirely by structural conditions—their settlement in inner-city slums, their concentration in low-paying occupations, and their experiences with racial prejudice and discrimination. Ronald Taylor uses the term *ethnogenesis* to refer to African American ethnicity generated by the structural conditions under which most African Americans have struggled for survival in American cities in the twentieth century.[48] Eugene Roosens expands the concept of ethnogenesis by emphasizing the role of ethnic leaders or "cultural brokers" in generating ethnicity.[49] From the perspective of ethnogenesis, ethnic identity, organization, and culture evolve and undergo dramatic changes, influenced by changing structural conditions. Members of an ethnic group selectively retain cultural patterns useful for survival and develop new cultural patterns to adapt to a changing social environment.[50]

Jews heightened the importance of Hanukkah to provide a Jewish alternative to the Christmas season, while African Americans created Kwanzaa to express their distinct ethnicity.[51] Hanukkah and Kwanzaa are good examples of how each ethnic group creates new cultural patterns to adapt to a changing world. Kwanzaa was created in 1966 by Maulana Karenga, a black cultural nationalist, who believed it was important for African Americans to create their own Christmas holiday. Observed for seven days between December 26th and January 1st, Kwanzaa emphasizes the importance of the family and is patterned after traditional African harvest festivals. In addition, the ritual of lighting candles each night symbolizes affirmation of seven principles: unity, self-determination, collective responsibility, cooperative economics, purpose, creativity, and faith.

While Hanukkah and Kwanzaa represent ethnic innovations that aimed to amalgamate the white Christian culture with individual minority cultures, other ethnic innovations in the U.S. were created to challenge the cultural, economic, and political domination of white Americans. The Nation of Islam for African Americans and the Ghost Dance for Native Americans are two such examples. Farrad Mohammed established the Nation of Islam in 1930 in Detroit by adopting Islamic teachings to provide blacks with an ideology antithetical to Christianity, which he considered "a whiteman's religion."[52] This pro-Arab movement of black Muslims also implies "an anti-Jewish feeling based on the ghetto experience of many blacks who perceive Jewish merchants as using sharp practices to take advantage of them."[53] The economic autonomy of blacks, along with the Buy-Black movement, has been an important aspect of the Nation of Islam.

The Native American Ghost Dance is based on the prophecy that dead Indians would be brought to life by the dance, while the white people would disappear. This religion, or ethnoreligious movement, started in the early 1870s in Nevada, then quickly spread to many Indian tribes in the western and Rocky Mountain states. It began to decline in the early 1880s, but was revived later that decade, culminating in the Sioux Outbreak of 1890.[54] The revival of the religion "can be understood only against the background of white domination, [Indians'] cultural confusion, the loss of the buffalo, and the inability to carry out the old rituals."[55]

As noted above, minority members sometimes create new cultural patterns either to provide ethnic alternatives to dominant cultural patterns or to challenge them. However, this does not mean that some minority members can escape successfully from the negative effects of prejudice and discrimination. In the development of identity and self-esteem, all minority members are powerfully influenced by how they are perceived and treated by the dominant group. In fact, for some minority groups in the U.S., such as blacks, their experiences with prejudice and discrimination largely determine their ethnic and racial identities. During the 1880–1924 mass-migration period, Jewish, Italian, and other non-Protestant immigrants were treated as inferior racial groups distinctive from Protestant white Americans;[56] this prejudice strongly influenced the identity formation of their children. With prejudice and discrimination against these non-Protestant white ethnic groups almost eliminated, many of their fourth-generation descendants have lost their ethnic identity. Thus, as Mary Waters indicates, ethnicity is a matter of option for white Americans.[57] But native-born blacks—no matter how many generations have lived here—do not have such an option because their racial category is externally imposed on them by the larger society. Empirical studies of ethnic identity show that even many children of Caribbean black immigrants identify as American black rather than as Caribbean American.[58] This proves the powerful influence of color-based prejudice and discrimination on the formation of ethnic identity among black children.

For Asian *immigrants,* native culture brought with them from their home country may provide the main source of ethnicity. For *second-generation* Asian Americans, however, their experiences in the U.S. are likely to determine their ethnic identity, although the ethnic culture practiced at home in their early years still has significant effects on their identity formation. Post-1965 Asian immigrants and their children are more favorably accepted in American society than their predecessors, who encountered many legal barriers and racial violence. The elimination of legal barriers against Asian Americans and the relaxation of anti-Asian prejudice may make many native-born Asian Americans feel comfortable with their lives in the U.S., and thus may reduce their ethnic and pan-Asian identities. However, the memory of how their ancestors suffered from racism in this country provides the basis for their ethnic identity. The memory of the internment of Japanese Americans in relocation camps during World War II has enhanced the ethnic identity of native-born Japanese Americans.[59] The Philippines suffered from a four-century colonization by Western powers, first by Spain and then by the U.S. Due to its group diversity and "colonial mentality," the Filipino community is loosely organized and many Filipino American young people suffer from identity crises and alienation. Linda Revilla suggests that knowledge of Filipino history and culture would help "foster a sense of pride for your Filipinos who are ashamed of their ethnicity."[60]

Although Asian Americans are now treated far more favorably than they were fifty years ago, as people of color they still encounter moderate levels of prejudice and discrimination. Despite the prevalence of the positive image,[61] many Americans still view Asian Americans as "strangers from a different shore," the title of Ronald Takaki's popular Asian American reader. Native-born Asian Americans are often embarrassed by such remarks as "What country are you from?" and "Go back to your country." These insensitive remarks reflect the belief of many white Americans that Asian Americans still do not belong fully to American society. The treatment of Asian Americans as "strangers" or "aliens" will certainly have negative effects on the psychological well-being and identity of younger-generation Asian Americans. Moreover, many Asian Americans, particularly new Asian immigrants, have recently become victims of anti-Asian violence. This anti-Asian violence is likely to heighten not only an ethnic but also a pan-Asian identity and solidarity, which will be covered in more detail in the next section.

SUBETHNICITY

Most white ethnic groups in the U.S. are nationality groups, which simplifies ethnic classification. However, some nationality groups consist of several subgroups that have significant differences in culture, religion, and/or history. Contemporary Iranian immigrants are a good example. The Iranian nationality group contains four ethnoreligious subgroups—Armenians, Bahais, Jews, and Muslims. Ivan Light and his associates found that the four subgroups differed significantly in self-employment rates and occupational and industrial clustering, and that they maintained co-ethnicity in partnership and employment relationships.[62] They concluded, "Each ethnoreligious subgroup had its own ethnic economy, and that these separate economies were weakly tied to an encompassing Iranian ethnic economy." The fact that the four groups maintained subethnic economies suggests that they also maintained subethnic social networks and identities. *Subethnicity* refers to differences within an ethnic group in culture, social networks, and identity. An ethnic group that has significant subethnic differences is severely disadvantaged for mobilizing broad ethnic collective actions and maintaining a collective ethnic identity.

While Korean, Japanese, and Vietnamese immigrants are highly homogenous in their native culture and place of origin, Indian, Filipino, and Chinese immigrants are characterized by varying degrees of subgroup differences based on language, religion, and/or place of origin.[63] Indian immigrants have more subgroup differences than any other Asian immigrant group. First of all, they have subgroup differences based on religion. Although Hindus comprise more than 80 percent of the population in India, members of minority religions— Sihks, Muslims, Christians, Jains, and Parsis—number more than 150 million. In India, Hindus, the dominant religious group, have a long history of conflict with minority religious groups—Sihks, Muslims, Jains, and Parsis. Though different religious groups do not conflict seriously in the Indian immigrant community, they certainly maintain separate cultural and social boundaries. To complicate matters, Indian immigrants suffer from a subethnic division based on place of origin and regional language, which is a legacy of long years of regional/linguistic movements in India.[64] Hindu immigrants from different states differ not only in native language and other cultural patterns, but also in economic activities and political identity. For example, an analysis of the 1980 U.S. Census showed that Gujarati Indians had a substantially higher self-employment rate than the rest of the Indian population.[65] In addition, Caribbean Indian immigrants, heavily concentrated in New York City, maintain physical boundaries separate from immigrants from India.[66]

The strong subethnic division of Indian immigrants has significant effects on their community organization and ethnic attachment patterns. Most ethnic organizations in the Indian immigrant community are regional or linguistic, while there are few pan-Indian organizations with political orientations.[67] Although Indian immigrants in New York City are far more fluent in English than Korean or Chinese immigrants, they are far less politically active than the other two Asian immigrant groups.[68]

A survey of Asian immigrants in Queens, New York, showed that most Indian respondents identified with their place of origin rather than as Indian, while almost all Korean respondents identified as Korean.[69] Many Indian immigrants seem to have multiple identities, adopting a religious identity (such as Muslim) in one situation, identifying with a regional language in another, and then identifying as Indian when engaged in political activities.[70]

Filipino immigrants also consist of a number of subgroups based on language and place of origin. The absence of a common native language and regional differences partly contribute to the factionalism and disunity that characterize Filipino American community organizations.[71] Most Filipino associations—largely based on place of origin, a common dialect, and kinship—serve mainly cultural and social functions rather than economic and political ones.[72] Filipino immigrants in the mainland U.S. have not established residential and business centers comparable to either Chinatowns or Koreatowns. Their group diversity, as well as their underrepresentation in small businesses, may be responsible for the absence of Filipino enclaves.

Traditionally, Chinese immigrants were described as maintaining strong ethnic ties.[73] However, this generalization is no longer applicable to contemporary Chinese immigrants, who are composed of several different nationality groups: Chinese immigrants from mainland China, Taiwan, Hong Kong, Singapore, and Vietnam. Immigrants from Taiwan and mainland China differ significantly in political ideology, socioeconomic background, and other characteristics.[74] Even immigrants from mainland China consist of several linguistic/regional subgroups who cannot communicate with one another because they have different native languages. Chinese immigrant churches in the U.S. often have problems holding services because of the linguistic diversity among members.[75]

Those ethnic Chinese who remigrated from a third country to the U.S. generally are not loyal to China. To measure the level of Asian immigrants' loyalty to their homeland, Chinese, Korean, and Indian immigrants in Queens were asked for which team they would cheer in an Olympic soccer match—the U.S. or the homeland team (Chinese, Indian, or Korean). Only 58 percent of Chinese respondents (in comparison with 96 percent of Korean respondents) said they would definitely or probably cheer for the homeland team.[76] This suggests that many Chinese immigrants from a country other than China have a divided loyalty between their country of origin and China.

PANETHNICITY

As reviewed above, many new immigrants identify with a region rather than with their national ethnic group. However, as a result of interactions with members of the dominant group and other minority groups, their identity will gradually transform from local and subethnic to ethnic. Further, the emergence of the second generation accelerates the ethnization of an immigrant group. Second-generation children identify with their nationality group rather than with their parents' region of origin mainly because society's perception of them—rather than their ethnic heritage—largely determines their ethnic identity. Children of immigrants from Taiwan or Gujarat (India) accept a Chinese or Indian ethnic identity because they are generally labeled and viewed as Chinese or Indian rather than as Taiwanese or Gujarati by both government agencies and the general public in the U.S.

Interactions with the larger society enhance not only an ethnic but also a panethnic identity and mobilization. In connection with the political construction of ethnicity, I emphasized previously the role of government policies in the rise of ethnic identity. Many researchers have indicated that U.S. government policies in the post–civil rights era may have contributed more than ethnic mobilization to a panethnic or a racial formation.[77] Government agencies and schools usually classify students as white, black, Latino, Asian American, and Native American for administrative and service allocation purposes. This racial classification—also utilized in various governmental programs such as affirmative action—have facilitated panethnic and racial formation. Felix Padilla shows that "[a]ffirmative action policy provided the critical base for the Mexican American and Puerto Rican leadership [in Chicago] to advance the interests of their populations collectively, rather than as individual or separate Spanish-speaking ethnics."[78]

The classification of all Asian students into one category by colleges and universities, and discriminatory measures in college admissions to restrict their numbers, have led to pan-Asian solidarity among Asian American students, community leaders, and faculty members.[79] Because agencies and school systems often allocate resources for Asian Americans as a single group, several pan-Asian organizations, including the Asian American Mental Health Center, were established in Los Angeles, New York, and other cities to provide services for Asian Americans. The federal and local governments have designated May as Asian and Pacific Islander American month, promoting the celebration of ethnic festivals and other cultural activities. These government-sponsored cultural activities enhance pan-Asian identity and interethnic interactions among all Asian Americans.

This practice of lumping all Asian groups together is not limited to government agencies and schools. Most Americans have difficulty distinguishing various Asian ethnic groups despite some observable physical differences, and thus often refer to Japanese, Koreans, and even Cambodians as "Chinese." Asian Americans have been physically attacked by white or black Americans who mistook them for members of other Asian ethnic groups. In 1982, for example, Vincent Chin, a Chinese American living in Detroit, was beaten to death with a baseball bat by two white factory workers who mistook him for Japanese.[80] The two white men reportedly blamed Chin for the loss of jobs in Detroit. In 1990, a Vietnamese immigrant was severely beaten by black gangs in Brooklyn because they thought he was Korean.[81] Each incident of violence led Asian Americans to realize that they could be targets of attack simply because they share Asian American physical characteristics. This, in turn, has enhanced a pan-Asian unity. When the two white men who killed Vincent Chin received light sentences, Asian Americans in Detroit and throughout the nation protested the verdict.

Asian Americans are greatly underrepresented in politics, far below blacks and Latinos.[82] Individual Asian ethnic groups in most cities, with the exception of those in Hawaii, are still small in number and thus not strong enough to influence politics or school boards, even at the local level. Yet the Asian American population in many West Coast cities and in New York City is large enough to influence city politics through a pan-Asian coalition. This practical need for a pan-Asian coalition in politics has also contributed to a moderate level of pan-Asian unity. For example, the Asian and Pacific Islander American population in Monterey Park, California, greatly increased throughout the 1980s, reaching 58 percent of the population in 1990. Chinese immigrants in Monterey Park formed a coalition with Japanese Americans, mainly native born, to elect Chinese Americans for mayor and city council.[83] Chinese and Korean immigrants in Flushing, the community with the largest Asian concentration in New York City outside of Chinatown,[84] have formed several coalitions since the late 1980s to get their candidates elected as school board members.[85] Also, Asian Americans in Los Angeles made political donations across ethnic lines to elect Chinese and Japanese Americans as city councilmen.[86] In addition, in 1991, Asian American political activists in Los Angeles, New York, and other key cities made pan-Asian coalitions to demand fair redistricting.[87]

The pan-Asian movement is probably felt most keenly at major universities that have a large number of Asian American students. By the early 1990s, the proportion of Asian Americans had already reached more than 30 percent of the student body at several University of California campuses, including Berkeley, Los Angeles, and Irvine, and more than 20 percent in many prestigious private and public universities, including Columbia, Cornell, and Harvard. Thus, these universities developed a critical mass of American-born, Asian American intellectuals who were conscious of their common destiny as Asian Americans in a white-dominant society. Following the Third World students' movement in the 1960s,[88] Asian American activists at these universities demanded that a Eurocentric curriculum be revised drastically to reflect more minority experiences. Through pan-Asian organizations, they pressured administrators to establish Asian and Asian American studies programs and to hire more Asian American faculty members.

As a result of a continuous increase in the proportion of Asian American students and pressure from Asian students, a number of major universities have established Asian American and/or Asian area studies programs and hired many new Asian American faculty members since the early 1980s. Other colleges and universities that have not established Asian/Asian American programs offer more courses related to the history and culture of various Asian countries and the experiences of Asian Americans. The institutionalization of Asian and Asian American studies programs, in turn, further facilitates a pan-Asian identity and solidarity among Asian American students. Asian American studies programs put a priority on raising the ethnic and pan-Asian consciousness of Asian American students through their various courses and extracurricular activities.[89] Often directed by the student activists of the 1960s, they also emphasize campus activism, social change, and providing culturally sensitive services to Asian American communities.

No doubt, the mobilizationist approach is far more useful than the primordial approach in understanding the construction of Asian panethnicity in the various areas reviewed above. However, by saying this I do not mean to suggest that primordial ties do not play any role. Asian ethnic groups are diverse in culture and physical characteristics, more so than Latino ethnic groups, who share a common language and religion. Yet, as previously indicated, some Asian ethnic groups—East Asian groups on the one hand and South Asians on the other—have stronger primordial ties than others. As a result, East Asians and South Asians separately can make a more effective panethnic coalition than all Asian groups combined. Unfortunately, however, most researchers, focusing on structural sources of Asian panethnicity and political identity, have not paid much attention to interactions between primordial ties and structural variables in creating pan-Asian ethnicity.[90] Let me elaborate below the similarities and differences within East and South Asian groups.

Three East Asian groups—Chinese, Koreans, and Japanese Americans—are physically and culturally similar. All of Mongolian origin, they look so alike that they often have trouble differentiating members of their own nationality. The three groups, along with Vietnamese, also have many cultural similarities that stem from Confucianism. Confucianism, which started in China, has had a powerful cultural influence on Korea and Japan. China's cultural influence includes the export of Chinese characters, which are still being used in both countries along with their own characters. Because of their physical and cultural similarities, members of these three Asian groups frequently interact socially, as reflected by their high intermarriage rates. On the collective level, Chinese and Korean immigrant communities in Los Angeles, New York, and other cities work closely to protect common interests.[91] Pan-Asian organizations in major cities and Asian student clubs at universities are represented largely by members of these three East Asian groups.

In contrast, Indians, Pakistani, Bangladesh, and other South Asians are physically and culturally similar to one another and distinct from other Asian groups, especially from East Asian groups. Probably because of their physical distinctiveness from East Asians, U.S. officials have had difficulty classifying South Asians throughout the twentieth century.[92] In addition, South Asian groups share culture, religion, and history. Until the end of World War II, these South Asian groups experienced British colonization for many years as a part of India. Most South Asian immigrants share a religious identity either as Hindus or as Muslims, although their home countries have a long history of religious and political conflicts with one another.

Yet South Asian groups do not have much in common with other Asian groups. Thus, even most younger-generation members do not feel they have strong connections with other Asian Americans. South Asian students at major universities socially interact mainly with one another through South Asian students' associations and identify more as South Asian or person of color than as Asian American.[93] South Asian scholars, critics, writers, and activists realize the importance of making a pan-Asian coalition to protect common interests. But they, too, agree that the cultural, racial, and historical divide between South Asians and the other Asians may be too great to bridge.[94] Moreover, they also feel excluded from and marginalized in pan-Asian organizations, the Asian American literary canon, and Asian American studies programs.[95] Their sense of marginalization in Asian America, their physical affinity with blacks, and the memory of how their ancestors suffered under white colonization and white racism may lead many South Asians to identify with blacks or other people of color. Indeed, a few articles in *A Part, Yet Apart: South Asians in Asian America* emphasized the importance of forming a coalition between blacks and South Asians.

REVIVAL OF ETHNICITY DURING RECENT YEARS

In his popular article "Symbolic Ethnicity" (1979), Herbert Gans disagreed with the scholarly emphasis on an ethnic revival, arguing that white ethnic groups had experienced a gradual assimilation over generations to such an extent that third- and fourth-generation white ethnics used only ethnic symbols to retain their ethnic identity. His generalization is valid as long as white ethnic groups in the 1970s are concerned. However, it is not applicable to multiethnic America in the 1990s. Ethnic phenomena—cultures, neighborhoods, networks, identity, and politics— are far more salient in the 1990s than they were two decades ago. Several factors have contributed to a revival of ethnicity in recent years.

First, the last thirty years have witnessed a mass migration of people from non-European, Third World countries. Until the 1970s, the period from 1880 to 1924 had been known in American history as the "mass migration" period. However, the enforcement of the Hart-Celler Act of 1965 ushered in another mass migration period. In fact, the U.S. will have received more immigrants—approximately eleven million—in the 1990s than in any other decade in American history.[96] The contemporary mass migration of mostly Latinos and Asians has made the U.S. far more multiethnic and multicultural than before. The influx of Latin American and Asian immigrants has had a significant impact on the ethnic diversity of American cities, particularly because the immigrants are heavily concentrated in several large cities such as Los Angeles, New York, Miami, and San Francisco.[97] The new immigrants in these cities have influenced major American social institutions—the government, the economy, the schools, the family, and religion—and culture as much as they have been influenced by the latter. The mass migration of people from periphery to core countries, not limited to the U.S., is a worldwide phenomenon, which has revived ethnicity in other major Western countries as well.

Second, since the early 1970s the Federal and state governments and educational institutions have changed policies toward minority members and immigrants from "Anglo conformity" to cultural pluralism.[98] The changes in policies were partly responses to various minority movements—the Civil Rights movement, the black cultural nationalist movement, the Chicano movement, and the Third World students movement—and the women's movement, and partly responses to the influx of new immigrants from Third World countries. In this connection, it is important to note the 1974 Lau vs. Nichols Supreme Court decision. In 1974, the Supreme Court declared that students with limited English language proficiency be given special remedial aid to facilitate their learning of English. Armed with the landmark Supreme Court decision, the Office of Civil Rights of the Department of Health, Education, and Welfare established a series of guidelines to require all school districts with non–English speaking students to provide bilingual education programs for "language minority children."[99] For new immigrant groups, especially Latino immigrants, bilingual education programs have served as a means to maintain their native languages and cultures. Since the early 1970s, the federal government and many state and city governments have provided funds for ethnic festivals and ethnic heritage studies programs as well as for bilingual education programs.

American universities and colleges also have gone miles to increase ethnic diversity over the last two decades. As a result of the influx of non-white immigrants and minority groups' improvement in education, colleges and universities have become far more racially and ethnically diverse than ever before. Employment through affirmative action programs and establishment of ethnic, area, and women's studies programs, along with the improvement in minority groups' and women's graduate educations, have also increased the number and proportion of minority and women faculty members. Under pressure from minority and women students and faculty members, many colleges and universities have revised the white male–oriented curriculum by including in traditional liberal arts courses more works by people of color and women, as well as adding numerous courses pertaining to their experiences.[100] The establishment of ethnic studies and women's studies programs in many campuses in particular has resulted in a significant revision of the traditional curriculum.[101] The multicultural education movement in colleges and universities, although severely attacked by conservative intellectuals,[102] has impacted all aspects of higher education—from the formal curriculum to methods of instruction and extracurricular activities.

The rise of ethnonationalist movements in Eastern Europe and other parts of the world since the late 1980s and the end of the cold war have also contributed to an ethnic revival in the U.S (as well as in other parts of the world). During the forty-year period following the end of World War II, communist and anti-communist ideological conflicts played a more important role than ethnonationalist movements in shaping the world order. During the cold war period, a nation state, based on a common ancestry, culture, and history, was often artificially divided into two politically opposing entities based on ideological differences, while a few nationality groups were fused into a political entity based on a common ideology. Germany, Korea, and Vietnam are examples of the former, and the former Soviet Union and Yugoslavia are examples of the latter. However, beginning with the unification of Germany in 1989, nationalist and ethnonationalist movements have turned these ideologically based, artificially created political entities back into pre–World War II nation states.[103] Ethnonationalist movements dissolved the former Soviet Union into fourteen different independent republics and Yugoslavia into three states. Minority ethnic groups in the newly independent, former Soviet republics have further tried to gain political autonomy, frequently leading to ethnic conflicts.[104] The success of ethnonationalist movements in Eastern Europe during recent years has encouraged ethnonationalist movements in other parts of the world. It has also led multiethnic societies, including the U.S., to change policies toward minority groups, allowing for more cultural autonomy, if not political autonomy.

L   Finally, transnational linkages between the host and home countries enable contemporary immigrant groups to maintain higher levels of ethnicity than earlier immigrant groups. Improvements in international travel, telecommunications, and the mass media have helped immigrants maintain strong ties to their home countries.[105] The accessibility of international air travel enables immigrants and their children to visit their home country far more easily than ever before. The increased convenience and affordability of long-distance telephone calls help immigrants to communicate with their relatives and friends in the home country on a regular basis. In addition, advances in media technologies have contributed to the development of active ethnic media, keeping immigrants and their children culturally, socially, and psychologically tied to their ethnic communities and home countries. Faster modes of international travel and communication, along with the end of the cold war and the mass migration discussed previously, have brought about changes that Arthur Schlesinger characterizes as the "cult of ethnicity."[106]

ETHNICITY, ASSIMILATION, AND SOCIAL MOBILITY

The previous sections provided an overview of concepts, theories, and trends related to the ethnic phenomenon. This section will examine the relationship between ethnicity and two related social phenomena, assimilation and social mobility, by reviewing relevant studies. Recent theoretical developments and discussions regarding these relationships will be emphasized.

Extending the classical assimilation theory, Milton Gordon (1964) made a distinction between cultural and social assimilation.[107] *Cultural assimilation,* he said, refers to the degree to which immigrants and minority members adopt the language, customs, and other cultural patterns of the host society. *Social assimilation* indicates the degree of their large-scale entrance into cliques, clubs, and institutions of the host society on the primary level. Gordon's distinction between the two types of assimilation is still important today for understanding the relationships between ethnic attachment and assimilation. Gordon pointed out that a minority group could achieve a high level of cultural assimilation, but that such cultural assimilation did not guarantee a similarly high level of social assimilation because social assimilation required acceptance by the dominant group.[108] In other words, members of a group that has achieved a high level of acculturation can maintain a strong social ethnic attachment either because they are not accepted by members of the dominant group or because they feel more comfortable interacting with co-ethnic members.

This phenomenon of high cultural assimilation without significant social assimilation was first observed in Jewish and Japanese Americans,[109] although both groups now have achieved a high level of social assimilation as reflected by their high intermarriage rates.[110] There is no question that children of post-1965 Asian immigrants are highly acculturated. The question, however, is whether they have achieved a similarly high level of social assimilation. For example, a survey conducted in New York City showed that Korean high school students, while well assimilated to American culture and weakly attached to Korean culture, were strongly involved in Korean social networks.[111]

Classical assimilationist theorists proposed a *zero-sum* model of assimilation.[112] In this view, an increasing acceptance of the new culture and greater social relations with members of the host society leads to a concomitant decline in an immigrant's native culture and his or her involvement in co-ethnic networks. To put it alternately, assimilation involves the gradual replacement of an immigrant's ethnic culture and social networks with those of the host society. Thus, in this model it is impossible for a well-educated, highly assimilated person to maintain a high level of ethnic attachment.

A zero-sum model may be useful as a description of the basic policy of the U.S. government toward minority and immigrant groups—and also the most prevailing ideology of assimilation in the U.S. until the 1960s—which has been characterized by Anglo conformity.[113] However, it is not helpful in understanding the experiences of immigrants and their children, particularly in the post-1965 era. That is, the mode of adaptation by contemporary immigrants to American society usually does not involve a zero-sum game in which a progressive acculturation and assimilation into the American social structure leads to a gradual decline in their ethnic attachment. For example, Hurh and Kim, based on data collected in Los Angeles, demonstrated that although Korean immigrants achieved assimilation in proportion to their duration of residence in the U.S., their strong ethnic attachment was largely unaffected by their assimilation rates.[114] They proposed an *additive* model of assimilation for Korean immigrants, indicating that "certain aspects of American culture and social relations are added on to Korean immigrants' traditional culture and social networks."

An additive model suggests that some immigrants can achieve a high level of acculturation while maintaining their ethnic culture almost perfectly. Contemporary immigrants—and even their children—can maintain a strong bicultural orientation especially because of transnational ties to their home country, as previously discussed. A number of studies have shown how Latino and Asian immigrants maintain high levels of biculturality and binationality. I can use my own case as a typical example to illustrate the bicultural and binational orientations of contemporary immigrants. I subscribe to *The New York Times* and a Korean ethnic daily, a satellite duplicate of a major daily published in Seoul. Almost every evening, I hear news edited by the Korean Broadcasting Station in Seoul and broadcast via satellite to New York City while regularly listening to news provided by major U.S. TV networks. I visited Seoul for at least one month in each of the last three summers.

Although children of immigrants are well assimilated into American culture, many of them, particularly many 1.5-generation children, remain highly bicultural.[115] Until the 1960s, academic and journalistic writings emphasized assimilation—acculturation in particular—as a prerequisite to social mobility for immigrants and their offspring.[116] They considered strong attachments to the ethnic culture and ethnic networks as a barrier to social mobility. Further, they assumed that being exposed to two languages at home would discourage the offspring of immigrants from learning English and thereby stunt their intelligence. In the ultimate analysis, they argued that children of immigrants should get rid of their parental culture as soon as possible and learn English and about the mainstream culture in order to succeed academically and achieve social mobility. This view was consistent with the U.S. government's monolithic assimilationist policy and the Anglo conformity ideology before the 1970s.

However, empirical research and theoretical works on immigrant children and children of immigrants since the late 1980s have rejected these traditional views about the relationships between ethnicity/assimilation and social mobility. The new theoretical viewpoints consider assimilation into some aspects of American culture harmful to their academic achievement and social mobility. They also emphasize that retention of the ethnic culture and involvement in ethnic networks can facilitate the economic mobility of immigrants and their children. To elaborate these theoretical viewpoints, I must introduce *segmented assimilation theory*, developed by Portes and his colleagues to suggest the modes of adaptation of the new second generation.[117] According to this theory, descendants of post-1965 immigrants will adopt three different modes of adaptation, depending on their race, residential locale, parents' socioeconomic status, and the family and community structure: (1) incorporation into the white middle class, with a high level of socioeconomic mobility; (2) incorporation into the minority culture with no mobility; or (3) retention of ethnic culture with mobility found within the ethnic community.

The first mode of adaptation is a replication of a path suggested by assimilationist theorists, while the other two challenge assimilationist assumptions. Children of lower-class immigrants, particularly those of Latino and Caribbean black immigrants, usually live in inner-city, low-income, minority neighborhoods. Their close contact with concentrations of native-born minorities is likely to lead them to assimilate into the "adversarial subculture developed by marginalized native youth," which, in turn, will block their academic achievements and thereby their social mobility.[118]

The idea of the adversarial, minority youth subculture was originally developed by Fordham and Ogbu to explain the poor academic performance of blacks.[119] In their view, many black students fail because their youth culture defines hard work and success in school as a "white" thing and because their desire to fit in with black peers weakens their efforts to excel academically. Therefore, the sector of American society into which immigrants acculturate partly determines the social mobility of their offspring. Some immigrant communities, such as the Korean and Cuban communities, have developed large numbers of ethnic organizations and ethnic businesses, which provide the second generation with a mobility ladder without assimilation into the white middle class. Proponents of segmented assimilation consider it another mode of adaptation open to the offspring of post-1965 immigrants.

No empirical study has tested the validity of the hypotheses derived from segmented assimilation theory concerning labor market opportunities for descendants of post-1965 immigrants. However, a number of empirical studies have examined the relationships between levels of ethnic attachment/assimilation and school performance using high school students.[120] These studies have consistently supported the view that second-generation and immigrant children who have strong ethnic attachments and ethnic identities are positively correlated with the motivations and behavioral traits conducive to successful academic performance. For example, Margaret Gibson showed that second-generation Punjabi students achieved a higher level of academic success than the majority of Anglo students mainly because they adopted only desirable American ways; they resisted full assimilation by maintaining their separate cultural identity and adopting their parents' values and attitudes.[121] She referred to this type of adaptation as "accommodation" without "full assimilation." Zhou and Bangston demonstrated that Vietnamese high school students in a predominantly black neighborhood who were more tightly bound to ethnic networks in the Vietnamese immigrant community were more academically successful and more college-oriented than those who were more assimilated into the local subculture.[122] In their study of Southeast Asian refugee students, Rumbaut and Ima found that a sense of ethnic resilience was positively correlated with grade point average.[123]

There are other findings that challenge assimilationist assumptions. The conventional wisdom of assimilation theory predicts that the longer immigrant children live in the U.S., the better they will perform in school. However, several recent studies of immigrant children have revealed that their length of residence in the U.S. is negatively correlated with their adjustment to school in terms of motivations, school performance, and desirable behavior.[124] Also, many studies have found that bilingual students from immigrant families outperform both English monolingual students and native-born white students.[125]

Bilingualism and/or strong ethnic attachment are positively associated with academic performance mainly because students with bilingual skills and/or those who are actively involved in the immigrant community retain parental and community values, such as a strong work ethic, aspirations for education and upward mobility, and respect for adults—all values conducive to good academic performance. All these findings clearly indicate that the wholesale assimilation of immigrants' offspring into American culture, particularly acculturation into the American minority youth culture, is detrimental to their academic performance. For this reason, researchers have recently emphasized *additive assimilation* or *selective assimilation* as a viable strategy for the successful adjustment of immigrants and their children to American society and schools. The other important reason, not emphasized by researchers,[126] that bilingual or bicultural students achieve a higher level of academic achievement is that schooling in the U.S. has placed a great emphasis on racial and cultural diversity during recent years, to the extent that they reward rather than punish bilingual and bicultural students.

Although empirical data are currently unavailable, descendants of post-1965 immigrants with strong bilingual and bicultural orientations are likely to be successful in their occupations as well. Values such as a strong work ethic and respect for adults seem to be as conducive to occupational mobility as to academic performance. Moreover, an emphasis on multiculturalism and transnationalism has opened up many professional jobs in the government and private sectors—particularly in academia—as well as within the ethnic community, for second-generation adults who are highly bilingual and bicultural. For example, many 1.5- and second-generation Koreans have found academic positions over the last several years mainly because they specialized in Korean studies or Korean American studies. Their Korean background, Korean language skills, and familiarity with Korean culture have helped them to find academic positions. Segmented assimilation theory, focusing on the ethnic market, has not suggested the possibility of second-generation adults using their ethnicity to find professional jobs in the general labor market.

ENDNOTES

1. Won Moo Hurh and Kwang Chung Kim, *Korean Immigrants in North America: A Structural Analysis of Ethnic Confinement and Adhesive Adaptation* (Madison, NJ: Fairleigh Dickinson University Press, 1984); Jack David Miller and Reed Coughlan, "The Poverty of Primordialism: The Demystification of Ethnic Attachments," *Ethnic and Racial Studies,* vol. 16 (1993), pp. 183–202; Milton Yinger, "Ethnicity," *Annual Review of Sociology,* vol. 11, pp. 151–180.

2. Pyong Gap Min, *Caught in the Middle: Korean Merchants in America's Multiethnic Cities* (Berkeley: University of California Press, 1996), p. 5; Francois Nielsen, "Toward a Theory of Ethnic Solidarity in Modern Societies," *American Sociological Review,* vol. 50 (1985), pp. 133–149.

3. Richard Alba, *Ethnic Identity: The Transformation of White America* (New Haven, CT: Yale University Press, 1990); Lola Romanucci-Ross and George De Vos (eds.), *Ethnic Identity: Creation, Conflict, and Accommodation* (Walnut Creek, CA: AltaMira Press, 1995); Philip Kasinitz, *Caribbean New York: Black Immigrants and the Politics of Race* (Ithaca, NY: Cornell University Press, 1992).

4. Milton Gordon, *Assimilation in American Life: The Role of Race, Religion, and National Origin* (New York: Oxford University Press, 1964); Robert Park, *Race and Culture* (New York: Free Press, 1950); W. Lloyd Warner and Leo Srole, *The Social System of American Ethnic Groups* (New Haven, CT: Yale University Press, 1945); Lewis Wirth, *The Ghetto* (Chicago: University of Chicago Press, 1928).

5. James McKay, "An Exploratory Synthesis of Primordial and Mobilizationist Approaches to Ethnic Phenomena," *Ethnic and Racial Studies*, vol. 5 (1982), pp. 395–420.

6. Harold Abramson, *Ethnic Diversity in Catholic America* (New York: John Wiley, 1973); Gordon, 1964; Andrew Greeley, *Ethnicity in the United States: A Preliminary Reconnaissance* (New York: John Wiley, 1976); Harold Isaacs, *Idols of the Tribe* (New York: Harper and Row, 1975); Nash Manning, *The Cauldron of Ethnicity in the Modern World* (Chicago: University of Chicago Press, 1989).

7. William Yancy, Eugene Ericksen, and Richard Juliani, "Emergent Ethnicity: A Review and Reformulation," *American Sociological Review*, vol. 76 (1976), pp. 391–403.

8. Michael Banton, *Racial and Ethnic Competition* (New York: Cambridge University Press, 1983); Frederick Bath (ed.), *Ethnic Groups and Boundaries* (Boston: Little, Brown, and Company, 1969); Edna Bonacich and John Modell, *The Economic Basis of Ethnic Solidarity: Small Business in the Japanese American Community* (Berkeley: University of California Press, 1980); Leo Despress, *Ethnicity and Resource Competition in Plural Societies* (The Hague: Mouton Publishers, 1975); Michael Hechter, "Group Formation and the Cultural Division of Labor," *American Journal of Sociology*, vol. 84 (1978), pp. 293–318; Min, 1996; Francois Nielsen, "The Flemish Movement in Belgium after World War II: A Dynamic Analysis," *American Sociological Review*, vol. 45 (1980), pp. 76–94; Susan Olzak and Joane Nagel (eds.), *Competitive Ethnic Relations* (New York: Academic Press, 1986); Jeffrey Reitz, *The Survival of Ethnic Groups* (Toronto: McGraw Hill, 1980).

9. George De Vos, "Preface: 1995," In *Ethnic Identity*, p. 28.

10. Nash, 1989, p. 5.

11. Charles Jaret, *Contemporary Racial and Ethnic Relations* (New York: Harper Collins College Publishers, 1995), p. 85.

12. Daniel Bell, "Ethnicity and Social Change," in *Ethnicity: Theory and Experience*, edited by Nathan Glazer and Daniel Moynihan (Cambridge, MA: Harvard University Press, 1975), p. 169.

13. Dino Cinel, *From Italy to San Francisco* (Stanford, CA: Stanford University Press, 1982).

14. Sidney Goldstein and Alice Goldstein, *Jews on the Move* (Albany: SUNY Press, 1996), p. 203; Arthur Goren, *The American Jews* (Cambridge, MA: Harvard University Press, 1982), p. 110.

15. Alba, 1990, p. 76.

16. Gillian Stevens, "Nativity, Intermarriage and Mother Tongue Shift," *American Sociological Review*, vol. 50 (1985), pp. 74–83.

17. Waters, 1990, p. 116; Alba, 1990, p. 94.

18. Alba, 1990, p. 94.

19. David Lopez, "Language: Diversity and Assimilation," in *Ethnic Los Angeles,* edited by Roger Waldinger and Mehdi Bozorgmehr (New York: Russell Sage Foundation, 1997), p. 151.

20. Alba, 1990, p. 91.

21. Herbert Gans, "Symbolic Ethnicity: The Future of Ethnic Groups and Cultures in America," *Ethnic and Racial Studies,* vol. 2 (1979), pp. 1–20.

22. D. B. Kraybill and M. A. Olshan (eds.), *The Amish Struggle with Modernity* (Hanover, NH: University Press of New England, 1994); M. Leon, *The Roots of Modern Mormonism* (Cambridge, MA: Harvard University Press, 1979).

23. For an overview of ethnoreligious conflicts, see Milton Yinger, *Ethnicity: Source of Strength? Source of Conflict?* (Albany: SUNY Press, 1994), pp. 270–300.

24. S. M. Tomasi and M. H. Engel, *The Italian Experience in the United States* (Staten Island, NY: Center for Migration Studies, 1970), p. 186.

25. S. Rosenberg, *The New Jewish Identity in America* (New York: Hipocrene Books, 1985).

26. Robert Mirak, "Armenians," in *Harvard Encyclopedia of American Ethnic Groups,* edited by Stephen Thernstrom (Cambridge, MA: Harvard University Press, 1980), pp. 150–154.

27. Georges Friedman, *The End of the Jewish People,* translated by Eric Mosbacher (New York: Doubleday, 1967).

28. Goren, 1982, pp. 108–110.

29. Parminder Bhachu, *Twice Migrants: East African Sikh Settlers in Britain* (London: Tavistock Publications, 1985); Yen Le Espiritu, "Beyond the Boat People: Ethnicization of American Life," *Amerasia Journal,* vol. 15 (1989), pp. 49–67.

30. Herbert Gans, *The Urban Villagers: Group and Class in the Life of Italian-Americans* (New York: The Macmillan Company, 1962).

31. Peter Kwong, *The New Chinatown* (New York: Hill and Wang, 1987); Joan Moore, *Going Down to the Barrio: Homeboys and Homegirls in Change* (Philadelphia: Temple University Press, 1991).

32. D. Y. Yuan, "Voluntary Segregation: A Study of New Chinatown," *Phylon,* vol. 24 (1963), pp. 25–265.

33. J. Desbarats and L. Holland, "Indochinese Settlement Patterns in Orange County," *Amerasia Journal,* vol. 10 (1983), pp. 23–46; Pyong Gap Min, "Korean Immigrants in Los Angeles," in *Immigration and Entrepreneurship: Culture, Capital, and Ethnic Networks,* edited by Ivan Light and Parminder Bhachu (New York: Transaction, 1993), pp. 185–204; Timothy Fong, *The First Suburban Chinatown: The Remaking of Monterey Park, California* (Philadelphia: Temple University Press, 1994).

34. Pyong Gap Min, "An Overview of Asian Americans," in *Asian Americans: Contemporary Trends and Issues,* edited by Pyong Gap Min (Newbury Park, CA: Sage Publications, 1995), p. 23.

35. Pyong Gap Min, "Cultural and Economic Boundaries of Korean Ethnicity: A Comparative Analysis," *Ethnic and Racial Studies,* vol. 14 (1991), p. 233; Yancy et al., 1976, p. 393.

36. Michael Hechter, "Political Economy of Ethnic Change," *American Journal of Sociology,* vol. 79 (1974), pp. 1151–1178; Michael Hechter, *Internal Colonialism: The Celtic Fringe in British National Development* (Berkeley: University of California Press, 1975); Hechter,

1978; Michael Hechter, D. Friedman, and M. Appelbaum, "A Theory of Ethnic Collective Action," *International Migration Review,* vol. 16 (1982), pp. 212–234.

37. Hechter, 1978.

38. Edna Bonacich, "A Theory of Middleman Minorities," *American Sociological Review,* vol. 35 (1973), pp. 583–594; Walter Zenner, *Minorities in the Middle: A Cross-Cultural Analysis* (Albany: SUNY Press, 1991).

39. Min, 1996.

40. Michael Hannan, "The Dynamics of Ethnic Boundaries in Modern States," in *National Development and the World System,* edited by John Meyer and Michael Hannan (Chicago: University of Chicago Press, 1979), pp. 253–275; Joane Nagel and Susan Olzak, "Ethnic Mobilization in New and Old States: An Extension of the Competition Model," *Social Problems,* vol. 30 (1983), pp. 355–374; Nielsen, 1980; Susan Olzak, "Contemporary Ethnic Mobilization," *Annual Review of Sociology,* vol. 9 (1983), pp. 355–377.

41. Susan Olzak and Joane Nagel, "Introduction, Competitive Ethnic Relations: An Overview," in *Competitive Ethnic Relations,* p. 2.

42. Alejandro Portes, "The Rise of Ethnicity: Determinants of Ethnic Perceptions among Cuban Exiles in Miami," *American Sociological Review,* vol. 49 (1984), pp. 383–397.

43. Cynthia Enloe, "The Growth of the State and Ethnic Mobilization," *Ethnic and Racial Studies,* vol. 4 (1981), pp. 123–136; Nathan Glazer and Daniel Moynihan, "Introduction," in *Ethnicity,* pp. 1–28; Joane Nagel, "The Political Mobilization of Native Americans," in *Majority and Minority: The Dynamics of Race and Ethnicity in America, Fourth Edition,* edited by Norman Yetman (Boston: Allyn and Bacon, 1985), pp. 457–463; Joane Nagel, "The Political Construction of Ethnicity," in *Competitive Ethnic Relations,* pp. 93–112.

44. Illsoon Park, "The Korean Minority's National Education in China," in *The Current Status and Future Prospects of Overseas Koreans* [in Korean], edited by Research Institute on World Affairs (New York, 1986).

45. Jyotirindra Das Gupta, "Ethnicity, Language Demands, and National Development in India," in *Ethnicity,* pp. 466–488.

46. Manju Sheth, "Asian Indian Americans," in *Asian Americans,* pp. 188–189.

47. For information about South Asians' ethnic and panethnic identities, see Lavina Dhingra Shankar and Rajimi Srikanth (eds.), *A Part, Yet Apart: South Asians in Asian America* (Philadelphia: Temple University Press, 1997).

48. Ronald Taylor, "Black Ethnicity and the Persistence of Ethnogenesis," *American Journal of Sociology,* vol. 84 (1979), pp. 1401–1423. See also Jaret, 1996, pp. 381–386 for an extended discussion of ethnogenesis.

49. Eugene Roosens, *Creating Ethnicity: The Process of Ethnogenesis* (Newbury Park, CA: Sage Publications, 1989).

50. Yancy et al., 1976; Roosens, 1989.

51. W. Gerson, "Jews at Christmas Time: Role Strain and Strain Reducing Mechanisms," in *Social Problems in a Changing World,* edited by W. Gerson (New York: Crowell, 1969), pp. 65–76; S. L. Madhubuti, *The Story of Kwanzaa* (Chicago: The Third World Press, 1977).

52. Eric Lincoln, *The Black Muslims in America* (Boston: Beacon Press, 1961).

53. De Vos, 1995, p. 22.

54. James Mooney, *The Ghost Dance Religion and the Sioux Outbreak of 1890* (Chicago: University of Chicago Press, 1965).

55. Yinger, 1994, p. 262.

56. Madison Grant, *The Passing of the Great Race* (New York: Charles Scribner's Sons, 1916).

57. Mary Waters, *Ethnic Options: Choosing Identities in America* (Berkeley: University of California Press, 1990).

58. Waters, 1994; T. M. Woldemikael, *Becoming Black American: Haitians and American Institutions in Evanston, Illinois* (New York: AMS Press, 1989).

59. Don Nakanish, "Surviving Democracy's 'Mistakes': Japanese Americans and the Enduring Legacy of Executive Order 9066," *Amerasia Journal,* vol. 19, no. 1 (1993), pp. 7–36.

60. Linda Revilla, "Filipino American Identity: Transcending the Crisis," in *Filipino Americans: Transformation and Identity,* edited by Maria P. Root (Newbury Park, CA: Sage Publications, 1997), p. 101.

61. For an extended discussion of changes from the negative to the positive image of Asian Americans, see Won Moo Hurh and Kwang Chung Kim, "The 'Success' Image of Asian Americans: Its Validity, and Its Practical and Theoretical Implications," *Ethnic and Racial Studies,* vol. 12 (1989), pp. 512–537.

62. Ivan Light, Georges Sabagh, Mehdi Bozorgmehr, and Claudia Der-Martirosian, "Internal Ethnicity in the Ethnic Economy," *Ethnic and Racial Studies,* vol. 16 (1993), pp. 581–597. See also Mehdi Bozorgmehr, "Internal Ethnicity: Iranians in Los Angeles," *Sociological Perspectives,* vol. 40 (1997), pp. 387–408.

63. Min, 1991.

64. Das Gupta, 1975.

65. See Kwang Chung Kim, Won Moo Hurh, and Marilyn Fernandez, "Intra-Group Differences in Business Participation: Three Asian Immigrant Groups," *International Migration Review,* vol. 23 (1989), pp. 73–95.

66. There are two Indian business districts in New York City, one in Jackson Heights and the other in Richmond Hill. The Indian business district in Jackson Heights, commonly called "Little India," was created mainly by immigrants from India while the one in Richmond Hill has been recently established by Guyanian Indian immigrants.

67. Pyong Gap Min, "A Comparison of Korean and Indian Immigrants in New York in Community Organization," Paper presented at the Annual Meeting of the Eastern Sociological Society, Philadelphia, March 1998.

68. Chinese and Korean immigrants in New York City succeeded in getting their candidates elected as school board members in the late 1980s and the early 1990s, respectively. However, Indian immigrants succeeded only in 1996. In the 1996 school board election, three Chinese, three Korean, and one Indian immigrants were elected as school board members in New York City.

69. Pyong Gap Min and Lucy Chen, "A Comparison of Korean, Chinese, and Indian Immigrants in Ethnic Attachment," Paper presented at the Annual Meeting of the American Sociological Association, Washington, DC, 1997.

70. See Das Gupta, 1975, p. 471; Maxine Fisher, "Creating Ethnic Identity: Asian Indians in the New York City Area," *Urban Anthropology,* vol. 7 (1978), pp. 282.

71. Antonio J. A. Pido, *The Philipinos in America: Macro/Micro Dimensions of Immigration and Integration* (Staten Island, NY: Center for Migration Studies, 1986), p. 95.

72. Pauline Agbayani-Siewert and Linda Revilla, "Filipino Americans," in *Asian Americans,* p. 154; Elena Yu, "Filipino Migration and Community Organizations in the United States," *California Sociologist,* vol. 3 (1980), p. 96.

73. Ivan Light, *Ethnic Enterprise in America: Business and Welfare among Chinese, Japanese, and Blacks* (Berkeley: University of California Press, 1972); Stanford Lyman, *Chinese Americans* (New York: Random House, 1974).

74. Kwong, 1987; Luciano Mangiafico, *Contemporary Asian Immigrants: Patterns of Filipino, Korean, and Chinese Settlement in the United States* (New York: Praeger, 1988).

75. Pengang Yang, "Tenacious Unity in a Contentious Community: Cultural and Religious Dynamics in a Chinese Christian Church," in *Gatherings in Diaspora: Religious Communities and the New Immigration,* edited by Stephen Warner and Judith Wittner (Philadelphia: Temple University Press, 1998), pp. 342–345.

76. Min and Chen, 1997.

77. Espiritu, 1992; David Lopez and Yen Le Espiritu, "Panethnicity in the United States: A Theoretical Framework," *Ethnic and Racial Studies,* vol. 13 (1990), pp. 198–224; Michael Omni, "Out of the Melting Pot and Into the Fire: Race Relations Policy," in *State of Asian Pacific America: Policy Issues to the Year 2020,* edited by LEAP Asian American Public Policy Institute and UCLA Asian American Studies Center (Los Angeles, 1993), pp. 199–214; Michael Omni and Howard Winant, *Racial Formation in the United States from the 1960s to the 1980s* (New York: Routledge, 1986); Dana Takagi, "Post-Civil Rights Politics and Asian American Identity: Admissions and Higher Education," in *Race,* edited by Stephen Gregory and Roger Sanjek (New Brunswick, NJ: Rutgers University Press, 1994), pp. 229–242.

78. Felix Padilla, "Latino Ethnicity in the City of Chicago," in *Competitive Ethnic Relations,* pp. 153–172.

79. Sucheng Chan, *Asian Americans: An Interpretive History* (Boston: Twayne Publishers, 1991), pp. 179–180; Takagi, 1994.

80. U.S. Commission on Civil Rights, *Civil Rights Issues Facing Asian Americans in the 1990s* (Washington, DC: U.S. Government Printing Office, 1992), p. 25.

81. Min, 1996, p. 79.

82. Stewart Kwoh and Mindy Hui, "Empowering Our Communities: Political Policy," in *The State of Asian Pacific America,* pp. 189–197.

83. John Horton, *The Politics of Diversity: Immigration, Resistance, and Change in Monterey Park, California* (Philadelphia: Temple University Press, 1995), Chapter 6.

84. In 1990, Asian Americans comprised 22 percent of the population in Community District 7, which encompasses Flushing, Whitestone, and College Point. See the New York City Department of Planning, *Demographic Profiles: A Portrait of New York City's Community District from the 1980 & 1990 Censuses of Population and Housing* (New York: New York City Department of Planning, 1992), p. 217.

85. In the 1990 school board election, Chinese voters made the Chinese candidate the first choice and the Korean candidate the second choice, while Korean voters reversed the order of choice. As a result, the two Asian candidates received the largest numbers of ballots among the seven elected school board members.

86. Espiritu, 1992, pp. 63–64; William Wei, *The Asian American Movement* (Philadelphia: Temple University Press, 1993), Chapter 8.

87. Kwoh and Hui, 1993, pp. 192–194.

88. Russell Endo and William Wei, "On the Development of Asian American Studies Programs," in *Reflections on Shattered Windows: Promises and Prospects for Asian American Studies,* edited by Gary Okihiro, Shirley Hune, Arthur Hansen, and John Liu (Pullman: Washington State University, 1988), pp. 5–15.

89. Wei, 1993, p. 135.

90. The exceptions are Stacy Lee, "Perceptions of Panethnicity among Asian American High School Students," *Amerasia Journal,* vol. 22 (1996), pp. 109–125; Lopez and Espiritu, 1990; and Shankar and Srikanth, 1997.

91. Despite commonalities in cultural and physical characteristics, the Chinese and Korean communities have had little contact with the Japanese community during recent years. There are two important reasons for this. First, anti-Japanese feelings are strong among Chinese and Korean immigrants who experienced Japanese colonization in their home countries. Second, in their values and positions on many social issues, Chinese and Korean immigrants differ significantly from Japanese Americans, who consist mainly of well-assimilated native-born citizens.

92. In the early twentieth century, the U.S. government awarded Asian Indian immigrants citizenship on the grounds that they were not "Mongolians." However, in 1923 the U.S. Supreme Court ruled that Asian Indians were not "Caucasians" and therefore not eligible for citizenship. In 1970, the U.S. Census Bureau included Asian Indians in the white category. After Indian community leaders lobbied for reclassification of Indians, the U.S. Census Bureau classified them as an Asian group in 1980. For information about how the U.S. census treated Asian Indians, see Sharon Lee, "Racial Classification in the U.S. Census: 1890–1990," *Ethnic and Racial Studies,* vol. 16 (1993), pp. 75–94.

93. Anu Gupta, "At the Crossroads: College Activism and Its Impact on Asian American Identity Formation," in *A Part, Yet Apart,* pp. 127–145. Of course, many South Asian college students are likely to have multiple identities, depending upon situations. An Indian American may identify him or herself as a Hindu, a Gujarat, an Indian, or a South Asian.

94. A number of essays by South Asian scholars, activists, and writers included in *A Part, Yet Apart* addressed the issue.

95. Lavina Dhingra Shankar and Rajini Srikanth, "Closing the Gap: South Asians Challenge Asian American Studies," in *A Part, Yet Apart,* pp. 1–22; Sumantra Toto Sinha, "From Campus to Community Politics in Asian America," in *A Part, Yet Apart,* pp. 146–167.

96. Ruben Rumbaut, "Origins and Destinies: Immigration to the United States since World War II," *Sociological Forum,* vol. 9 (1995), pp. 583–612.

97. Raynold Farley, *The New American Reality: Who We Are, How We Got Here, Where We Are Going* (New York: Russell Sage Foundation, 1996); Robert Manning, "Multiculturalism in the United States: Clashing Concepts, Changing Demographics, and Competing Cultures," *International Journal of Group Tensions,* vol. 25 (1995), pp. 117–167; Alejandro Portes and Ruben Rumbaut, *Immigrant America: A Portrait, Second Edition* (Berkeley: University of California Press, 1996). Already in 1990, minority populations (Latino, black, and Asian) comprised the majority of the population in each of the four major cities listed above.

98. David Theo Goldberg, *Multiculturalism: A Critical Reader* (Cambridge, MA: Basil Blackwell, 1994).

99. Linda Chavez, *Out of the Barrio: Toward a New Politics of Hispanic Assimilation* (New York: Basic Books, 1991), Chapter 1.

100. Evelyn Hu-Dehart, "P.C. and the Politics of Multiculturalism in Higher Education," in *Race*, pp. 242–256.

101. Jonnella Butler and John Walter, *Transforming the Curriculum: Ethnic Studies and Women's Studies* (Albany: SUNY Press, 1991).

102. For conservative critiques of the multicultural movement in higher educational institutes, see Allan Bloom, *The Closing of the American Mind* (New York: Simon and Schuster, 1987); Dinesh D'Souza, *Illiberal Education: The Politics of Race and Sex on Campus* (New York: Free Press, 1991); Arthur M. Schlesinger, *The Disuniting of America* (New York: Norton, 1992).

103. At present, Korea is the only country that is still ideologically divided into two political entities, the legacy of the cold war period.

104. Graham Smith (ed.), *Federalism: The Multiethnic Challenge* (London: Longman, 1995).

105. Linda Basch, Nina Glick Schiller, and Christina Szanton-Blanc (eds.), *Nations Unbounded: Transnational Projects, Postcolonial Predicaments, and Deterritorialized Nations* (New York: Gordon and Breach Science, 1994); Steven J. Gold, "Transnationalism and Vocabularies of Motive in International Migration: The Case of Israelis in the United States," *Sociological Perspectives,* vol. 40 (1997), pp. 409–426; Michael Kearney, "The Local and the Global: The Anthropology of Globalization and Transnationalism," *Annual Review of Anthropology*, vol. 24 (1995), pp. 547–565; Pyong Gap Min, *Changes and Conflicts: Korean Immigrant Families in New York* (Boston: Allyn and Bacon, 1998), Chapter 7; Nestor P. Rodriguez, "The Real 'New World Order': The Globalization of Racial and Ethnic Relations in the Late Twentieth Century," in *The Bubbling Cauldron: Race, Ethnicity, and the Urban Crisis,* edited by Michael Peter Smith and Joe Feagin (Minneapolis: University of Minnesota Press, 1995), pp. 211–225; Nina Glick Schiller, Linda Basch, and Christina Szanton-Blanc (eds.), *Toward a Transnational Perspective on Migration: Race, Class, Ethnicity, and Nationalism Reconsidered* (New York: New York Academy of Science, 1992); Constance Sutton, "The Caribbeanization of New York City and the Emergence of a Transnational Socio-cultural System," in *Caribbean Life in New York City,* edited by Constance Sutton and Elsa Chaney (Staten Island, NY: Center for Migration Studies, 1987), pp. 25–29.

106. Schlesinger, 1992,

107. Gordon, 1964, Chapter 3.

108. Gordon, 1964, p. 77.

109. Harry Kitano, *Japanese Americans: An Evolution of a Subculture* (Englewood Cliffs, NJ: Prentice Hall, 1976); M. E. Spiro, "The Acculturation without Assimilation," *American Journal of Sociology,* vol. 66 (1960), pp. 275–288.

110. Steven Cohen, *American Modernity and Jewish Identity* (New York: Tavistock Publications, 1985); Harry Kitano, Wai-Tsang Yeung, Lynn Chai, and Herbert Hatanaka, "Asian-American Interracial Marriages," *Journal of Marriage and the Family,* vol. 46 (1984), pp. 179–190.

111. Min and Choi, 1993.

112. Gordon, 1964; S. G. Cole and M. Cole, *Minorities and American Promise* (New York: Harper and Brothers, 1954); Robert Park, *Race and Culture* (New York: Free Press, 1950); Warner and Srole, 1945, pp. 283–296.

113. Gordon, 1964, pp. 88–114; Jaret, 1995, pp. 400–405. The U.S. government tried to strip Native Americans and immigrants of their native cultures and force them into the

Anglo-Saxon culture with great rapidity. The major goal of public education was to indoctrinate children, immigrant children in particular, into American customs and values based on Anglo-Saxon culture. The Anglo conformity ideology was most prevalent in the first two decades of the twentieth century, culminating in the establishment of discriminatory immigration quotas based on national origin in the early 1920s.

114. Hurh and Kim, 1984.

115. For a discussion of the strong bicultural orientations of children of contemporary immigrants, see several essays in Thomas Dublin (ed.), *Becoming American, Becoming Ethnic: College Students Explore Their Roots* (Philadelphia: Temple University Press, 1997).

116. Alejandro Portes and Richard Schauffler, "Language and the Second Generation Bilingualism Yesterday and Today," *International Migration Review,* vol. 28 (1994), pp. 641–643; Alejandro Portes and Min Zhou, "The New Second-Generation: Segmented Assimilation and Its Variants," *The Annals of the American Academy of Political and Social Science,* vol. 530 (November 1993), p. 82.

117. Alejandro Portes, "Segmented Assimilation among New Immigrant Youth," in *California's Immigrant Children,* pp. 71–76; Portes and Zhou, 1993; Waters, 1994; Min Zhou, "Segmented Assimilation: Issues, Controversies, and Recent Research on the New Second Generation," *International Migration Review,* vol. 31 (1997), pp. 975–1008.

118. Portes, p. 73.

119. S. Fordham and John Ogbu, "Black Students' School Success: Coping with the 'Burden of Acting White,' " *The Urban Review,* vol. 18 (1986), pp. 176–206; S. Fordham, "Racelessness as a Factor in Black Students' School Success: Pragmatic Strategy or Pyrrhic Victory," *Harvard Educational Review,* vol. 58, pp. 54–84.

120. Gibson, 1988; Margaret A. Gibson and John Ogbu (eds.), *Minority Status and Schooling: A Comparative Study of Immigrant and Involuntary Minorities* (New York: Garland, 1991); Mari E. Matute-Biangchi, "Ethnic Identities and Patterns of School Success and Failure among Mexican-Descent and Japanese-American Students in a California High School," *American Journal of Education,* vol. 95, pp. 233–255; Rumbaut and Cornelius, 1995; Ruben Rumbaut and Kenji Ima, *Adaptation of Southeast Asian Refugee Youth: A Comparative Study* (Washington, DC: U.S. Office of Refugee Resettlement, 1988); Zhou and Bangston, 1998.

121. Gibson, 1988.

122. Zhou and Bangston, 1998.

123. Rumbaut and Ima, 1988.

124. Grace Kao and Marta Tienda, "Optimism and Achievement: The Educational Performance of Immigrant Youth," *Social Science Quarterly,* vol. 76 (1995), pp. 1–19; Rumbaut and Ima, 1988; Carol Suarez-Orozco and Marcelo M. Suarez-Orozco, *Transformations: Migration, Family Life, and Achievement Motivation among Latino Adolescents* (Stanford, CA: Stanford University Press, 1995).

125. Robert Fernandez and Francois Nielsen, "Bilingualism and Hispanic Scholastic Achievement: Some Baseline Results," *Social Science Research,* vol. 15 (1986), pp. 43–70; Ruben Rumbaut, "The New Californians: Comparative Research Findings on the Educational Progress of Immigrant Children," in *California's Immigrant Children,* pp. 17–69; Zhou and Bangston, 1998.

126. The exception is Mia Tuan, "Korean and Russian Students in a Los Angeles High School: Exploring the Alternative Strategies of Two High-Achieving Groups," in *California's Immigrant Children,* pp. 107–131.

Part Two

Ethnic Culture
An Identity in Conflict

THE FIRST THREE essayists—all Korean American—are highly critical of their parents' native culture. Ruth Chung and Rose Kim base their criticism of Korean culture on its patriarchal traditions and gender stereotypes. For them, ethnicity and gender identity are inextricably intertwined. "Some of my earliest memories are of suffering the degradation of being female, and for a long time I could not help but associate Korean culture with the oppression of women," Kim writes. "My parents encouraged my brothers to attend the best universities and to become lawyers and doctors. My sister and I were only groomed for marriage—constantly being told to look pretty, talk softly, and sit properly."

Alex Jeong is also critical of Korean culture, but his thoughts have been shaped by the culture's ostracization of the physically disabled. In Korea, the physically disabled lack the rights they have in the U.S. Jeong's partial paralysis, caused by an automobile accident in law school, stripped him of his standing in the Korean immigrant community. After initially being regarded as a potential leader within his church, after his accident Jeong was treated like an infant by fellow parishioners. Jeong eventually stopped attending church for this reason. Now working as an assistant district attorney in Brooklyn, New York, Jeong is helping to reshape the community's perception of physical disabilities.

To a greater extent than the other contributors, Chung and Kim tried to hide their ethnicity and to act like their white peers. Acutely aware of the differences between their lives and those of their predominantly white classmates, Chung and Kim rebelled against the Korean values of their parents. Their resistance to their parents' values stemmed both from the pressure to fit in with their white peers and from their rejection of Asian gender stereotypes. They both describe the feeling of wanting to be white as children. Yet, as they grew older, they realized that they were unable to escape their physical differences and grew more interested in and accepting of their ethnic past. They now describe their identities as being a hodgepodge of Asian, Korean, and American influences.

My Trek

THE LATEST INCARNATION of "Star Trek," the legendary science-fiction television series, premiered just a day after I was asked to write this essay describing my experiences as a Korean and an Asian American. For the first time in the history of the show that has spawned so many spin-offs, a woman—actress Kate Mulgrew—took the helm as the calm, reassuring, and commanding captain. Curiously enough, a prominent member of the U.S.S. Voyager was named Ensign Harry Kim, ostensibly a Korean.

The casting caught my attention because the television series had been the source of some of my fondest childhood memories—early Saturday evenings after dinner, with my sister and two brothers. Our parents forbade us to watch television on nights before school because they thought it would interfere with our studies. So, as soon as Friday evening arrived, we would be glued to the TV, or "the Devil's Box," as my grandmother called it.

As a child, I deeply resented my parents' prohibition on television because I missed popular shows such as "My Three Sons," "Alias Smith and Jones," and "Batman." But over time I've grown to appreciate their decision and would impose the same restriction on my own children, if I ever have any. As a result, I read more and daydreamed more often—and when I did get to watch television, I paid closer attention.

But beaming back to the Enterprise, I alternated between admiration for and infatuation with Captain James T. Kirk, the commander of the U.S.S. Enterprise. I wanted to be one of his conquests, but I also wanted "to explore new planets and new civilizations, to boldly go where no man has gone before."

The show's benevolent 1960s-ish themes of equality and respect for different cultures helped shape my social conscience—despite the constant violations of the Prime Directive to not meddle in other societies and the relegation of women to secondary roles as nurses, switchboard operators, and love objects. The show was unique in having a multiracial cast, including Uhuru, the African communications officer, Sulu, the Asian helmsman, and Chekhov, the Russian navigation officer.

The debut of a female captain in 1995 made me realize how much the world had changed since I was growing up. For though I longed to be like Kirk, when I was a child it seemed impossible, since I was female and Asian in a white, male-dominated society. For a while in my early teens, my loftiest goal was to become Secretary of State, a state office held by a Chinese American woman, March Fong Eu, in California in the 1970s. As late as my freshman year in college, I wished to be a white man so I could achieve my dreams of being an astronaut or president of the United States.

I did hang onto my dream of being a writer, and worked for six years as a journalist for a major daily newspaper in New York City. I've grown to appreciate my Korean heritage and my gender, and feel lucky to have been exposed to two cultures. But it is an outlook that has taken most of my life to achieve. The fact that Ensign Kim was played by a Chinese American actor, Garrett Wong, made me realize how much things still needed to change.

SOME OF MY earliest memories are of suffering the degradation of being female, and for a long time I could not help but associate Korean culture with the oppression of women. I believe that my reaction was inevitable in a culture where women primarily held domestic, nonpublic roles as housekeepers, mothers, wives, and prostitutes.

When guests arrived at our house, my sister and I were shuttled into the kitchen and forced to assist in preparing food for the guests. My brothers, meanwhile, were allowed to sit with the adults in the living room. Though I now enjoy cooking, I actively resisted learning even the basics as a youngster. A virtually straight-A student, I proudly received my first D in sewing in the eighth grade. Girls were forced to learn the domestic arts, a fact that I despised. I longed to be in wood or auto shop.

As the youngest daughter in a Korean family, I often found myself on the lowest rung of the social order. My parents encouraged my brothers to attend the best universities and to become lawyers and doctors. My sisters and I were only groomed for marriage—constantly being told to look pretty, talk softly, and sit properly. A bachelor's degree was considered essential for a suitable match.

The world outside my home seemed so much more open and inviting.

I WAS BORN and raised in a middle-class neighborhood of single-family houses in central Los Angeles. The lawns were well groomed, and fruit trees filled the spacious backyards. The neighborhood once had been predominantly Jewish, but was now divided mostly among second- and third-generation Japanese Americans and

African Americans. There were also a few second-generation Chinese Americans. My Korean family stood out as new immigrants.

My father was born in North Korea, and was the only surviving member of his family. He had been a journalist in Korea, and came to the United States in 1959 on a student visa. He attended Brigham Young University in Salt Lake City, Utah, to study English, and my mother joined him on a student visa two years later. They eventually moved to Los Angeles, where I was born in January, 1962. Though they talked about returning to their homeland, they were lured into staying by the good salaries and the prospect of owning their own home. They also preferred the American schools and the higher quality of life. My mother thought that the Korean schools were too restrictive and high-pressured. She told me years later that an older brother whom she'd been close to had committed suicide after failing to get into a good university.

In Los Angeles, my father worked as the editor of the *Shin Han Il-bo,* the city's oldest Korean newspaper. It was a one-man operation. Not only did he edit the newspaper, he wrote nearly all of the articles and did the typesetting himself. Eventually, in the early 1970s, he and my mother started a lucrative wig business. My mother recently commented on how tiny the Korean community had been in the early 1960s. "There was just a handful of us," she said. "We all knew each other. Nothing like today."

Though the only family I knew as an infant consisted of my mother and father, I had two brothers and a sister in South Korea. My parents had left them in the care of my maternal grandmother and other relatives. They saved money, bought a home, and then sent for their children. My older brother, Steven, then eight, and my sister, Sophia, six, came to the United States when I was about a year and a half. My older brother, Edward, came two years later with my maternal grandmother when he was about five.

My siblings were at the forefront of the modern wave of Koreans to immigrate to the U.S., and other students teased them for their stumbling English and different appearance. I was spared such harassment because I was assimilated and able to read English when I entered kindergarten. Still, I felt the stigma of being different. While my classmates had meat loaf and fried chicken for dinner, I ate pungent, spicy foods like *du-bu chi-gae* (soybean casserole) and *kimchi* (pickled cabbage). The smells of garlic and fermented soybean paste permeated the house, and I was embarrassed to invite my friends over.

Since most of our relatives were in South Korea, we lacked an extended family and rarely celebrated holidays, neither American ones such as the Fourth of July nor Korean ones such as *Chu-suk* (Harvest Festival). When my parents visited my school on Open House nights, I felt self-conscious and ashamed of their English, a reaction that embarrasses me today. I wish that I had been more generous toward my parents, but again, as a child, there was an enormous pressure to blend in or be "normal."

In the sixth grade, I entered a lottery to attend an affluent, oceanside junior high school, and was among the ten or so winners. The school was near a college campus, and many of the students were the children of academics or professionals. The junior high school closest to my home was in an impoverished section of the city and had poor academic scores. My parents tried to send all of us to better schools outside our zoned district.

My father drove me to school in the morning, and I would catch three public buses—an hour-and-a-half ride altogether—to get back home. After saving up some money, my parents started a coat factory in Seoul, Korea. As the business took off, they became more preoccupied with their work. My mother began spending months at a time in South Korea, eventually returning to the U.S. only once a year to maintain her resident status. My father, meanwhile, often traveled throughout the United States on business. By the ninth grade, I was waking up at 6:30 A.M. to catch the bus to school by myself.

Except for one Chinese American boy whose father was a mathematics professor, I was the only Asian at the junior high school. All the other lottery winners were black. Everyone else was white. Again, there was a sense of being different. While other students remained after school for extracurricular activities, I boarded the bus for the long trip home. I was in the school orchestra and lugged my cello back and forth to school each day. I was very fat and had only a few friends. Outside of a few of the others who were bussed, I hung out with Laura, the daughter of an Italian American romance languages professor. Still, I appreciated the superior education. The school had a state-of-the-art computer system that was unavailable in the inner city.

When it was time for high school, I was uprooted again. This time my parents moved to Montebello, a middle-class suburb in the San Gabriel Valley, directly east of L.A. The neighborhood was middle- to upper-middle-class and predominantly Asian American and Latino, with a smattering of whites. The school's academic scores were average, and there were several honors-level courses.

As awkward as my junior high school experiences had been, for some reason I sentimentalized them. Somehow, I had developed the notion that white students were superior, and felt disdainful toward my classmates. I never participated in school events, spent lunches in the school library, gained even more weight—peaking at 181 lbs. in my senior year—and daydreamed constantly about going away to college. Many years later, I recognized these feelings as being the possible result of living in a society where Asian Americans were not regarded as members of the mainstream. When I read about the concept of internalized racism, the replication of racist prototypes within one's own mind, I finally was able to come to terms with my past, conflicted feelings. It also occurred to me years later that I might have carried all that extra weight to obscure my gender.

Though I felt alienated from my classmates, I found friends elsewhere by volunteering in local political campaigns. As a teenager, I participated in NAACP-led marches for school desegregation, worked to gain voting rights for migrant farm-workers through Cesar Chavez's United Farm Workers, and also volunteered in the gubernatorial and presidential campaigns of Jerry Brown, the former governor of California. In my junior year of high school, I rode the bus after school to Brown's campaign office, which was on the outskirts of downtown L.A. My father's office was nearby, and he would pick me up at 8:00 or 8:30 P.M., at the end of his work day. We would often have dinner at a Korean restaurant before returning to our empty house. My siblings were all away at college.

Being involved in politics helped ground me, and I credit my childhood enthusiasms to my brother Steven, who was seven years older. Though my father played a strong role in my early education by teaching me how to read and grilling me on mathematics, he grew more detached as I grew older. My parents worked long hours, often six or seven days a week, so we were raised primarily by Steven and my grandmother, who lived with us until I was about eight. She fed us, kept house, and tended the garden, while Steven educated us. Under his direction, we read aloud Shakespeare's plays during winter breaks. He took us to museums, foreign films, and summer concerts at the Hollywood Bowl. During the summer, he and I used to read aloud poetry in our backyard. Another summer when I was about twelve, he made me write a college-style research paper, requiring footnotes and at least five different sources. My topic was "communal utopias," and he gave me a month to complete the assignment.

Working during Brown's second gubernatorial campaign, I formed one of my first teenage relationships with an Asian American. Cheryl, a first-generation Chinese American, was starting her junior year at the University of California at Los Angeles when we met. She had just completed a summer internship working for the U.S. Congress, and impressed me with her worldliness. Both of us worked in Brown's press office, which was headed by Bobbie Metzger, a deputy press secretary on leave from the governor's office. She was in her early thirties, and the five of us in the office, including Elise, the administrative assistant, and Holly, another college volunteer, were all female. We once calculated our average age to be about twenty-three.

Since elementary school, I had shunned Asians and girlfriends. I hated to talk about clothes, makeup, and boys, and preferred to hold discussions on politics, literature, and films. Most of my school acquaintances were guys, particularly white guys. Cheryl changed that. She exposed me to vast, unknown parts of Los Angeles—trendy restaurants, neat bookstores, and shops galore. We spent hours driving around at night, going to the beach, and hanging out in twenty-four-hour diners. I had a lot of freedom as a teenager—my parents were often away on business and my siblings were at college. My dad had bought me a brand-new, four-door Fiat sedan when I got my driver's license at sixteen.

I was a good student, and only began ditching classes in my senior year. Even then, I did harmless things like go to a matinee, browse in bookstores, or read a book at the beach. My teachers trusted me implicitly, and never questioned my sporadic absences.

When it was time to consider college, I applied to the University of Chicago, Barnard College in New York City, Reed College in Portland, Oregon, Cornell University in Ithaca, New York, the University of California at Berkeley, and maybe two others. I was accepted by all except Cornell, and decided to attend Chicago, which had been my first choice. I was attracted to the school's emphasis on the classics of western civilization and its reputation for being hard-nosed and serious about intellectual pursuits. I was the first child to attend an out-of-state college. (My sister had attended Scripps College near L.A., and both my brothers had gone to the University of California at Berkeley.)

When I arrived at the University of Chicago in the fall of 1979, I discovered the community that I had been searching for. Chicago did not attract the Ivy League crowd. The students were more middle- and upper-middle-class, serious about academics, and often emotionally maladjusted. For the first time, I felt as if I fit in. Without any effort, I shed much of my excess weight.

I formed a close relationship with my first-year roommate, Neeta, whose parents came from India as graduate students. My other friendships—male or female—were mostly with whites. I consciously and unconsciously avoided associating with East Asians, particularly Korean Americans. It was a blind effort to blend in, I think. Meanwhile, I stayed in touch with Cheryl and others I knew through my political activities.

Though the first year was exhilarating, I became discontented in the second year. I grew disenchanted with the school's rigorous ten-week quarters and harsh winters. The impoverished ghetto that surrounded the university was depressing and contradicted the college's oft-repeated platitudes regarding equal opportunity and access. I sank into a deep depression and stayed inside my room for days at a time. I had always been a responsible student, but I yearned to break loose and do whatever I wanted—to travel, to be a novelist—without any accountability to my parents. I finally dropped out at the beginning of winter quarter.

I postponed telling my parents for as long as I could, about two months, until just before the next quarter's bill was to be mailed. They were as angry and disappointed in me as I had thought they would be. They had never wanted me to attend an out-of-state college, and I had fought and begged to leave. Steven had helped persuade my parents that it was a wise move. But once they got used to the idea, they—especially my dad—were proud that I attended a prominent college. Dropping out meant losing face, and was disgraceful.

I transferred to the University of California at Santa Cruz, one of the state system's most liberal campuses. I thought a different campus might renew my interest in school, but I ended up staying for just one session. After Chicago, Santa Cruz seemed intellectually impoverished. I wrote fiction and worked as a waitress in an omelette house in Santa Cruz. After a year, I moved to Los Angeles, where I continued to write, working again as a waitress, this time in a twenty-four-hour coffee shop. The working life was exhausting, and after a year I was ready to return to Chicago. I applied for loans to cover my tuition.

Returning to Chicago provided relief from the drudgery of work. I took several enjoyable classes—particularly in studio art. I became friends with Aubrey, a first-year student from Washington state and a gifted poet. School was intellectually stimulating, but it was impossible to finance a second year. The college slashed my financial aid, and I couldn't meet the college's projection of my contribution. But I wasn't too upset by the turn of events; I was restless and ready to leave. I had been developing this notion that I would return to college only when my mind needed stimulation, that I would deliberately avoid getting a college diploma, which I regarded then as an evil symbol of social conformity. My parents were increasingly dubious about my future, so it was easier and easier to do whatever I wanted. I saw them maybe once a year. I wore eccentric, second-hand clothes and shaved my head with a razor.

I moved to Providence, Rhode Island, because I had always wanted to live in the northeastern United States. I worked as a waitress in a downtown crab house and was the lone Korean in a town full of blue-blooded WASPs and first- and second-generation Italian, Irish, and Portuguese Americans. The city also had small pockets of recently immigrated West Indians, Africans, and Hmongs as well as Ivy Leaguers at Brown and art students at the Rhode Island School of Design. I became acquainted with some local writers and artists, practiced meditation, experimented with prayer, and spent a lot of time reading, writing, and exploring the city.

Life in Providence was pleasant, but after more than a year of not getting published, I grew increasingly nervous about not making it professionally as a novelist. I decided to return to Chicago to get my B.A.—a degree seemed essential for any sort of white-collar job with basic health-care benefits. My parents' ethic to be a social success had been deeply ingrained in me. I was frightened by a life of manual labor, of being a waitress for the rest of my life.

Deciding to return to school was easy, but financing it was difficult. I had unknowingly defaulted on my previous educational loans and had to pay them off in full in order to register. My scarred credit history prevented me from getting any more loans, so I decided to work full-time as a secretary in the university's fund-raising offices to get 50 percent off tuition. At $1,500 per quarter (paid out every three months), it was still a stretch on a secretary's salary. I supplemented my income by writing for a variety of local newspapers and magazines. Working during the 1980s for the gay weekly, the *Windy City Times,* stirred my interest in journalism. So much was happening in the gay community—gays and lesbians were gaining historic, legal rights, while at the same time being ravaged by AIDS. The *Windy City Times* played a vital role in informing the community about all of these events and fueled my interest in journalism.

Obtaining my college degree was exhausting, but the upside was that it taught me a lot about self-discipline. For three years, I took two classes a quarter, the maximum number allowed an employee. Though I had always shunned rituals, I attended the graduation ceremony at Rockefeller Chapel and was happy to receive my diploma from the college president Hanna Gray in December, 1990. The photo of that moment sits near my desk even today.

Since I enjoyed working as a freelance journalist, I decided to seek a full-time position at a daily newspaper. One of the newspapers I had been freelancing for was the English section of the *Korea Times* in Los Angeles. My sister was an assigning editor at the paper, which was edited for some time by K. W. Lee, a pioneering Korean American newspaperman. Both of them encouraged me to become a journalist and stoked my interest in covering the Korean American community. Journalism seemed like the perfect way to combine my interests in writing and public service.

I was in the process of accepting a summer internship at the *Tacoma News Tribune* in Tacoma, Washington, in the spring of 1991, when I learned that I was one of ten finalists in the *Los Angeles Times*'s Minority Editorial Training Program (METPRO). I was the first Korean American to be accepted into the program, and struggled with the decision of whether to accept. In recent years, Korean Americans had figured prominently in the news with the Brooklyn boycotts of 1990–1991 and the fatal shooting of Latasha Harlins in Los Angeles in 1991. The lack of Korean American journalists had resulted in a distorted, incomplete picture of the Korean American community. I wanted to fill that void, but also wondered whether being affiliated with a minority advancement program would stigmatize me. Ultimately, it was an offer that was impossible to decline. METPRO provided the graduate-level training in journalism that I lacked, as well as lots of hands-on experience; after one year in L.A., interns were placed at one of six Times Mirror newspapers across the country. A permanent job was assured at the end of the second year, if you didn't screw up. Entering METPRO was a decision that I never regretted. It was exhilarating to work for my hometown newspaper, even for a year, and my subsequent assignment to *Newsday* in New York was just as exciting.

More than 120,000 Koreans and Korean Americans live in New York City, and more than 350,000 in the New York metro area. It's the second-greatest concentration of Korean Americans in the country, following Los Angeles, and newspapers, as well as other businesses, are trying to tap this market. With my cultural and language skills, I was able to break stories and to obtain exclusive interviews within the Korean community. For years the only Korean-speaking news reporter at a mainstream daily in this city, I regularly included Koreans in a variety of stories and suggested covering little-known aspects of the local community, such as second-generation voter-registration drives. I also spoke out when my paper misrepresented or stereotyped Korean Americans. One of the most egregious examples was an article that covered the raid of a Queens brothel. The brothel was run by a Korean woman and the article quoted police sources who claimed that *ah-joom-mah,* the Korean word for aunt or older woman, was the Asian word for a brothel madam. It was mind-boggling that someone would think in this day and age that there was a pan-Asian language.

My fears of being stigmatized did not materialize, but more than once I have felt self-conscious about being a product of a minority advancement program. In recent years, the newspaper industry and journalism in general have undergone corporate downsizing and reorganization. After *Newsday* closed its city edition in 1995, the staff shrank considerably. With such economic pressures, there seem to be undercurrents of resentment toward ethnic and racial minorities and the suspicion that we were somehow second-rate and robbing others of their rightful jobs. The reduction in staff no doubt negatively effects the depth and variety of news being reported. It also threatens the diversity of the newsroom by the sheer reduction in staff.

In a recent interview, the newspaper's chief executive, Mark Wiles, said he was trying to build up readership in minority communities. He suggested that quoting more minorities and using their photographs more frequently would win their loyalty. I think that in-depth reporting on minority communities, through bilingual reporters who are sensitive to different cultures, is a better strategy.

In the summer of 1998, a few months before the publication of this book, I decided to leave my full-time reporting job to seek a graduate degree in sociology. I was growing disenchanted with the quick processing of facts required by journalism, and wanted the chance to do more in-depth research. I am interested in further exploring questions and issues raised in this essay and this book. As a child, for so many years I denied my ethnicity. Now here I am planning to devote years of study to it.

Though there may not be a common language uniting all of Asia, there definitely is a pan-Asian identity taking shape in this country. Korean Americans on their own form a tiny subset, yet, coupled with Japanese, Filipino, Chinese, and Indian Americans, they can achieve a significant political mass. In this country, we share a physical or geographic resemblance, whether we think so or want to. I participate in the New York City chapter of the Asian American Journalists Association, and am well acquainted with other minority journalists, especially blacks and women. My friends are of diverse backgrounds, but recently I have grown to know more Asians and other ethnic minorities.

I USED TO tutor two Korean boys, ages fourteen and twelve, who immigrated to New York City in their early teens. The older one once chastised me for owning a Honda Accord, a Japanese car. He said he preferred American or Korean cars, and evoked Japan's brutal occupation of Korea as the reason for his position. I admitted that Japan and Korea had a violent and tragic history, but chided him for regarding one nationality or race as being morally superior to another. There are good and bad Japanese, I told him, whether he understood or not.

We have this illusion of shaping or directing our lives, but, just as strongly, life imposes its circumstances upon us, requiring us to adjust. As I have attempted to explain, my perception of my ethnicity and identity has undergone many permutations and it is difficult to predict how I will feel in another thirty-six years.

I'm grateful to have been exposed to two cultures. Some of the Korean or Asian ideas that have influenced me are a respect for elders, a reverence for scholarly achievements, and an appreciation for formality in social interactions. I love all sorts of international cuisines, but still rank Korean as one of my favorites, and have introduced it to many of my non-Korean friends. But American meals—broiled meats and tossed salads—are more convenient to prepare and eat on a daily basis.

American influences, meanwhile, seem to be my belief in the importance of self-reliance and public service, as well as the virtually limitless possibilities of the individual. I always have been thankful that my parents immigrated to this country. America, despite its setbacks, has offered me opportunities that would have been virtually impossible in Korea.

My parents were at the beginning of a massive emigration of Koreans, and I consider myself to be a transitional generation, marking that jump. To a great extent, they have retained their Korean culture. Though my mother's English skills are weak, she embraces this country. My father, on the other hand, is more fluent, yet he longs to return home. I cannot ever imagine leaving this country, as my parents left theirs. Yet, neither do I feel comfortable or fully accepted here. I expect that my children will feel far less conflicted than I do about their ethnicity, and I hope they will assimilate more effortlessly.

When I tell them stories about my life, perhaps they will seem as strange and fantastic as the stories of my parents—of living in a war-torn city, of dodging gunfire, and of hiking across mountains and jumping on railroad cars to visit friends in distant villages. Korean Americans, after all, have been making enormous advancements and popping up in the most unexpected places. Comedian Margaret Cho had her own TV sitcom, and former presidential candidate, Senator Phil Gramm (R-Texas), is married to a Korean American economist. As a transitional generation, settling into a new land, I must say that I sometimes feel like a space traveler, boldly going where no one has gone before.

Captain, out.

Reflections on a Korean American Journey

Coming to America

I peered out the oval window of the 747 jumbo jet as it made its final descent to Los Angeles International Airport. Tired and dazed from the long journey, I wondered what this new world would hold in store for me. My mother, brother, and I, then eight, came with high hopes and expectations, but on that autumn day we had not even begun to imagine how profoundly our lives would be changed by our transpacific migration from South Korea.

America was a bewildering place at first. As we entered the terminal reception area, a strange man rushed up to me and smothered me with hugs and kisses. The stranger turned out to be my father, whom I had not seen in three years. I felt so dwarfed in this new place. From my father to the freeways, the buildings, and even the facial features of Americans with their big eyes and big noses, everything loomed large and strange. Such a strange place with strange people, I thought. And this was to be my new home. Even the trees didn't conform to a Korean child's notion of what they should be. I thought palm trees were telephone poles until I looked up and saw the strange, featherlike protrusions on the tops.

One aspect of living in America that I looked forward to the most was having our own car. I was so proud that my father owned one. In Korea, only the wealthiest families did. As he drove us to our new home, I failed to notice that it was an old, faded blue Rambler with cracked plastic seats that had tufts of browning foam oozing out from the fissures. I sat proudly in the rear right seat, the seat of honor in Korea, and imagined that I was a little princess being chauffeured to my new home.

My father came to America on a visitor's visa with only twenty dollars and the dream of studying in America and then returning to Korea. When the visa expired, he lived the fearful life of an illegal alien until he managed, eventually and miraculously, to get a green card. He then sponsored us to join him. Now, when I hear negative sentiments expressed against illegal aliens, I think of my father and what he must have experienced. It is difficult to reconcile the stereotypes and images of illegal aliens with him and to think that not so long ago, he was perceived in the same way. The faces of illegal aliens now may be different from his, but their hopes and dreams for a better life are not. It seems that the best of what America stands for is in the hearts of those who come to its shores.

I thought I looked like a Caucasian

By the time my mother, brother, and I arrived, my father had paved the way so that we could bypass the usual stopover in L.A.'s Koreatown and settle directly in the suburbs. Growing up in a predominantly white environment forced me to learn the language and adapt quickly. It also didn't take long before I became painfully conscious of being different. I quickly experienced the consequences of being a minority in America. One day in the second grade, I looked wistfully at the blond hair of a classmate who was sitting in front of me, wondering why couldn't I have been born in America to white parents, why couldn't I have blond hair and blue eyes like her, and a "normal"-sounding name like Smith. Instead, I was subject to a litany of well-intended but humiliating questions such as "Where are you from?" "How come your eyes look different?" "What do you eat at home?" There were also the taunts, pairing my last name Chung to some form of sing-song rhyme that was derisive of the Chinese. It failed to impress my tormentors that I was Korean, not Chinese.

As I grew into adolescence and entered high school, the impact of being a minority and being different became more complex. I had acculturated rapidly and was thus able to disguise the more obvious tokens of my difference. I had mastered American language and culture enough to act like a typical American teenager when at school and with my white friends. But the reality was that I lived a double life. At school, I was an outgoing, all-American teenager, but at home I was a good, quiet Korean girl who spoke Korean and ate Korean food. The shift from one to the other was immediate and automatic as soon as I opened the front door of my house. It was also largely unconscious.

My family was financially established and lived in a nice house in a middle-class, suburban neighborhood by the time I started high school. Still, I was ashamed to bring my friends home. I felt as if I had some deep, dark secret to hide. I was afraid that my friends would find out how different I really was. I didn't want them to have to take off their shoes at the door, to notice the smell of *kimchi* that lingered in the air, and to ask questions about the Korean wall hangings and calendars that adorned every room. I was ashamed of my Koreanness and anything that hinted at my difference. I believed that I had to reject my culture and deny who I was if I wanted to be accepted by my friends and American society. No one ever said this to me; no one needed to. The message oozed in through my pores in the faces and images that represented America and its notion of female beauty. There was little there that was reminiscent of me. By virtue of being non-white, I was excluded from society's perceptions of beauty and value. And yet I tried desperately to be white and actually came to believe that I was successful, until one day during my sophomore year.

I was walking down the mirror-paneled hallway of my high school, talking and laughing with a group of friends. For a brief moment as we walked past the mirrors, I caught my reflection in the midst of my friends. What struck me at that moment was how visibly different I was from them. Because most of the faces that I saw around me were white, I had come to believe that mine was too. In that devastating moment of truth, I was confronted with the reality that no matter how much I tried to deny it, I was inevitably who I was and that it was useless and foolish to ignore that fact. I recognized that in my desire to belong and fit in, I had been deluding myself to the point of thinking that I was actually white.

This incident served as a catalyst for painful soul-searching and marked the beginning of an inner journey toward greater self-acceptance. Until that point, my struggle with ethnic identity and the denial of my Koreanness had been largely unconscious, but I began to see that the cost of my denial was too high a price to pay. I accepted the reality of my biculturality, that I was inevitably both Korean and American, and that I had a unique opportunity to learn from both cultures, rather than rejecting one for the other. For the first time since that moment in the second grade when I wished I was a blond-haired girl with the last name Smith, I began to see my bicultural experience as a blessing and an opportunity rather than a curse.

College provided different issues and challenges as I continued to come to terms with my ethnic identity. Going away to college and living in the dorms made me confront my previous dualistic life: now my home and school environments were the same. I found that while the culture of high school was that of conformity to a narrowly defined notion of what is socially acceptable and desirable, the culture of college was that of finding and expressing one's individuality and uniqueness. I consciously tried to be more integrated and culturally balanced. And in my friendships I sought out the company of Korean Americans as well as that of whites. I experienced newfound enjoyment and pride in my ethnic heritage. However, echoing my earlier dualistic life, the two cultural worlds remained unintegrated, not because of my own design but because the two spheres were so distinct.

Most of my Korean friends associated with other Koreans, and my white friends socialized among themselves. When I spent too much time with my white friends, I worried that my Korean friends would think that I was too good for them or that I was trying to assimilate. On the other hand, if I spent too much time with my Korean friends, I was afraid that my white friends would think me too cliquish. As I shuttled back and forth between my two segregated worlds, trying to maintain a balance, I was painfully reminded that I resided in the crevice between two worlds, not fully belonging to either. The cost of complete belonging would be the surrender of one for the other. I knew I did not want to do this, nor could I. I realized that I had to create a new space, a unique place of my own, forged by selecting and integrating the best of both worlds.

My awareness of this hybrid and hyphenated nature of my in-between existence left me with a profound sense of alienation and aloneness. It made me wonder if anyone else would share that peculiar space with me. Would I find someone to share my life who would understand this part of me? At that point, the prospect seemed dim. I had yet to encounter anyone else who seemed to be struggling with these issues. My fellow Koreans, who tended to be more recent immigrants, seemed content to be just Korean, and obviously none of my white friends seemed to struggle with their ethnic identity. I wondered why I was the only one grappling with these issues, and if there was something wrong with me. Eventually, I learned that many other 1.5- and second-generation Korean and other Asian Americans struggle with these issues; but, like me, they maintained an exterior that belied that inner struggle. I appeared to them as unaffected as they did to me. Only later, after the fact, would we give word and voice to that which we had kept hidden.

Defining my ethnic identity is an ongoing process. I operate from two basic principles of balance and integration. I try to maintain a balance of my two worlds and to integrate what I deem to be the best of both, but this is easier said than done. When I graduated from college, I thought I had resolved my "ethnic identity crisis," but then I realized I had other related questions to consider. No sooner had I achieved a comfortable state than I was confronted with still other unexplored dimensions and challenges. How would my ethnic identity affect who I would marry—would I marry a Korean American as I was told to, or marry a non-Korean, as I was inclined to do? Once married, how would I negotiate gender-role expectations within the marriage? How far would I go to instill Korean culture and identity in my children? I realized that the questions were endless and varied, according to the task and issues particular to a specific stage of life. I was forced to abandon the notion of a static ethnic identity and to reconceptualize it as a dynamic process that I would address on an ongoing basis.

In talking to some of my Korean and Asian American students, I realize that, while we share similar experiences, they—separated by a decade or so—have grown up in a different environment. The broader American society, at least in Southern California, is now more culturally diverse and tolerant than when I first arrived. Because of this, there is less of a stigma attached to being a minority. Even the Korean American community is more open than the one I grew up in.

When I returned to Korea for a visit, I made the surprising discovery that the Korean American culture I grew up with was much more conservative than the one in Korea. The Korean culture practiced by the first generation of immigrants tends to be the one that existed at the time of their migration. For many, culture is frozen at this point in time, preserved with great passion and determination and increasingly idealized. Unfortunately, just as *kimchi* that is pickled and buried in jars in autumn turns sour and unpalatable as the winter wears on into spring, so does a static, preserved Korean culture appear to the next generation, particularly if it is rigidly imposed upon them. In my experience of working with Korean American families, parents who enforce Korean values without any regard for the different reality in which their children live can cause tremendous pain and suffering for their children and themselves. And children who are devoid of a sense of their own history and background often fail to appreciate the sacrifices that their parents have made and the values that they have imparted. Better communication, openness, and a desire to understand each other can go a long way toward achieving reconciliation and harmony.

I was told that I couldn't marry a non-Korean

As I entered adolescence, my parents began to tell me how important it was to marry a Korean. Even without their direct prohibition, I was already fully aware of the shame and stigma associated with out-marriage. The price would be ostracization for me and the loss of face for my family within the Korean community. The problem was that I was more attracted to white men than Korean men. This was due in part to my resentment of what I deemed to be oppressive patriarchy within Korean culture. It seemed that most of my Korean American male counterparts favored traditional gender roles (not that American culture is immune from this). This is understandable from their perspective: They are privileged in this system and stand to benefit from it. As I observed the inequality between men and women in Korean culture, I was determined not to perpetuate the pattern. When I was thirteen, I was given the dubious title of a "woman's libber" by my brother when I refused to get up from the dinner table and get him a glass of milk. I believe the precise phrase that proclaimed my liberation was "Get it yourself!"

Another reason for my attraction to white men had to do with my ethnic identity. During my I-want-to-be-white phase, dating white men symbolized my arrival as an American, and proved that I could fit in. Dating was one thing, but marriage was quite another. Even as I was more interested in white men, I found it difficult to ignore the deeply ingrained script of "don't marry a non-Korean." Thus, I would inform any potentially serious prospect that our relationship could not continue beyond a certain point. In retrospect, I think the warning was more for my benefit than theirs. Despite this, one relationship did get serious enough to test the boundaries of the out-marriage taboo and the limits of parental love. Needless to say, my father was quite displeased when I asked for permission to marry a non-Korean. He bombarded me with all the familiar arguments against interracial marriage that I already knew: whites were not as committed to marriage as Koreans, thus more likely to divorce; cultural differences would doom the marriage to failure; our "half-breed" children would be rejected by both cultures; other Koreans would look down upon me (and my parents).

When these arguments didn't achieve their goal, my father uttered the worst sanction that he could think of: He threatened to disown me. The threat of being disowned meant not only separation from my family, but also from Korean culture. It seemed as if I were being forced to choose, once again, between the two cultures. Even without this ultimatum, I knew that I would inevitably drift further from Korean culture if I married a non-Korean. Furthermore, while I could "pass" to a large extent in his world, he couldn't pass in my Korean world.

I eventually ended the relationship for reasons of interpersonal incompatibility, but parental objection and the fear of losing my culture were undeniable factors in the decision. I still wonder sometimes if my father really would have carried out his threat if I had married a non-Korean. I'll never know for sure, because I eventually met and married a second-generation Korean American who shares with me that in-between place of biculturality. He was the second Korean that I dated. In contrast to my past relationships with non-Koreans where I felt like a cultural tour guide, I found it refreshing not to explain so much of myself. I also appreciate the fact that my parents can easily relate to him and, vice versa, even if he doesn't speak Korean fluently.

In retrospect, a powerful factor in my lack of interest in Korean men had to do with negative stereotypes. Just as I had internalized a white standard of female beauty that made me resent my "Mongoloid" (the technical term used to describe the Asian race) features, I also bought into the prevailing image of masculinity that precluded Asian American men. In keeping with stereotypes about them, I dismissed Korean guys as passive, wimpy, nerdy, and socially inept.

Stereotypes about Asian Americans not only affected my attraction to Korean men, but also my own self-perception and self-esteem. Without knowing it, my brother and I had actually bought into the stereotypes, and appropriated them to salvage a positive sense of self. For example, my brother didn't know anything about martial arts when he was in Korea, but not long after his arrival in the U.S. he began to develop a real interest in it and became quite skilled at it. I don't think it is coincidental that the only positive Asian male role model at the time was Bruce Lee—or that he was the only Asian male I found attractive. As for myself, I wanted to fit the "Suzie Wong" China-doll image. Unfortunately, I was tall, not short and petite. I also had frizzy, curly hair that wouldn't lend itself to a short, blunt, face-framing cut; to no avail, I slept each night with big plastic curlers in my hair, trying to straighten it. And no matter how hard I tried, I was never very convincing at the shy, demure act. Both my brother and I bought into the externally defined and static notions of what an Asian American should be to gain greater acceptance. Left with limited alternatives and few positive role models, we did the best we could by appropriating the few, seemingly positive images available to us.

Stereotypes also had an interesting and contradictory impact on my social life. On the one hand, there have been white men who have been interested in me only because I am Asian; on the other hand, there have been those who excluded me from their realm of possible relationships for exactly the same reason. In both cases, my race—and stereotypical notions about my race—prevented them from knowing me as an individual and not just as a member of the Asian race. Those who were interested because I was Asian (commonly known as Asian woman fetish) seemed to operate from their own preconceived notions. Their ideas of me were based on common stereotypes, such as those portraying Asian women as demure and passive. They became somewhat puzzled and eventually lost interest when I didn't live up to their expectations.

I never doubted that it would be ideal to marry within my culture—I was simply skeptical and distracted. Not that I believe in any of the arguments against interracial marriage, nor do I oppose it, but to the extent that one is steeped in a particular culture, marrying someone who shares that culture would, all other things being equal, ensure a greater degree of commonality and compatibility. While I preferred to marry a Korean American, I'm not so sure that it will matter as much, nor should it, for the next generation. I know that I will not brainwash my child with the same expectations with which I was raised. Intermarriage cannot help but be a critical issue between the first and second generations. It is the contested ground upon which our identities and our hopes and dreams are played out. My research on Asian American families confirms this, revealing that the issue of dating and marriage is one of the greatest sources of conflict between college students and their parents.

For immigrant parents, intermarriage may symbolize the ultimate loss of their children to America. While they immigrated with hopes and dreams for a better future for their family, they failed to realize that an unintended consequence is the Americanization of their children. As they work hard to provide a stable financial base for the family, their children rapidly acculturate. Parents see all too late that acquiring the house in the white suburbs with the good schools also means that their children want to become like those around them—like whites. Immigrant parents fear not only the loss of Korean culture but also the loss of their children. Outmarriage may be perceived as the final step in this process. On the other hand, for teenagers and young adults who grew up in this culture and accept it, it can be difficult to subject matters of the heart to the artificial constraints of race.

"Are you sure you don't want to become a doctor?"

Being a Korean American has certain advantages. For example, your life is neatly laid out for you. All you have to do is just follow the prescriptions and you are rewarded with approval. Your parents get to brag about you to their friends; they, in turn, use you as their comparison standard when they turn to their own children, saying "Why can't you be more like so-and-so?" We are expected to aspire to one of the few clearly identified status professions: doctor, dentist, lawyer, or engineer. The problem arises when you don't want to or can't enter these fields.

As a female, I was under less pressure than my older brother; if I couldn't become one of the above, I could always marry one. While I was encouraged to strive for academic achievement and to pursue a high-status career, I also received conflicting messages that led me to believe that my education and career were a pretense to make myself more "marketable" as a wife and to add to my dowry, so to speak.

My parents supported me and encouraged me to choose my own career. However, upon hearing that I wanted to major in psychology, they were immediately skeptical. They were the first to ask the often-repeated question "What are you going to do with that degree?" Needless to say, there were no role models for me and I had only a vague notion of what I would do as a psychologist. My mother in particular encouraged me to go into nursing, if not medicine. She said it was a good, respectable profession for a woman and a "safe" one because I would be able to support myself if anything should happen to my husband. I knew she meant well, and that security and stability were the most important values for her, but they were not the determining ones for me. As uncertain as I was about my career path, I was certain of a few things. I wanted to have a career of my own, regardless of my marital status, and I wanted it to be meaningful and fulfilling.

I must confess, there were many times when I considered more traditional careers like medicine and law, especially because most of my Korean American friends were committed to that route. They seemed to have the benefit of a clearly defined path while mine was not so clear. I had only a vague notion of what I wanted to do and a little better sense of what I *didn't* want to do. But as I continued in the general direction of my chosen path, things became clearer to me and I experienced greater intrinsic confirmation that I was indeed on the right track. At times I felt out of place and less valued within the Korean American community because I didn't aspire to one of the more recognized careers, but I felt compelled to find my own way. I suspect that my parents' friends stopped using me as a positive model in their comparisons and may have even used me as a negative model of what not to become. Eventually, despite my own doubts and fears as well as those of others, I obtained a Ph.D. in counseling psychology. Ironically, now that I'm a professor, I've been revived as a role model—educators are highly respected in Korean culture and somewhat rare in the immigrant community.

My overriding motivation to pursue a career in psychology directly relates to my bicultural experience. I saw that immigrant families faced many difficulties in the dislocation and adaptation process, and had few avenues of support. There were few trained mental health professionals who could speak their language or understand the nuances of their culture. Cultural and intergenerational differences, exacerbated by a language barrier, caused many immigrant families to lead separate and alienated lives. Given the importance of the family and its tremendous impact on both the individual and society at large, I felt that I could have the greatest impact by promoting healthy families. As a Korean American psychologist and as a member of the 1.5 generation, I see my role as being a facilitator and educator for the first and second generations, bridging the gap to help each better understand and accept the other.

In my educational process, I struggled, as an Asian American woman, to speak out and be assertive. In college, I wanted to participate in class discussions, but felt that unless I had something truly profound to say, I shouldn't waste other people's time. But many of my fellow classmates, particularly white males, didn't hesitate to speak up, even when what they had to say wasn't particularly insightful or profound. In graduate school, I realized that, contrary to my socialization, I needed to be more assertive and expressive if I was going to survive in academia. The social and behavioral skills that I eventually acquired to help me succeed were not only those of the predominant white culture, but also those traditionally seen as masculine. It is a challenge to maintain my femininity in an environment that sees it as a weakness. While for the most part I value the newly acquired behaviors, I resent the cultural and gender hegemony in academia and the fact that I had to transform myself in this way to survive.

Being an Asian American woman professor has its advantages and disadvantages. Because there aren't many like me, I get more attention. This helps bring notice to the issues I fight for, such as the establishment of Asian American studies and the challenge to institutions to be more inclusive. But I also have received some unwanted scrutiny in the form of racial and gender stereotypes. I have been referred to as "a nice, Oriental lady," and asked, "How did you learn to speak English so well?" I also have received unwelcome comments about my appearance in professional settings; despite the fact that they were complimentary, they undermined my intellectual qualifications. My assertiveness and articulateness seem to surprise and threaten some because I don't fit their stereotype of an Asian woman. Others ignore these traits altogether and treat me in a condescending and paternalistic way.

I find that I have to compensate for my race, gender, and age, and have to prove myself in ways that my fellow white, male, older colleagues do not. While they are automatically given a certain level of respect and authority, I have to earn every bit of mine. I am often mistaken for a student or a staff member on campus and treated accordingly. A few times when checking out books from the library, I had to ask for faculty borrowing privileges even though they should have known that I was a faculty member by the type of ID that I had. In another situation, I went to get my photo ID upon arriving at a new campus. They mistakenly gave me a student ID even after I told them twice that I was a new faculty member.

Despite these challenges, I enjoy my profession immensely. One of the most rewarding aspects of being a professor is serving as a role model. For most of my students, I am the first Asian American woman professor they encounter. Many Asian American students have told me how refreshing and empowering it is for them to see me in front of the classroom. I can only hope that my presence gives them a sense of possibility for their own dreams and aspirations.

From a stranger to an American

Ron Takaki, in his book *Strangers from a Different Shore,* refers to George Simmel's notion of being a "stranger" as a central motif in his historical overview of Asian migration to America. I arrived in America almost thirty years ago, a stranger from a distant shore. Just as I was seen as a stranger, I, too, found this to be a strange place. Now, I call this place home; that which was strange has become familiar and comfortable. The personal experiences that I have shared chronicle key moments in the transformation process.

I call America home not because it is a perfect place, but because there is enough space and freedom here for me to define my own version of America—a Korean America, an Asian America. Although many people may still regard me as a stranger, and may continue to do so, my very presence is helping to reconceptualize what it means to be an American. I am contesting the narrowly defined notion that only white Americans are Americans, and striving to establish a new national identity that includes all those who have come and will yet come to its shores, regardless of race and skin color. In doing so, I feel that I and others like myself exemplify the true spirit of what America stands for.

A Handicapped Korean in America

ANY KOREAN PARENT taking a look at my résumé would want me for a son-in-law. I'm twenty-nine, single, and an assistant district attorney in New York City. I'm a graduate of Colgate University and George Washington University Law School. But if they were to meet me in person, perhaps they might feel differently. A traffic accident six years ago left me paralyzed below the chest, and irrevocably altered the perception of most Koreans of not only my eligibility as a husband, but also my most basic identity as a man.

In all societies, the physically handicapped are subject to some prejudices and discrimination. Yet the bigoted attitudes I have encountered in the Korean community far exceed anything I have encountered in American society at large. In Korea, individuals with disabilities are shunned and locked away. Unlike America, there are no laws ensuring equal access and opportunities. Many Korean Americans share this prejudice. When strangers see me on the street, they pity me without even knowing who I am. They think that I deserve their pity just because I cannot walk. Even my own parents have told me that they would rather see me as an able-bodied ditch digger than as a disabled attorney.

When I became disabled, my status within the Korean community suddenly diminished. Before the accident, I served as a Sunday school teacher and as the president of my church's students' association. Church members viewed me as someone who could make valuable contributions and often consulted me on ecumenical affairs. After the car accident that disabled me, they treated me more like an infant than a grown man. When church members approached me after Mass, they would only discuss my physical condition. "How are you doing, Alex? I hope you improve soon." I stopped attending church because of the closed minds of some of the parishioners. These days, I remain reluctant to attend any Korean social function because of the uneasy reception I'm bound to receive. It's a pity that people make such assumptions about me without even having a clue as to who I am inside.

* * *

IN 1976, WHEN I was nine, my entire family immigrated to New York City. I am the only son and have two sisters. We lived in a high-rise apartment building on a relatively quiet stretch of Kissena Boulevard in Flushing, Queens. My cousins lived in the same building and we spent a lot of time together, along with other Korean kids in the building. Flushing—where I still live today—has the second largest enclave of Koreans in the U.S., following Koreatown in Los Angeles. Even in 1976, there was a sizable Korean population, with several Korean markets and stores, many with signs posted in Korean. In my class, there were four other Koreans. Although there were also Chinese and Japanese Americans and a few African Americans, at least 70 to 80 percent of the students were Caucasian, and of Italian, Irish, or Jewish descent.

Some of my most vivid childhood memories are of the hardships that my parents endured when they first came to this country. My father, a graduate of Korea University, worked in real estate before emigrating. In Korea, we owned our own home; in America, we didn't even have furniture or carpets. I was embarrassed by our living conditions and resented my parents' decision to leave Korea.

My parents came to America for the reason shared by so many immigrants: more economic opportunities, a higher quality of life. We were misled by false perceptions, I think. Several of my uncles already lived in the U.S.—two were doctors and the third, a pharmacist. We imagined that we would live as they did. Instead, my parents held an assortment of manual labor jobs. As soon as my mother recovered from her jet lag, she got a job as a seamstress in a garment factory. She left for work early in the morning before we left for school and came home when it was dark. Her ankles swelled like balloons from pressing the pedal of the sewing machine ten hours a day. My father endured similar struggles, driving a taxicab and hauling boxes in a warehouse.

Despite the physical labor that consumed their lives, my parents never forgot the importance of a good education. Like many other Korean parents, they strongly believed that America provided a higher quality of education for their children. I was given a lot of freedom as a child, but never strayed into delinquency. For as long as I can remember, my parents impressed upon me the fact that I had to take care of them when they grew older. Being successful in school and becoming a professional, white-collar worker were essential to achieving that goal.

My parents suffered many financial ups and downs, but they always managed to find money for school-related activities. I belonged to a number of sports teams and they made sure that I had the uniforms and athletic equipment I needed. Seeing how hard my parents worked motivated me to do my best in school. I concentrated on my studies, more or less continuously attending school from the third grade until my graduation from law school.

When I started the third grade shortly after my arrival in America, I didn't even know the English alphabet. A Korean boy was assigned to serve as my interpreter, but he was rather aloof and we never really got along. I recall sitting through entire lessons, not understanding a word of what was going on. There were a few Korean girls in my class and they were much more helpful. In and out of school, I mingled only with other Koreans. It was convenient, because they all knew Korean, but my exclusive association with them hindered my acquisition of English.

Two years after we emigrated, my family moved to Alameda, California. One of my father's friends asked him to manage his liquor store, and he accepted, hoping the change would bring better economic opportunities. I loved living in northern California. Alameda was a predominantly white, upper-middle-class suburb outside of Oakland. Though there were a few Asians in the neighborhood, most were native-born Filipino or Chinese Americans. Suddenly thrust into a very different environment, I was nervous about being teased and harassed by the other kids for not speaking English perfectly. However, few kids teased me, perhaps because of my bigger-than-average size. In fact, I made friends easily. Kids were more athletic than in New York and I enjoyed playing sports. I was a sprinter in junior high school, and also played a lot of baseball. Dating, however, was a problem. There were enough Asian American girls, but the good-looking ones often paired off with non-Asian guys. Approaching white girls, meanwhile, was difficult because I was not among the school's social elite. I used to attend school dances in junior high school, but eventually quit going when I started high school.

When I entered the tenth grade, my parents moved back to Flushing. I didn't want to move, but the liquor store went out of business and my dad had difficulty finding another job. We moved back to New York and lived in Co-op City, a huge complex of apartment buildings in the Bronx. It was a depressing change from California. The local high school, which was predominantly black, was considered a rough school—the type of place where you could get killed over a leather jacket—and had a poor academic reputation. My parents decided to enroll me in a private Catholic school they picked out of the phone book. There were fewer than 800 students at the school, most of them from blue-collar, Italian and Irish American families. I caught a public bus to and from school every day. Unlike me, most of the students did not even think about going to college. I participated in soccer, but had only a few acquaintances from school. I developed other friends through a Korean church. On weekends, my church buddies and I would attend Korean parties at local colleges. The first time I attended one of these affairs, I was stunned and exhilarated by the sheer number of Koreans.

Back in New York, I discovered that I spoke better English than a lot of other Korean kids. I even knew more English than some kids who had immigrated at a younger age than I. If I had remained in Flushing, I suspect I would never have gained my current mastery of English, a skill that is essential to my job as an assistant district attorney. The trade-off, however, was that my Korean language skills lagged behind those of my Korean friends.

Most of the Korean I know today is the result of being forced to speak it at home. My parents never punished me for not speaking Korean, but I had no choice since my mom didn't speak any English. When I was a child, I was embarrassed that she was unable to converse in English. Today, I consider it a blessing, as it has helped me retain my native tongue. Though I feel most comfortable speaking in English, I'm glad to have some Korean.

By the eleventh grade, I had settled on becoming either an attorney or a doctor—the only two careers that most Koreans seemed to know about. I just knew that I wanted a job with social prestige, and that I had to earn enough money to take care of my parents as they grew older. A Korean priest I knew from my church encouraged me to become a lawyer. He was an activist priest, and often talked about how the knowledge of law could empower the Korean community. My father had majored in law in college, but never became an attorney. Perhaps that also influenced my decision.

I had my doubts about becoming an attorney. My greatest fear was that I didn't write or speak English well enough, a skepticism echoed by my twelfth grade English teacher. She was a good, sensitive teacher, but thought I simply lacked English skills. The absence of Korean attorneys to serve as role models or mentors didn't make it any easier to imagine myself holding such a position. Despite these doubts, I graduated from law school and passed the New York State Bar Examination in November 1993.

As an undergraduate, I attended Colgate, a small, liberal arts college in upstate New York; for my law degree, I went to George Washington University Law School in Washington, D.C. Like many Koreans, my parents equated going to a prestigious university with getting a good education. So, with little regard to my family's financial situation, I chose the best schools possible. Today, I would do it differently, focusing on practical considerations such as financial aid and scholarships. Unlike in Korea, people in America can graduate from top-ten law schools with mediocre grades and still end up unemployed, while others who graduated from mediocre schools with excellent grades can make close to six figures right out of school.

Life in law school was miserable. I lived with two college friends in the Foggy Bottom section of the Capitol, a yuppie neighborhood near George Washington University. There wasn't much of a life beyond going to class, reading casebooks, and taking tests. I was just waiting for law school to be over.

The car accident that paralyzed my lower body occurred at the end of my second year of law school. It was the first day of summer vacation and I was driving with a friend to Texas, which was where my parents were living. Four or five hours into the trip, in Virginia, just miles from the Tennessee border, it happened. A car cut me off, and to avoid crashing, I drove into a grassy median. I hit a ditch and the car flipped over. My injuries were severe and emergency crews transported me to a local hospital, then airlifted me by helicopter to an even larger hospital. For five months in 1991, from May until October, I underwent rehabilitation at New York University's Rusk Institute. The Institute was a premier rehabilitation center and a relative of ours worked there.

In the summer of 1993, I completed my final year of law school at Queens College. My first full-time job out of law school was as an assistant district attorney in the Kings County District Attorney office in Brooklyn, New York, a position that I have held now for approximately five years. My job involves all aspects of criminal prosecution, from interviewing crime victims and witnesses, negotiating plea bargains with the defense, and preparing for trial to ultimately trying cases in court. I enjoy the legal profession and feel lucky to have chosen a career well suited to my personality. Despite the moderate income, I am fulfilled by my job, particularly because of its potential to make an impact on society.

MY PARENTS DID the best they could to offer me a bright future, but little did they realize that the traditional Korean family structure—the only one they knew—might sabotage my future in the American workplace. While my parents emphasized and practiced a strong work ethic, they paid scant attention to developing the social or conversational skills that can be so crucial to advancing in the workplace. My job evaluations always have highlighted my strong work ethic, and I think that's an edge I have over most of my colleagues—nearly all of whom are non-Korean, native English speakers. But if I am competent on the job, it's a completely different story when it comes to mingling with my colleagues outside the office.

I feel uncomfortable and often tongue-tied at work-related social gatherings, whether it's a formal office party or an informal get-together at a local bar. At the last office Christmas party, an executive assistant district attorney approached me. After our initial hello, I couldn't think of anything else to say. We silently sipped our drinks, then went our separate ways. On such occasions, the ability to banter and tell humorous stories is far more important than the ability to formulate brilliant legal arguments. Though I keep up with current events and am an avid sports fan, I have always had a hard time shooting the breeze.

My lack of communication and social skills is the result, I think, of the Korean cultural patterns that prevailed within my family. We rarely talked with one another. Dinners often lasted less than fifteen minutes since we never uttered an unnecessary word. We loved and still love each other very much, but, unlike Americans, we did not physically or verbally express our feelings. In traditional Korean society, a child was considered virtuous if he or she was silent and obedient to his or her parents. Because of my parents' own experiences in traditional, authoritarian families, they lacked the knowledge of how to create a warm, familial atmosphere where open verbal exchanges flourished. In fact, we were discouraged from pursuing any type of discourse. I remember that my sisters and I once overheard our parents discussing a juicy piece of gossip about a relative. When we inquired about it later, my parents reprimanded us for being nosy. Nosiness was not an attribute of well-behaved Korean children, they told us over and over again. Because of the way I was raised, I have difficulty talking with my parents even today.

My inability to banter has also caused difficulties in my relationships with the opposite sex, especially during college. There were few Asians at Colgate or in any of the neighboring towns. Social activities revolved around fraternity parties and two downtown bars; no other social outlets existed. At a party or over cocktails, the ability to tell a funny story is crucial.

Korean social situations were easier to navigate. When I hung out with my Korean friends, we often went to Korean parties at local colleges. It was easy to meet Korean women. They often found me attractive and, for some reason, small talk was unessential. A lot of Koreans I've known feel more comfortable among one another. One Korean friend of mine doesn't have any non-Korean friends.

THOUGH I AM often quick to find fault with some aspects of Korean or American culture, I realize that I am the result of both, and feel, all in all, culturally assimilated. Sometimes the Korean and American characteristics are so intertwined in my personality and identity that they are impossible to separate. I feel fortunate to have been exposed to two different cultures, and I strongly believe that diversity breeds tolerance.

Racism, I have come to believe, is something that exists outside of us. It only begins to become a problem when one starts internalizing racist concepts and develops feelings of inferiority. Being a Korean immigrant has caused me to feel insecure about myself at times, but I have developed my self-esteem, first by excelling in sports, and then later in other endeavors. Superior skills make race—and physical condition—a nonfactor.

I plan to open my own law firm in the future. I want to provide Koreans with reliable, effective legal services at reasonable costs. I am particularly interested in helping Koreans because of the difficulties my own parents faced. As newcomers to this country, Koreans can be taken advantage of easily because of their inability to speak English and their unfamiliarity with the American legal system.

If I lived in Korea, my opportunities, no doubt, would be restricted by the ill-informed perceptions that most Koreans have about the disabled. By functioning effectively as an assistant district attorney, I have helped to alter the perceptions of many Koreans.

Part Three

Building Coalitions
A Pan-Asian or Non-White Identity?

THE NEXT THREE essayists are grouped together partly because they hold varying degrees of pan-Asian and/or Third World identity and partly because their ethnic and racial identities had a strong impact on their academic and professional careers.

As children, Kavitha Mediratta, David Wang, and Phuong Do were often the sole Asians at their schools. Wang and Do experienced racist taunts and physical violence, while Mediratta felt set apart by her physical appearance and her Indian name. Victimization by racial prejudice and racial violence during early years led them to develop a kinship with African Americans and to hold varying degrees of Third World identity. Though they had predominantly white friends, Mediratta, Do, and Wang also developed close friendships with African Americans and/or Latinos, empathizing with their exclusion from the white mainstream. Searching for role models for battling racism, Wang said he looked to African Americans, such as Medgar Evers and Martin Luther King, for inspiration. Mediratta developed her identity as a person of color in part through her realization that dark-skinned South Asians were discriminated against and targeted for racial violence in ways similar to African Americans. "Even with their economic privilege, Indians remain dark skinned and vulnerable to the vagaries of cultural and ethnic discrimination," Mediratta writes.

The essayists' awareness of their ethnic and racial identities affected their choice of college majors and careers. Mediratta's sense of kinship with African Americans led her to abandon her parents' dream of her becoming a doctor in order to work instead as a public school teacher in a black neighborhood in urban New Jersey. Do's decision to volunteer at a refugee agency in Denver and to obtain a graduate degree in social work were closely related to the formation of her ethnic and racial identities as a Vietnamese and an Asian American. Wang's ethnic and pan-Asian identities also influenced his decision to work as a liaison to Asian communities for the Office of the Manhattan Borough President. "I will continue to deepen my connection within the Asian American community. It is an obligation I willingly accept," Wang writes.

How Do You Say Your Name?

> Sometimes I visualize grace as a
> black, tropical bat,
> cutting through dusk on blunt, ugly wings.
> —From "Angela," a short story by Bharati Mukherjee

THROUGHOUT MY LIFE I've felt like an outsider, self-consciously aware of standing out and apart, a lone Indian in the largely Anglo American communities in which I grew up and have worked. As an adult, I delighted in discovering Bharati Mukherjee.[1] There, littered among the lines of her stories, were the details of living in a foreign land—images that captured an awkwardness that is all too familiar to me. I imagined that I knew what it felt like to cut through the dusk on blunt, ugly wings.

Perhaps it seems strange to talk about one's life this way—to choose to highlight a sense of awkwardness as the centerpiece of a story. But more than any other image, this one truly captures the immigrant experience for me. Writing now, I'm struck by how difficult it is to weave together in a single narrative the wealth of experiences that have shaped my understanding of my life. What follows is a glimpse of who I am, illustrations and thoughts about a journey that is very much in process.

My Name

My mother named me *Coveta* (pronounced Cu-vee-tha) because I was humming a song when I was born. In Sanskrit my name means poem. I am a singer of songs, a poetess. But if this name is meant to sound graceful, it has always felt more like Mukherjee's dark, awkward bat than the poised elegance my mother meant to bestow upon me. When my name rolls off the American tongue, it sounds heavy and ugly. *Ca-vetta . . . Cav-i-tha . . . Cuv-uda . . .* I have a name that never fails to draw attention and that no one can pronounce.

For much of my life, I've struggled to find the beauty in my name. Why has this struggle loomed so large for me? How is it that the act of naming one-self—and, conversely, of having one's name trivialized—can be so powerful and consuming?

My struggle to come to terms with my name traces my exploration of my dual cultural identity. It has led me to rename myself at points in my life, to alter-nately embrace and reject my Indian and American identities. I've been Coveta, Cavetta, Cov, and now Kavitha. At thirty-one, I've come to understand this jour-ney as a search for a sense of belonging. And now I recognize in my journey the common experience that I share with other first-generation "hyphenated" Amer-icans who, like me, must continually renegotiate the boundaries of identity, cul-ture, and community.

Immigrating to America

My twin brother and I were born in Buffalo, New York, in 1965 while my mother was visiting the U.S. We lived in India, where my sister was born, until I was three. My parents officially immigrated here in the hopes of continuing their professional careers unfettered by the lumbering bureaucracy prevalent in Indian society.

Although the United States was experiencing dramatic social change in 1968, one would never know it from my family in those early years here. We were insulated from the world around us, separated by the difference between our tra-ditions and mainstream American tradition, and by our own need for the familiar space of homelife.

During this time, my younger brother was born. My father worked briefly with an aerospace engineering firm on Long Island. My mother, a practic-ing physician for over a decade in India, took care of my siblings and me until I was five. My parents then switched roles and my father took care of us while my mother resumed her career.

The new domestic arrangement between my parents challenged both Indian and American norms of family life in ways they were ill-prepared to handle. Their choice to structure our family life this way was precipitated by the difficulty my father found in pursuing a research career in the U.S. defense industry as an Indian national. Perhaps if my parents had made this role reversal in India it would have been easier for them to cope with the conflicting expectations and frustrations they experienced. But in the U.S., without support or security from family and friends, and in the midst of enormous cultural and economic transi-tions, my parents found it difficult to cope, and there was often tension between them at home. This tension hung over my life as a child, and manifested itself in the often conflicting feelings I had about my parents' expectations for me.

Negotiating Life at Home and in School

For many immigrant families, school serves as a frontier between cultures. Children must mediate expectations for achievement and rules for behavior that differ widely between the home and school.

Both of my parents valued learning in school, but my father was particularly focused on our academic achievements. His own professional aspirations on hold in his new role as caretaker, he sought to instill his ambition in his children. He had confidence that we would be just like him, achieving academically in school, becoming doctors or engineers, and maintaining a sense of our Indian heritage. Duty, discipline, and tradition underlied his vision for us. My mother, in contrast, was less focused on these qualities and less concerned about our Indian heritage overall. Since she was often working, we felt my father's hopes and expectations much more acutely.

For much of my life, it has not been clear exactly what the Indian heritage is that my father prized so highly. There were often conflicting messages at home about what it meant to be Indian. My parents come from different parts of India. My mother is an upper-class Catholic from South India. She grew up in the city of Bangalore and was shaped by European traditions bequeathed by the Portuguese and the legacy of Britain's long occupation. In contrast, my father is an upper-caste Hindu from North India. He grew up in a tiny village in the Punjab, in an area that is now part of Pakistan. India for him meant Hindu traditions even though he does not practice the religion. These differences of geography and religion are not minor details; together, they give shape to completely different experiences of Indian identity.

My family practiced a mix of Christian and Hindu traditions that revolved mostly around holidays, food, and clothes, which were the lowest common denominators between my parents' different traditions. We celebrated Christmas and the Indian ceremony *Raksha Bandhan*,[2] we ate Indian food at home, and for important events (like parent-teacher night at school) my mother always wore a *sari* and my father a *churithar kurtha*. Although each of my parents speaks several Indian languages, the only language they have in common is English.

In my family, this cross-cultural experience was made more complicated by my family's mobility during our early years in school. My twin brother and I attended four different public schools in New York state before my family settled down on Long Island for my third grade. I remember feeling very detached from both my peers and teachers for much of elementary school. It was easier to stick by my brother than to venture forth into the sea of unfamiliar white faces who stared at my two long, oiled braids, which my father carefully bound every day, and sniffed at the scent of Indian spices that clung to my clothes.

I've always considered my Indian heritage important, but throughout grade school I found that being Indian made life both complicated and uncomfortable. My color, my hair, my clothes, even my name, set me apart from everyone around me. I dreaded the days in school when we had substitute teachers who, while taking attendance, would inevitably pause, stutter, and then call out a name barely recognizable as mine. Because my father insisted that I introduce myself by my full name, I seemed to be forever engaged in coaching people on how to pronounce it.

As my siblings and I grew up, our inevitable Americanization brought us into conflict with my parents' expectations for maintaining our Indian heritage. My father often railed against the American customs we began to assimilate. He comes from a world in which respect means obedience, but we were born American—and American children are independent; they speak their minds, raise their voices, and disagree openly with their parents. For the most part, we hid behind my mother, who was less concerned about our transformation. Perhaps this was because of her own westernized upbringing, or perhaps it was because she, too, in her professional life as a doctor, was trying to assimilate into American culture.

Fighting Invisibility

For high school, my parents sent my brother and me to Choate Rosemary Hall, a private New England boarding school for the wealthy. Boarding school began a whole new chapter in our life. Choate was built upon assumptions of white, Anglo-Saxon, Protestant culture and privilege; it was not an inviting place. Nevertheless, away from the familiar space of our family for the first time, my brother Ajata and I cautiously began to explore this new world. We ate pizza and listened to the Doors, which we saw as daring acts of rebellion against my parents' Indian tastes.

The urge to fit in among peers in high school is powerful, often irresistible. But how do you fit in when you have a name like Coveta, a hairstyle like Pocahontas's, and a wardrobe from Sears in a school outfitted at Bloomingdale's? To the extent that we were visible during our first two years at Choate, it was as *curios*—defined by our differences from our classmates. We were completely invisible both socially and intellectually. The adults and students around us didn't probe beneath the image of strangeness they perceived in our different customs in order to learn who we were and what we were saying.

My transformation began with my name: I became *Cov*. My brother and I were given nicknames by our roommates on the very first day we moved into Choate, and we seized these names with enthusiasm. In retrospect, it was a pragmatic response to the torture of hearing our names mispronounced. For years I had been surrounded every day, all the time, by people who never pronounced my name correctly. After a while their mispronunciations seeped into my most private thoughts so deeply that, sometimes, I called myself *Ca-vetta*.

The next step in my transformation was my appearance: I stopped wearing my hair in braids and began wearing lipstick and eyeshadow. It seemed that the more I conformed to the conventions of beauty around me, the more my social

standing among my female and male peers increased. It's true that these transformations began, in a sense, to make me visible at Choate, but the image they
brought into focus wasn't me. It was a distorted notion of hypersexualized femininity that had been popularized by media images of dark-skinned women with
long hair: Jennifer Beals in *Flashdance,* Lisa Bonet in *Angel Heart.*

To the extent that Choate facilitated an exploration of my identity, it was
almost exclusively an exploration of my cultural identity in the context of wealthy,
white America. Much of what being Indian meant to me I understood in terms of
how it differed from WASP culture. My friends were mostly wealthy, Jewish, New
Yorkers, and I felt a level of kinship with their feeling of marginalization at Choate.

In retrospect, I've often wondered why I didn't think about my identity in
terms of color. Choate had but a handful of students and faculty of color—mostly
black—and I didn't know them very well. Once I was invited by my African American art teacher to attend a students of color meeting. I was eating breakfast at the
time, and I remember wishing he would go away so I could finish my pancakes in
peace. Since I wasn't black, I didn't understand why he would invite me to the
meeting. I saw being Indian as very different from being black, even though the
exotic images of beauty that benefitted me were images of black women.

Later, in college, I began to take the idea of my own visibility more seriously, and consequently, to understand my status as "not-white" much more profoundly. I experienced this growth on a variety of levels: I developed a political
identity as a woman and defined my cultural identity as an Indian American.

On college campuses, the defining social space is the dining hall; there we
are forced to reveal ourselves by the choices we make about where to eat and who
to sit with. Amherst was more diverse than Choate, and the lunchroom had been
staked out by the school's various ethnic and identity groups. I felt little connection with the handful of Asian students, who were mostly East Asian and culturally quite different from me. Since my previous school experiences had left me so
conversant in Anglo American culture, I moved comfortably—or so I thought—
back into that social context. I introduced myself as *Cov,* still caught up in a
Choate-inspired mission to assimilate into American culture in which being Indian
was seen as exotic. My long, black hair, dark skin, and the *kajal* I wore for eye
makeup set me apart from my blond, preppy classmates.

I began dating for the first time in college, although my mother had
encouraged me to date boys for years. Although most of my friends were white, my
first boyfriend was biracial—black and Jewish. I suppose I felt a sense of kinship
with his experience of being somewhere in-between cultures at a place like Amherst.
After that, I met Clay, my future husband. Preppy, popular, a freshman hockey star,
he reminded me of the people I had gone to high school with. I remember being
surprised by his genuine interest in me; at the time, it made me feel truly visible.

Maybe because I started college on a more comfortable footing—the
American culture was familiar to me—I was able to see the cultural assumptions

that shaped my interactions with my peers more clearly. Maybe it was that, for the first time, I was separated from my brother and so I felt more strongly how *minority*—a word I had previously used rather glibly to refer to myself—could mean marginalization, not just difference. In any case, I became increasingly irritated at constantly being seen as the exotic other, which I perceived as little more than a male sexual fantasy and a continuation of my invisibility.

With this growing awareness of my invisibility, I became much more insistent on being taken on my own terms, as a woman and as an Indian. My friendships with women became much more important to me, and became a space in which to explore my sense of gender identity. This evolving political identity created a lot of conflict with Clay. It became increasingly difficult to understand each other across the enormous differences between how we looked at the world, as man and woman, as Anglo American and Indian American, as white and non-white.

My growing politicization also transformed my academic interests. I began college with the regimen of math and science courses expected of a pre-med student. My parents tell me that I had wanted to be a doctor since I was a child, although I can't separate out what I wanted for myself from what they wanted for me. As I began to find my own voice, I felt more of an urgency to learn about the culture and history of India. In part, I wanted to make sense of the stories my parents had told me as a child and the many conflicting expectations they seemed to have for me. But, most of all, I wanted to figure out exactly what being Indian meant to me.

So I majored in Asian studies and English, hoping this would create a broad enough arena for me to explore all of my questions about my identity. But by senior year I was feeling the boundaries of Amherst's limited perspective and values, particularly its shallow treatment of non-European cultures. My thesis advisor informed me that only two writers (Rudyard Kipling and E. M. Forster, both colonial-era) had written enough about India in English to support a thesis. His colonial perspective enraged me. It made me question the ways in which I had allowed the expectations and assumptions of people around me (including my parents) to define the possibilities for what I did.

A full recognition of the limitations of my academic environments, and my continued invisibility within them, made me want to be a teacher. I wanted to affirm children—particularly non-white children—in the way I had never been as a student. And, I wanted to get as far away as possible from overprivileged, white environments like Choate and Amherst.

Finding My Voice

I left Amherst and my parents' dreams of my future as a doctor to teach seventh grade life sciences in urban New Jersey. Teaching was supposed to be a brief stop on my way to figuring out what I really wanted to do, but East Orange changed all that. I enjoyed teaching and found an easy camaraderie with my students.

My year there challenged my naive, liberal assumptions about teaching and race relations in America. I was struck by how poor my school was compared to the Long Island schools of my childhood. Built to provide an "open learning" environment for students, it looked like an airplane hangar that had been hastily partitioned into rows of officelike cubicles. Children were stuffed everywhere. A banner extolling the virtues of learning hung over the entryway to the school. But, as my students frequently noted, anyone who built a school like that clearly had no academic expectations for the children who attended it. I don't think I had fully understood before then just how powerful racism is in this country, and how deeply it has devastated the prospects of entire communities.

At the same time, in neighboring Jersey City, Indians (doctors and lawyers) were being repeatedly beaten by a band of young white men who called themselves "dotbusters."[3] These attacks brought home for me how naive the assumptions of upper-middle-class immigrants—like my family—are about the possibilities for assimilation into American culture.

A level of affluence and mobility is afforded by the particulars of individual and familial economic status. But even with economic privilege, Indians remain dark skinned and vulnerable to the vagaries of cultural and ethnic discrimination. It is ironic how, even when faced with this discrimination, so many Indians cling to a centuries-old prejudice based on color and class in India, and refuse to acknowledge their different status here. (Years later, my parents, when rejected by a co-op board on Manhattan's Upper West Side, could not believe that racism was at play despite the mountains of evidence proving it was so.)

During my year in East Orange, I began to identify myself as a person of color, although I still introduced myself socially as *Cov.* This transition was precipitated not just by my sense of kinship with my students and my new African American friends, but also by my discovery of African American writers like Toni Morrison. More than any of the Asian writers I had read at this time, Toni Morrison's writing unlocked a world that seemed oddly familiar, even though she wrote about lives and experiences of black people that were very different from mine.

After my year in East Orange, I traveled briefly in West Africa, visiting Clay, who was in the Peace Corps in Liberia. This visit rekindled our friendship, and the steady stream of letters over the years following this trip helped to build a bridge between our different worlds. Liberia had transformed Clay. It had opened him up to a whole different culture and equipped him to cope with ambiguity, with being isolated and alone. By the time he came to see me in India two years later, it was clear that we were not only heading down a similar path but also that we had found a way to forge that path together.

After West Africa I went to India for two years to teach fourth grade in an international school for South Asian children drawn primarily from the subcontinent and the Middle East. Teaching in India gave me a chance to explore the country on my own terms, without the constraining social expectations of living with relatives and the emotional upheaval of traveling with my family. I had the time, space, and freedom to learn about my parents' India and to understand how different their individual experiences of India had been from each other, and how collectively their experiences of being Indian differed from mine.

In India I began to insist that people pronounce my name correctly. It might seem funny that India would be the place I first took this stand, but I was teaching in a South Indian international school for South Asian children that had a number of American and European staff members. When I wasn't teaching, I spent time with relatives and traveled through villages and cities, exploring almost every region of India. Everyone was confused by the strange spelling of my name, my mix of North and South Indian looks, and by my Indian and American mannerisms. I wanted a name that would make my Indian heritage clear, and *Kavitha* (pronounced Ka-vee-tha), the more traditional spelling and pronunciation of my name, did just fine.

My Indian friends and colleagues alternately marveled at my "modern image" as a New Yorker and were amused by my interest in Indian things. Indians have an expression for Indian Americans like me: I'm an "ABCD"—an American-Born Confused *Desi* (a Hindi expression for Indian.) During my two years teaching, I thought a lot about my cultural identity and why I've been so consumed with figuring out what it is. Who decides one's cultural identity? Is it imposed by the larger society or family, or is it ours to define? What does it mean to be an Indian? Can I choose to be both Indian and American? Is this choice mine to make?

It has become clear to me that although I may know little about the ancestry of my family and cannot speak any Indian language fluently, I'm connected to India in a number of intangible ways. It's hard to give words to the familiarity I felt being in India, and even harder to explain why I felt such ease being there. At some point, while sitting in the dark, incense-filled temple chambers or walking through the marketplace, the pungent aroma of familiar spices brought home to me just how much Indian tradition had seeped into my upbringing, even though I had been raised a million miles away.

Still, during this time in India, I also became conscious for the first time of how truly American I am—especially as a woman. I found myself alternately accepting and rebelling against what was expected of me, even as I longed to fit in. I traveled alone, challenged my colleagues in school, and wore above-the-knee skirts when I felt like it. I justified these rebellions as my birthright precisely because I am both Indian and American. But this freedom came at a price. Frequently I was told—often by complete strangers—that I was less than desirable: I was too dark, too thin, too independent, and too outspoken. In the end, how I lived in India exemplifies the many contradictions I felt about being there: feeling like a stranger in my supposed homeland, being a witness to a culture that is both mine and not mine.

Coming Home

Many of the transitions I've made in recent years reflect the understandings that became clear to me in India. I formally changed the spelling of my name to Kavitha, but have been less concerned about whether or not people pronounce it correctly. Most Americans are not used to listening carefully, are not used to cultural difference—but whether or not they pronounce my name correctly has little bearing on my connection to India.

I have followed my interest in urban education by obtaining a master's degree in education, working as a staff developer with New York City public school teachers, and serving as a visiting fellow in school reform at a national foundation. I now work at an education research and policy institute, where I assist parent and community groups that are working to improve their neighborhood schools.

It's ironic that all of these academic and professional environments have been predominantly white, even though their purpose is to serve communities of color. Often, in spaces like these, it is easy to fall (and to be forced) into playing the role of spokesperson, as a South Asian, or even more ridiculously, for people of color in general. Marginalization, in its most blatant and insidious dimensions, is always present. I've been told that I was hired only because of an employer's fancy for exotic women and misguided commitment to workplace diversity. I've been called "angry" because I openly discuss issues concerning people of color and, consequently, have been ignored because my perspective is "too limited."

As in India, I find myself engaged in a daily struggle to mark out my own space, to make explicit the ways in which the expectations of people around me differ from my own, and to not let these expectations limit what I believe is possible and worthwhile. Resistance has been such a powerful dynamic in my life, and has lain beneath much of my struggle to claim both an identity and a community. But sometimes resistance can create its own sort of limiting space—especially if it never moves beyond reacting to what surrounds us. Such reactive resistance defines one in simplistic either/or ways, rather than proactively giving voice to the full range of our complicated, often contradictory identities.

Of late I have consciously begun to build nurturing spaces for myself that are not marked by resistance to the assumptions of people around me. My marriage is one such place where I have the freedom and support to be all the different and often conflicting parts of who I am. My white women friends from college, and the women of color I've met in the years since then, have helped me to explore what it means to be a woman who is both Indian American and "of color" rather than "not white."

In the past few years I have met more Indian Americans than in all the time I was growing up. New York City is now home to a vast array of South Asians, from all sorts of socioeconomic and cultural backgrounds. Indians drive taxis and run newspaper stands, restaurants, and clothing boutiques. Although there is now a thriving social scene among young, upper-middle-class Indian

Americans, I rarely spend time in those circles. How easy it is to take something for granted when you have it in abundance.

TODAY, PEOPLE ASK me about my cultural and ethnic identity in all sorts of awkward ways. They count off the Indians they know, comment on how articulately I speak, or tell me I can't be Indian because I don't "sound Indian." In fact, a white man recently told me that I can't be a person of color because I don't sound like one. Americans in general seem to have difficulty accepting complexity and ambiguity. I'm either Indian or American, white or black . . . I can't be both and neither.

What does it mean to be Indian in America? On what grounds does one stake a claim on identity, and by extension, on community? My Indian and American experiences and my gender identity and class background collectively shape the way I see the world. These are not distinct identities that can be separated out under close examination. Frustratingly, perhaps, there are no roadmaps on this journey of self-definition. Finding the intersection of one's multiple identities—cultural and otherwise—is different for each of us.

For much of my life I've felt an urgent need to definitively stake out where I am from and where I belong. This need has pushed me to write about my Indian heritage before, and is what drives me to talk about my Indian-American heritage now . . . as if, in doing so, I'll come to some simple but climactic answers about who I am. But in the end, being both Indian and American is a tightrope, a delicate balance, that I must cross and maintain everyday. This search to know, define, and connect the strands of identity and culture, to establish a sense of community and belonging, is an experience I share with other first-generation immigrants. And while at times I feel uncertain and uneasy, my dual cultural heritage also brings with it an ungainly beauty that's very much like that of a black tropical bat flapping awkwardly, but strongly, on the distant horizon.

ENDNOTES

1. Bharati Mukherjee is a twentieth-century Indian novelist who writes about the Indian immigrant experience in the United States and Canada.

2. *Raksha Bandhan* is a ceremony celebrated in late August, in which brother and sister renew their pledge to care for each other.

3. *Dotbusters* refers to the *bindi* that Indian women wear on their foreheads.

Beyond the Golden Door

> Give me your tired, your poor,
> Your huddled masses yearning to breathe free.
> The wretched refuse of your teeming shore.
> Send these, the homeless, tempest-tost to me.
> I lift my lamp beside the golden door!
> —"The New Colossus" by Emma Lazarus

WHEN I WAS ten years old, my Baba began to subject me to a unique form of punishment. Whenever the chores went undone, or whenever anything in the house was discovered broken, he sentenced me to produce one hundred handwritten copies of Emma Lazarus's "The New Colossus." At the time, I couldn't understand Baba's vindictiveness, but with each shattered bowl and broken toy, the poem began to grow on me and I gradually came to realize that this poem held a particular significance for my father.

Baba was a civil servant for a New York City government agency. Every night after dinner, he would recount stories from work of injustices faced by people struggling to make it in New York—the Chinese seamstress slaving in sweatshops for subminimum wages, the single mother fighting to get wintertime heat in her drafty tenement. These people, he declared, never had the opportunity to make a better life for themselves and their families.

Nevertheless, New York City remained a place of hope for Baba. In his own country of Taiwan, he explained, he had been treated like a second-class citizen in a society dominated by the Japanese dictatorship. The situation hardly improved when mainland China's Kuomintang took over after Japan's surrender at the end of World War II. The Kuomintang imposed martial law and executed thousands of dissidents.

In the early 1960s, Baba got the chance to leave Taiwan on a student visa. He left my mother, whom he was dating at the time, and traveled to Oklahoma to study for his master's degree in economics. After graduating, he moved to New York City and obtained resident status. He had difficulty finding secure employment in his field. Ultimately, he took and passed a civil service exam and got a city job. In the meantime, he corresponded with Mama frequently, eventually exchanging over 230 letters with her in six years. In 1968, Baba wrote and proposed to my mother. She quickly wrote back and accepted. He then arranged for Mama to come from Taiwan. Their first few years in New York were hard. Lunch was often a single slice of pizza shared between them.

Yet Baba loved New York City. He loved strolling down Broadway, visiting the Metropolitan Museum of Art, and watching the sun set over the Hudson River. He told me that he had accepted the city job out of a sense of gratitude for all the opportunities the city had offered him—a job, a secure home, and a new life. He explained that he wanted to help others secure similar opportunities promised at "the golden door." Through his unflagging enthusiasm in the promise of America—which found expression even in my punishments—Baba passed his beliefs on to me when I was very young.

Soon after I was born, my parents settled in Maspeth, a neighborhood in the heart of Queens that had welcomed earlier waves of Irish, Italian, German, and Polish immigrants. It was the kind of place where one could buy a house, raise a family, and grow tomatoes in the backyard. The local bank distributed "Maspeth is America" bumper stickers and cosponsored the annual Memorial Day parade. My family was one of only a handful of Asian families in the neighborhood, and over the years my parents developed friendly relations with our mostly white neighbors.

Like many other mothers in the neighborhood, Mama stayed home and took care of the children (in my case, just me). We learned English together from "Mr. Rogers" and "Sesame Street." Mama taught me how to fold origami, make pork buns and egg noodles from scratch, and celebrate Taiwanese holidays like the Moon Festival and the Chinese New Year. We used to cook for days during these holidays, filling the house with the aroma of pastries, ginger chicken, and steamed fish. Mama was also my private tutor, helping me with homework and giving me extra arithmetic exercises.

My relationship with Baba was more distant. After we watched the evening news, Baba would withdraw into the den to complete work he had brought home. Mama sat with him, balancing the family budget and reading the newspaper. I was not to disturb them. In fact, I rarely ventured into the den, except to ask for permission to go to the movies, get my weekly allowance, submit my report card, or be punished for being disobedient.

Baba's word was law, and I frequently ran afoul of it. Whether coming home late from the park, snickering inappropriately at dinner, or arguing with Baba when assisting with household repairs, I was often breaking some new family rule. When I was old enough, he would assign "progressive" punishments like copying the Lazarus poem. Then, when I talked back, he would invariably assign another more traditional one, such as kneeling for hours on a hard wooden floor—and did I talk back!

"You don't love me!" I'd yell.

"I pay for school!" he'd answer.

"Yeah, just throw money at me, not love!" I'd retort.

Then I would get grounded for weeks. It was not until I was much older that I came to realize that Baba expressed his love for me by making sure that I had a baseball mitt, food on the table, and warm clothing. More importantly, both Baba and Mama made sure that I did my homework, frequented the public library, and got a good education.

Because I got good grades, my parents assumed everything was fine at my mostly white parochial school—but I knew otherwise. My classmates taunted me incessantly. "Hey, Bruce, you know kung-fu? Teach me your ancient Chinese secret," I often heard. I soon grew to hate Bruce Lee. Every day at lunch, the boys would bring their tables together and then vote on whether or not I could join them. I usually ate alone.

Adding injury to insult, Brian, a classmate since first grade, would frequently smack me on the head. "Go back to China." he'd say.

"I'm as American as you are!" I'd protest.

"Shut up, you stupid Jap," he'd reply.

Many classmates treated me the way Brian did, sometimes with respect when we were alone, but with contempt in a group. Even those not in the popular group lashed out verbally or physically in order to enhance their social status. An all-too-familiar routine would begin with John saying, "Hey Chinaman, what are you doing?" And without fail, John and his friends would surround me.

"Leave me alone," I'd plead, but John would just bow his head, squint his eyes, and bray, "Ahso." I'd raise my hands to protect myself from what I knew was coming, but I was usually too late and the glob of spit would hit my neck and then ooze down into my shirt. I began to spend my lunches in the computer room.

As bad as it was for me, the Peruvian kid had it worse. While I got spat on occasionally, Juan, a thirteen-year-old who had recently arrived in the States, got spat on and kicked almost every day. The other boys gave him charley horses and called him "a dirty spic." He was my first friend who was neither Asian nor white. We were bound together by the racist barrages we both endured. From Juan, I learned to deflect the verbal assaults with self-deprecating humor.

Despite my sense of isolation at school, I shunned my Asian American classmates, Jenny and Richard. My white classmates insisted on writing "David loves Jenny" in all my books, and I bristled at the idea that we were made for each other just because we were both Chinese. I helped Jenny with her schoolwork, but only over the phone. I did not want to be seen with her or Richard at school. It made me uncomfortable that they spoke English with a slight accent—they were not like me.

During those days, I had a recurring nightmare in which my mother would give a tour of the house to my white classmates. In her broken English, she would show them the delicately painted Chinese scrolls and the Chinese curios in the cabinets. They would examine my Chinese textbooks and try their hand at Chinese calligraphy using my ink and brush. They even seemed to be not at all condescending toward my mother, but as they entered my room, I would start to panic. I became terrified that they would drop their cordial façade and start teasing me about how different my family and home were from theirs.

At this point, I would wake up frenzied, jump out of bed, and pull on a pair of pants. Only when I was ready to rush out and throw my classmates out of my house would I realize that it had been just a dream. Dazed, I would return to bed. The nightmares continued for years.

As an escape, I dove into my schoolwork. I began visiting the public library regularly and became an avid reader. My teachers encouraged me academically, urging me to submit my essays and science and social studies projects in districtwide competitions. My fourth-grade teacher asked me to give annual presentations on the Chinese New Year. My schoolwork and projects gave me confidence and I eventually graduated eighth grade as valedictorian.

My academic success in parochial school was not mirrored in Chinese school, however. Every Saturday when I was eight years old, my parents sent me to Mandarin classes in Chinatown. I hated the class from the beginning. I sat with the younger students at long tables in front, while the adults, who were mostly white, sat in the back. The three-hour class was devoted to rote memory and penmanship and was conducted entirely in Mandarin.

Because all the other Chinese students already spoke Mandarin at home, they had a much easier time learning the language. I spoke a Taiwanese dialect and was hopelessly lost. By the middle of the year, I was trying to whine and cry my way out of class every weekend. At the year's end, my report card was a column of red Fs. I had gotten the worst grades in the class. I was so demoralized that I did not attempt another Mandarin class until college. My inability to speak Mandarin made me feel alienated from my Chinese roots.

It was only in high school that I began to feel comfortable with my Chinese American identity. Stuyvesant High School specialized in science and mathematics and drew a relatively diverse student population from across the city. Asians from just about every origin represented fully 40 percent of the student body. At the freshman orientation, I discovered to my astonishment that the student body president was actually Korean American!

I felt accepted at Stuyvesant. Interracial friendships and dating were common. I quickly became good friends with students from a variety of backgrounds and ethnicities. I became involved in student government, running community service programs and school spirit activities. However, I joined neither the Asian American nor the Chinese American clubs, still bristling at the assumption that just because I shared the same ethnicity with other people, we would have an instant connection. When I ran for the office of student president during my junior year, I tried to distinguish myself from my clean-cut Asian American opponents by growing a ponytail. As student president, I felt that I needed to represent the concerns of the entire student body, not just Asian Americans.

AFTER SOPHOMORE YEAR, my family and I traveled to Taiwan for a two-month visit. I had not been there since I was four years old, when my parents presented me to my grandparents. I remember constantly screaming out, "Stupid Taiwan! Stupid Taiwan! I want to go home!" At the time, I thought Taiwan was just a stiflingly hot, humid place with no drinkable water and a major mosquito problem.

During my second visit, we stayed with Ah-Gu (uncle) Abing and his family in Pei-tou, a neighborhood near Taipei. On my third day there, a passerby asked me in Taiwanese where the Taipei train station was. I replied in Taiwanese, "Sorry, miss, I don't know."

"Aiya, of course you know!" she snapped.

She stalked off, and it dawned on me that I must have looked like a native to her! For the first time I thought, "Maybe I fit in here."

I was pleased to discover that I already knew many of the Taiwanese customs and courtesies. They were small things, like greetings, table manners, and how to accept gifts, but they helped strengthen the bond I was beginning to feel. I also spoke the language, albeit hesitantly at first, letting my parents do most of the talking. As I practiced, however, I gained confidence and began to chat away with my relatives, most of whom were extraordinarily pleased that I could speak so well. Afterward, I spent days traveling alone throughout Taipei, conversing with people I met.

Baba and Mama showed me the neighborhoods where they grew up. We shopped at the night markets. I paid my respects to Ah-Gong (grandfather) at his grave on a mountainside near Taipei. My Ah-Gau (aunt) told me stories about how Ah-Gong fought for equal rights for Taiwanese during the Japanese occupation and how Baba biked to visit Mama every weekend before coming to America.

My relatives also admired the American in me. According to Ah-Gu Abing, I seemed more creative and independent than my cousins. He told me that Taiwanese education was very competitive, with only about three out of ten applicants being accepted to college. Since admission was based solely on an exam, much of Taiwanese education revolved around exam preparation. The teacher's duty was to cram as much information as possible into their students through memorization and rote learning; students were even taught to copy essays from textbooks rather than write their own. Smiling, Ah-Gu said that Taiwanese children needed a little "America" in their lives.

One morning, I got up at 4:30 to hike up a mountain with my seventy-year-old Ah-Ma (grandmother) and her friends. We walked through narrow streets lined with low houses and up a steep, winding road past a Buddhist temple and a farmer harvesting bamboo shoots. I told stories about high school and admonished Ah-Ma for smoking. Ah-Ma explained how walking up the mountain invigorated her, keeping her fit and at peace with herself. At the top, we did stretching exercises and marveled at the panoramic view of Taipei and its surrounding neighborhoods.

Back in New York, I discovered that I had left the United States as an American and returned two months later feeling that I was more than that—I was Taiwanese American, from a large family grounded in a distinct history. Eager to share my Taiwan experiences with Asian American friends, I talked for hours with friends about our respective histories. A friend talked about visiting her birthplace, Hong Kong, for the first time since she arrived in New York ten years before, and how wonderful it was to see relatives and childhood sites again. Another recounted a similar experience to mine at an all-white elementary school. I felt closer to my Asian American friends.

At the end of our senior year, my friends and I followed the news coverage of the gathering of thousands of students in Tiannanmen Square, Beijing. Every day, we rushed to lunch to eagerly discuss the student hunger strikes, the support they received from factory workers, and the statue of the Goddess of Democracy that was erected across from the portrait of Mao.

I was exhilarated by student leader Wu'er Kaixi, who, although weakened by his hunger strike and clad only in pajamas, spoke eloquently and defiantly to top government officials. On a map ripped from the newspaper, I plotted the advance of the People's Liberation Army to the outskirts of Beijing from all over China. On June 4th, I watched TV with confusion and then horror as the Army stormed into the square and massacred the student protesters. I cried for hours.

In school the next day I met with friends to make sense of what had happened and to sort out our feelings. A few days later, we marched with thousands of other New Yorkers from the United Nations across town to the Chinese consulate, wearing black ribbons and carrying shrouded coffins, our fists raised, protesting the student massacre.

While walking with many Chinese Americans who had witnessed the tragedies of Taiwan's "Two-Two-Eight" massacre and the Chinese Cultural Revolution, I realized that, most importantly, I was marching that day in support of my family in Taiwan who had been disenfranchised and silenced. If my parents hadn't left Taiwan, my life would have been very different. With much resolve, I began to attend teach-ins and candlelight vigils supporting the democracy movement in China. My involvement continued during my first year at Harvard University.

I was extremely fortunate that my parents were willing to take out loans, scrimp and save, and spend their savings in order for me to go to Harvard. At the time, I wanted to attend Yale; my parents insisted I go to Harvard because "everyone in Taiwan knows Harvard." Unconvinced, I visited Harvard during spring of senior year. Arriving in Harvard Yard, I instantly fell in love with its red brick buildings surrounded by lush grass and canopied by elms. I decided Harvard might not be so bad after all.

Well, I was wrong. I had a rough first two years. I learned in an English expository writing class that I couldn't write. I was too brash in taking the accelerated Introduction to Chemistry. I discovered that many Mandarin-speaking classmates were cruising past me to easy As in my Mandarin language class. I was dogged by the suspicion that the admissions office had made a mistake in accepting me, even though I had done well in high school.

I spent many hours talking to my freshman advisor, agonizing over what subject I should major in. Ever since I was very young, my parents had wanted me to become a doctor. They believed it was a prestigious profession, as well as lucrative, secure, and a service to the community. I agreed with my parents and wanted to fulfill their wishes. However, American government fascinated me. I decided to major in government while taking pre-med classes, reasoning that pre-med studies balanced with a government background could raise my chances of getting into a good medical school. Those plans lasted two years.

The summer after sophomore year, I interned at the mayor's Office of Federal Affairs in Manhattan. During the administration of Mayor David Dinkins, I helped organize a proposal to raise funds for collaborative federal lobbying efforts among nonprofit organizations. The proposal eventually got funding, and these organizations banded together in raising funds to improve their neighborhoods. This experience showed me that government could make a difference. At summer's end, I decided against going to medical school. Instead, I would concentrate in government and then attend law school. When my parents tried to persuade me to reconsider my decision, I told them that if they wanted a doctor in the family, one of them should take the MCATs.

That fall, I took challenging classes in American government, urban politics, and international relations. I also became more involved in Phillips Brooks House, the student public service organization, teaching a weekly civics course to young people in Dorchester, an impoverished and racially segregated area of Boston. I also began to attend more plays, movies, and other student productions. My roommates noted in retrospect that my days at Harvard brightened only after I abandoned my pre-med ambitions.

At the invitation of several friends, I joined a newly created campus magazine devoted to Chinese American issues. I was drawn to the magazine's policy of expressing the diversity within the Chinese American community. I edited an article written by a Chinese American law student. The article took the form of a conversation with his mother explaining to her for the first time that he was gay. I was struck by how personal and honest the piece was. The author wrote about his fears that his mother would reject him for being gay. He also expressed his doubts and his own internalized racism: He admitted never having had a boyfriend who was not white. His piece was a plea for acceptance of his individuality.

After long weeks of editing, the first issue was printed. It contained articles on the supposed self-segregation of Asian American students, interracial dating, and profiles of prominent Asian Americans. The article I edited had been printed, but a disclaimer had been tacked on the end, stating that the author's views did not necessarily reflect those of the magazine. Aside from editorial pieces, no other article had a disclaimer.

I could not help feeling that my writer's article was singled out because of its subject. I had become sensitive to gay issues because of my suitemate Steve. Steve was more than my first openly gay friend; he was one of my best friends. We helped one another as we adjusted to college life, dealt with the pressures of our schoolwork, and the emotional roller-coaster rides that I had with my girlfriends and he had with his boyfriends. We were suitemates throughout college.

I learned that the disclaimer was a compromise among the magazine's board. It was my understanding that the article was going to be excluded from the magazine, but since I was so enthusiastic about the article, a few board members pushed for its publication. While I was pleased that the article was published, I was angered that the board seemed to be distancing itself from the article. I asked for an apology in the following issue but none was ever published. Disillusioned, I soon left the magazine.

I became more involved in public service activities. During a discussion on community conflicts in my civics class, one student told me that a friend of his had been knifed in a dispute over gang colors. Even though I myself had grown up in a neighborhood where fights were common, it was shocking to hear about thirteen-year-old children confronting one another with such hostility. Deciding that I would try to help them find a better way of resolving their conflicts, I eventually organized Peace Games in my senior year. As director, I assembled a group of public school teachers and education experts to draft a conflict resolution curriculum. I also pulled together 110 volunteers to teach more than 1,200 middle school students. Directing Peace Games helped me develop my organizing skills and gave me experience in community problem solving.

In recognition of the program's success, the Stride-Rite Foundation offered me a post-graduate public-service fellowship to establish Peace Games at Columbia University, to teach young people in Harlem, Washington Heights, and the Upper West Side. I hesitated at first in accepting the one-year fellowship. By accepting it, I would be doing something completely different from my classmates, the majority of whom were either working in consulting or financial services, or attending graduate or professional schools. I was deeply concerned that, unlike my classmates, there wasn't a clear career move once I completed the fellowship. I could instead decline the fellowship and attend law school. I was unsure of what my next step should be.

After a particularly unproductive night of soul searching, I called my parents. Baba answered, and we talked briefly about President Clinton's cabinet choices. Then we both paused.

"Baba, what am I doing?" I suddenly wished that I had not asked, expecting a long lecture about the importance of going to law school. Instead, there was silence.

"I mean, what would you do if you were in my situation?" I asked again.

Baba began to tell me a story. When he had finished his master's degree mid-semester, he left immediately to find a job. He said that, in retrospect, he should have stayed in school and spent more time with his friends. Slipping into Taiwanese, he said, "You should not forget what is important to you."

Baba paused and said, "I know you work very hard, and your mother and I are thinking of you and are proud of you." My jaw dropped. Baba had never before said that to me. Mama had always been the cheerleader in the family. Whenever I brought home a report card, I would show it first to Mama because she would gush over it. A raised eyebrow was all that would express my father's satisfaction.

His voice changed. "All right, talk to your mother," Baba murmured. Mama was always the "emotional" half of my parents while Baba tried to be the "rational" half, and I realized for the first time that whenever Baba told me to speak to Mama, it was because he knew she could better express what he wanted to say.

"Thanks. I love you, too," I whispered.

"All right . . . here's your Mama," he said.

What was important to me, I realized, was Peace Games. I immensely enjoyed directing a community service program, teaching young people, and working with volunteers. Also, my academics and experiences had taught me the best way to identify and solve public problems was to work on the grassroots level. The fellowship would give me the opportunity to apply this lesson and, more importantly, help address the epidemic of violence in my hometown. I decided to delay law school and instead accept the fellowship.

When I began organizing Peace Games in New York City, public school officials looked at me with suspicion, as if to ask, "What does a twenty-one-year-old Chinese kid from Harvard know about conflict resolution for African American and Latino kids in Harlem?" Thankfully, many principals took a chance on me with the program and I worked with school officials and educational advisors to refine the curriculum that would meet the students' needs. The program eventually taught 1,600 students.

During the fellowship, I conducted a three-day conflict resolution workshop with a tenth grade class at a high school in the Bronx. On the first day, I entered a classroom of mostly African American and Latino/a tenth graders, introduced myself, and answered questions.

I began my lesson. After an icebreaker, we went through activities that introduced the concepts of conflict and conflict resolution. The students were rowdy. One student interrupted by saying that he knew a Chinese American who owned a grocery near his home. Another student asked me whether or not I was a doctor. I noticed that some students were mimicking my fast-paced manner of talking. I was confused. Why were these students teasing me as my white elementary school classmates had done?

I was puzzled because I had always felt comfortable with the African American community. While growing up, I did not have any Asian American role models aside from my parents. In the ridicule and prejudice that I fought in grade school, I turned instead to African Americans like Medgar Evers and Martin Luther King, and Hispanic Americans like Cesar Chavez for strength and guidance. Later, in high school and college, I learned that as an Asian American and person of color, I had much in common with many African American and Latino/a friends: experiences of discrimination, confusion about racial identity, and progressive political views.

I gained my bearings and realized that my students probably had little clue where I came from. I stopped the class. I asked them who they thought I was. One student said that I was the grocer's son; another said that I was born in China. Still another said that I was very rich. I asked them how they arrived at these conclusions. One explained that the only Chinese people he saw owned grocery stores. Another said that since many of her teachers lived in Manhattan, she assumed I did, too.

I spent a minute or two talking about where I came from, what I was doing, and why I was teaching conflict resolution. Then we continued as planned. After class, a student came over to me and said I shouldn't have taken the taunts from the other students. I smiled and told him I should have done a better job introducing myself.

When the fellowship was over, I was recommended for a position at the office of the Manhattan Borough President, Ruth W. Messinger, a progressive Democrat who is a social worker by training and has spent the last twenty years in public life. I learned about Ruth when I volunteered for the re-election campaign of David Dinkins, the first African American mayor of New York City. I believed in her vision of an inclusive city whose strength lay in its diversity. Her intellect, public policy expertise, and thoughtful, savvy, compassionate style impressed me immensely.

The job with the Borough President was to work as a liaison to the neighborhoods of the Lower East Side, Chinatown, and downtown Manhattan and with the Asian American communities. At first, I was a little hesitant about accepting the position as an Asian American liaison. Like my childhood fears of being separated from the mainstream, I feared that the position would make me be considered merely an "ethnic voice" rather than someone acknowledged for his expertise in community organizing. Nonetheless, I decided to accept the job, feeling up to the challenge of working with the Asian American communities and working on both grassroots and government levels to create public policy.

In my first few months at this job, I attended a merchants' meeting in Chinatown. The meeting was conducted in Cantonese, and as the meeting proceeded, I could feel my cheeks burning with embarrassment because I didn't know what was going on. I felt as if I had been transported back in time to one of my parents' dinner parties where I had been an uncomprehending child. After fifteen minutes, I spoke up and asked that someone translate the discussion for me in English. The participants looked annoyed, but when I explained that I spoke Taiwanese, they smiled and nodded sympathetically. Someone then translated the discussion for me.

Also during my first month on the job, a community activist named Izzie gave me a tour of a mammoth housing project near Chinatown where 2,000 predominantly Latino/a and Chinese American families live. While touring the complex, he told me that most of the Chinese American residents were recent immigrants who spoke little English and worked long hours in restaurant and garment factories. Many were regularly preyed on by muggers.

When we reached the sixteenth floor, Izzie insisted on trudging up the stairs to the roof. Opening the broken, graffiti-covered fire door, I was overwhelmed by the sharp stench of old urine. We finally reached the fresh air. Pointing to a nearby building, Izzie mentioned that a woman had been raped on its rooftop the previous year. I looked over to the Empire State Building and the majestic East River bridges, one of which I crossed every day on my bicycle. When I saw these buildings from the bridge, I used to wonder who lived there.

Interrupting my reverie, Izzie asked, "Do you have the same problems where you live?"

"Different issues," I mumbled. In comparison with many of these residents, I was fortunate. Baba had a stable city job with full benefits; Mama took care of me. In the comfort of my home in Maspeth, social problems were merely ideas, merely Baba's stories from work. After the tour, I thought, I would go home to escape the poverty, unemployment, and violence.

But the things I had seen followed me home. I saw my family in the project residents I met. Like my parents, many had come to this country to seek a better life. They confronted many of the language and cultural barriers that my parents had. Their children were probably having the same tough time I had living in a dual society—one grounded in Asia, the other here in New York. Unlike my parents, however, the immigrants hadn't yet realized their dreams for a better life. I realized that it was my duty to work with the community in order to help make their hope possible.

In my four years at the borough president's office, I have tried to do just that. In my position, I lobbied for vigorous enforcement of labor laws in the restaurant and garment industries, fought for increased police patrols in China-town, and urged investigations into racially motivated attacks against Asian Americans, such as the alleged police beating of a South Asian taxi driver orga-nizer. I helped found a neighborhood improvement team composed of Latino and Chinese Americans and worked to save two Latino cultural institutions on the Lower East Side. I've worked with my colleagues to help fund Asian American family advocacy organizations and to develop low-income housing. In order to increase Asian American participation in government, I organized the Asian American Advisory Group to inform the borough president on policy matters and helped increase the number of Asian Americans appointed to local commu-nity boards.

My advocacy for New York's Asian American communities has been one of my most satisfying career experiences. I welcome the challenges of learning about the needs of each community and its political complexities and organizing the communities to meet their needs. I enjoy working with community leaders to win victories, such as the defeat of the proposed deregulation of New York rent laws, which, if enacted, would have thrown thousands of Asian Americans and others out of their homes and into the streets. Most importantly, I have learned that I can serve as an advocate, problem solver, and enabler in Asian American communities.

I CONTINUE TO learn more about my Taiwanese roots. At the end of Ruth Messinger's term as borough president, I spent six months in Taiwan visiting my relatives and studying Mandarin. During my trip, a large group of relatives and I visited my ancestors' graves during Tomb-Sweeping Day. The grave plots were arranged in a haphazard fashion up and down a mountain. At first, we struggled to find the grave of my great-grandfather (Ah-Tso); eventually, Ah-Gu spotted the tree that had been used by my family as a marker. Ah-Tso's plot was shaped like a typical Taiwanese grave, enclosed by a knee-high wall decorated with mosaics of scenes from folk tales. The tombstone was etched with Ah-Tso's name, my great-grandmother's name, the name of the town in China where my family was from, and the names of my great-grandparents' offspring.

When we finished clearing the knee-high grass surrounding the grave, Ah-Gu lit incense sticks and handed them to me. I bowed three times in front of Ah-Tso's tomb. There was so much I would have liked to say to Ah-Tso: What was life like a hundred years ago? What were your parents like? Why did our family come to Taiwan from Fujin Province in China? I also wanted to let him know how his granddaughter, my mother, has been a great mom and instilled in me values that my family holds dear—familial piety, education, and community. I whispered a word of thanks to Ah-Tso for making it all possible for me. I placed the burning incense sticks at his tombstone.

Afterward, we trooped back to town and shared a huge lunch. There, I learned more about my mother from my relatives. Because Mama was the oldest daughter, she had to watch over her siblings and cousins. According to her sister, Mama let you know immediately when something was wrong. She also had a quick temper. Mama was beautiful when she was my age (and still is) and had many suitors. She worked at a bank in Taipei, and after Ah-Gong died she became the breadwinner of the family. Ah-Gu explained that during the warm months, he and Mama would often see a movie and eat flavored shaved ice.

I appreciated hearing these stories about Mama. I have not spent much time with my relatives—most lived in either Canada or Taiwan. To be sure, I asked my parents about my family history, but had few opportunities to get the perspectives of others. And now, I was sitting among my relatives. Most had never seen me before and it was only because of my relationship to Mama and by extension my relationship to them that they were opening their lives to this stranger.

But then again, maybe I was not such a stranger. I was shocked to visit relatives' homes and find childhood pictures of myself in their albums. Most relatives knew of my whereabouts over the last ten years. And this knowledge was, of course, due to my parents. While conversing with relatives, I became worried that as my parents' generation passed away, I might lose touch with my relatives and Taiwan. I resolved to strengthen these fragile links with my relations.

I also wondered how I would pass along all I've learned about my family and its traditions and history. What if my children are as stubborn as I was when I was a child, disliking everything Chinese and wanting so much to be what I used to think was American—white, mainstream American? Would they hate Mandarin classes and not want to hang out with other Asian Americans and or learn family traditions, just as I had done? I would hate for my children to realize later in life how much they had lost through ignorance or stupidity.

Among the things I would teach my children are the values my parents taught me—some traditionally Taiwanese, others uniquely American. I would try to help them understand the continuity of their father's family history, from Taiwan to America. I would hope my wife would do the same with her family history, so that our children could be grounded with a sense of who they are and where they belong. I would tell them about my life. I would explain how I have come to understand how fortunate I have been in my family life, schooling, and career, and how through these experiences I've developed pride in my history, my heritage, and myself.

I no longer dream of being different.

* * *

THIS PAST FALL, I returned to the U.S. and started my legal studies at George-town University. I finally decided to attend law school because I learned from my government experience how legal assistance can change lives. When I worked with the Legal Referral Service to set up a free, multilingual clinic day in China-town, more than 250 people came to seek advice on housing, immigration, and business law. Many feared the changes in the recently enacted federal welfare and immigration reform laws, expressing concern about losing their welfare benefits and not being able to feed their families. Others felt helpless to keep their loved ones from being deported. I was inspired by the volunteer attorneys who helped these people simply by arming them with knowledge of the law. I realized legal training will help me assist the people who feel that there is no one with the power to help them—and there are many such people.

At Georgetown, I receive a public interest law scholarship, which pro-vides scholarship assistance, curricular and career advice, and an academic course to those committed to practicing public interest law. I am interested in studying how the law can be used to promote civil rights, political representation, and empowerment. I believe that legal training will improve my advocacy and policy-making abilities and will be a very powerful tool enabling me to continue helping individuals and their communities. After graduation, I intend to return to New York City and practice and formulate policy as a public interest lawyer.

The other day, Baba drove me to the subway station. We talked about the news items in the Chinese-language press—my parents love to cut out articles in which I might have an interest. Baba said, "Back in the 1960s, Orientals—I guess we now call ourselves Asian Americans—did not have any power. Now, we still are too few in numbers to make a difference."

We talked about the pro-immigrant rally at City Hall that occurred a few months ago. The rally was in response to a comment by a Queens elected official, who stated that Chinese and Koreans in her district were colonizers taking jobs from American citizens. I had joined an ad-hoc Asian American group to plan the rally. I told Baba that despite differences in ethnicity, language, and heritage, Asian Americans came together in solidarity, along with African Americans, Latino/as, liberal whites, and other leaders and groups. I explained that, later that day, the elected official apologized for her comments. I suggested to Baba that as we unite both within and outside the Asian American community, we will become a more powerful force in city, state, and national politics, and fully share in the American dream.

Baba raised his eyebrows in that cool, thoughtful way he has, and didn't say anything for a moment. Then he lowered them and smiled.

A Girl Called Hoai*

DURING MY FIRST year in New York City, it was difficult for me to shop at the Korean grocery stores, especially if there was an older man behind the cash register. I would leave the store carrying a weight of guilt and depression, reminded of my own father's long hours in the convenience store my parents owned in Colorado and how I had not been around to help. Over the past fifteen years, my parents have been harassed and threatened by their customers, held up, and shot at; fortunately, they have never been physically hurt. I have often wondered what my father felt and thought about all day at the store—fifteen hours a day, seven days a week, 365 days a year, unless my mother convinced him to rest on Christmas Day by reminding him that there would likely be only a few customers.

I know little about my father and his side of the family because he does not talk much about himself. His world is one that no one in the family seems able to penetrate. His face often projects a sense of fatigue, worry, and frustration. When he does smile or laugh, his whole being springs to life. It is as though he carefully guards his joy, freeing it only for a moment and then carefully locking it back up. Most of what I have learned comes from stories recounted by my mother and her relatives or from old photographs. My aunt told me that when I, his first daughter, was a toddler, my father took care of me, toting me everywhere while my mother was at work. I have no memory of those early years when he spent the most time with me.

As long as I can remember, it has been difficult for me to communicate verbally with my father. Cultural and gender role expectations undeniably influenced how he related to his children, for he only spoke to me from within his role as a father. Our communication was also hindered by my poor Vietnamese and his limited English. But deeper than cultural reasons, my father's painful experiences with his own family during his youth caused him to isolate himself emotionally. Even before he got married, he was rarely in touch with his family. When I was two, his

---

* Pronounced *why*

mother died. Over the years, my mother has been the one trying to maintain contact with his brothers and sisters, who still live in Vietnam. To this day, I have not met my relatives on his side of the family. I grew up believing that my father's reticent nature was just part of his personality. But through the introspective process of seeking my own sense of self and identity, in recent years I have begun to understand his silence and to recognize how strongly he has influenced me.

My father was a creative and talented man who abandoned his love of music to provide for his family. When he was young, he belonged to a band and played several instruments. His favorite was the French accordion, which has buttons on both sides of the bellow, rather than a keyboard. I have a vague memory of hearing him play, but never fully realized until much later how much the instrument meant to him. When we left Laos in 1975, all we could bring was some clothes and food. My mother told me that he tried several times to have a friend in Laos send him his accordion after we resettled in Denver. He was deeply disappointed when his friend did not, and felt as if he had lost an important part of himself.

When I was in the seventh grade, my father bought three accordions: a small, beginner's one, a medium, and a full-size one. I took beginning band, but the accordion was not taught in class. The teacher gave me a school clarinet, offering to give me accordion lessons after school. Before I knew it, my father had bought me a clarinet. When I began playing the guitar, he bought two of them. And when I learned photography, he gave me his camera. My father never attended any of my band performances or competitions because he had to work, but he would drop me off and pick me up after practices and performances. In his nonverbal way, he was sharing a part of himself.

When I was preparing to enter college, my father, for the first time, discouraged me from pursuing music as a study. Although he had been a musician, he never viewed it as a career choice. For him, it was an interest that he had to abandon as soon as he started a family. He did not want to see his life repeated in me. If I had decided to pursue music, however, I think he would not have objected, though he might have been concerned. My father did not try to restrict my sisters and me from certain pursuits because of our gender. He expected all of us to be college educated, mainly because he wanted us to have a different life from his and my mother's.

Although I have not touched my instruments in ten years, I am enriched by the experience of having studied music. It will always be a part of me. I am grateful that my father did not completely abandon his love for music, and that he shared it with me. I am saddened, however, by his sacrifices and the silence within which he holds his life's hopes, passions, sadness, and pain.

* * *

MY MOTHER, WHO is fifty, recently earned her travel agent's license. In a few months, she will also receive her American high school diploma. While many who know my mother often admire her incredible strength for survival and her will for self-realization, I have taken these qualities for granted. Only in recent years have I begun to recognize and appreciate my mother's spirit of courage and determination.

When we arrived in Denver in 1975, my mother knew only a few words of English. She attended English classes during the week, and worked as a cashier at a small Asian food store on weekends. A year later, she began managing the store; in 1978, the owner decided to sell the store to my parents. For the next six years, my mother managed the store by herself. My father would help her in the evenings after his nine-to-five job at a window-making shop. When Asian food stores became more commonplace, my parents turned the business into a general convenience store. My father then quit his job and began working at the store full-time. My mother, who had always managed the financial aspects of the business, maintained that role but began to develop other interests, such as continuing her education.

In Vietnam, my mother was forced to abandon her studies after middle school because public education did not exist and private schools were very expensive. In addition, as the eldest female in a poor family, she was expected to work to support her family and to earn money for her siblings' education. Her sisters also quit school to support their brothers. When she was in her early teens, my mother and her family moved from central Vietnam to a small village in northern Laos, searching for better living conditions. Many other Vietnamese—including my father—had also come to this village, seeking refuge from the French war in Vietnam.

When my mother reached the marriageable age of sixteen, my grandmother arranged her marriage to another man, unaware that my mother had met and fallen in love with my father. On the day of the engagement ceremony, she went into hiding with my father and did not return for several days. They got married but did not have a celebratory wedding. My mother gave birth to me when she was eighteen. Four years after I was born, she had two more girls, one year after another. Four years after that, she gave birth to a boy. A year later, at twenty-nine, she found herself starting all over again in a far away and unfamiliar country. Though she and her husband faced great uncertainty, she was filled with hope for her children's future.

Like my father, my mother wanted all of us to have college educations; it didn't matter what we wanted to study. When I decided to pursue French, she was uncertain how it would serve my future, but was happy I could speak the language. I have had many opportunities to study abroad since I chose to major in a foreign language. Initially, my mother was hesitant and frightened that I would be far away, but she adapted and supported me because it was part of my education. In her family, it was unheard of for an eldest daughter to go off on her own. My aunts who lived in France criticized her harshly for allowing me to live alone in college and to travel as much as I did.

Since I began traveling in college over ten years ago, I have not lived at home for any length of time. My exposure to different cultures and languages in Europe and Asia has played an invaluable role in shaping my sense of self, as well as my view of the world and of humanity. It is my mother's courage in trusting me and letting me go that has allowed me to develop my potential. She has instilled in me the determination that has given me the strength to move forward despite uncertainties.

MY UNDERSTANDING OF my parents' lives has provided me with the anchor that I long needed to establish a stronger sense of self and identity. It has taken a long time for me to arrive at this point, at the age of thirty-two, to be able to feel good about my ethnicity and who I am. The journey that brought me here has been one filled with many unpredictable yet seemingly purposeful twists and turns. It was a journey that began twenty years ago in Laos when I was awoken one morning by my mother and told that we were leaving for the U.S.

It was in July, three months after the fall of Saigon, when my father found a way for us to escape. It was an opportunity, but also a risk. That morning the sky was gray and pouring huge, heavy drops of rain. A Volkswagen bug arrived and took my mother, my siblings, and me to the Mekong River at the border between Laos and Thailand. My father left separately to avoid raising suspicions; he also thought officials might be more lenient if they arrested a woman with young children. We arrived at the riverbank several miles away from the patrolled border and waited for my father. Much to our relief, he arrived safely. Under the forceful rain, we boarded a small motorboat and crossed the turbulent waters to Thailand.

We all had new names and I had to remember to respond when I heard mine. My parents had purchased American papers from a family that did not want to leave Laos. We exchanged our family's fate for theirs. The family size was a perfect match and the ages were close. However, the genders of the children did not correspond; they were three boys and one girl, while we were three girls and one boy. But it was not a problem since we were all young enough to pass. Once in Thailand, my father submitted the paperwork to the American embassy. He went to the embassy every day and anxiously waited for us to be called. To our relief, we jumped another hurdle when our new names were called within a week.

We were flown to the Philippines and kept on an American military base for one week, then flown to Guam. We stayed there for another two weeks, continuing to get processed and receiving more medical checkups, before being flown to a military base in southern California. We spent three months there waiting for sponsorship to get resettled. Through decisions beyond our control, we were resettled in Denver, Colorado.

One of my sisters was lucky to get the sole female name. At home, we would address each other by our real names; outside, we would maintain our aliases. We had to keep our real names a secret because my parents were afraid that we might be prosecuted in the U.S. or sent back to Laos if the truth was known. At the time, I thought I had to carry the new name indefinitely. The few Vietnamese friends I had thought it was strange that I had a male name and that my "nickname" at home was female. When we became citizens five years later, we were able to assume our real names. My assumption of a different identity to enter the U.S. was a foreshadowing of the identity struggle I would contend with years later.

My introduction to life in the U.S. at the age of eleven began with the harsh reality of poverty and racial conflict. We lived in Sun Valley, a housing project in Denver where the majority of the residents were poor Hispanics and blacks. Unable to speak English, I was faced with hostilities that were incomprehensible to me. The name-calling and physical attacks I endured in and out of school were provoked by my Asian facial features and the language I spoke. From fourth to ninth grade, fear and anxiety permeated my daily life. I dreaded boarding the school bus in the morning and leaving the school building in the afternoon. The classrooms were the only places where I felt somewhat safe from the pushing, hair-pulling, and name-calling. At home, our house and car windows, so often smashed by rocks, were sealed with plastic and tape. We felt safer when we moved to the suburbs six years later, but the racial epithets did not cease.

The physical harassment finally subsided when I entered high school. Although I belonged to the school's band, played in the citywide marching band, and was active in a photography class, I formed my one close friendship with a girl I met in math class. She became my most important source of support during high school. Being black and having the maturity to share with me her struggles with racism, she provided me with the comfort and strength to withstand difficulties and self-doubts. She was the first person I met who expressed an interest in learning about Vietnamese culture and showed compassion and respect for my experiences.

At this time, I began losing contact with the few Vietnamese friends I grew up with. They either attended different high schools or got married. The Southeast Asian students at my school, meanwhile, were mostly newcomers. I tried to help a few of them with their schoolwork, but really could not identify enough with them to develop any friendships. In addition, my tastes in music, movies, and pastimes were diverging from the Vietnamese young people I knew. Not realizing it at the time, I was growing more independent and quietly rebelling against my own ethnicity and culture. As my English progressively improved, my Vietnamese deteriorated. The end of high school marked a significant departure. I left home for college, leaving not only the physical and cultural environment of my home, but also my identification with my ethnicity and the pain associated with it.

I deliberately selected a college that was far enough away so I could live in a dormitory, but close enough to be acceptable to my parents. It was also a college with only a few Vietnamese or Asian students. The minority student population was approximately 5 percent or less. My attempts to escape my ethnic identity and to assimilate, however, were futile. The overt name-calling experienced in childhood was replaced with "Where are you from?" or "Where are your parents from?" Sometimes I would be given a choice of being either Chinese or Japanese. My father once told me that I could never be American, no matter how hard I tried, because people would only acknowledge my face as Asian. I did not realize how powerful these words would be; even today, they ring in the back of my mind. His words not only expressed the racism he had experienced, they were also a reminder for me to think about where I had come from.

I spent only my freshman and senior years at my college. In between, I participated in a semester-long exchange program in Florida, and spent the rest of my time studying in France. During the summers, I traveled extensively. My conscious reason for studying French was that it was the second international language and an essential skill for working in the international arena (although I was unsure the exact field I would enter). Unconsciously, I was desperately trying to search for a new self. My travels were a tremendous learning experience, but they also introduced a new phase of loneliness and isolation. The question "Where are you from?" became more complicated and frustrating to answer because I could not expect people from other countries to accept me as an American when America itself did not.

I returned to Colorado to complete my senior year and decided to take on a second major in international relations. As a diversion, I joined the college newspaper as a staff photographer. Between my two programs and my newspaper activities, I found myself socializing in a mixed group of artists and political activists, all of whom were Caucasian. Although I made a few good friends, I never felt completely comfortable with them at social gatherings. As the only Asian in a group, both by choice and circumstances, I found myself in a constant emotional and psychological state of ambivalence. I could only connect with my friends through the westernized or Americanized part of me. The Vietnamese part of me, meanwhile, had been too fragmented to either communicate or share.

At that time, my identity was not developed enough to serve as an anchor to provide me with the confidence I sought. The remnants of the caustic racist slurs I had experienced during my early years gnawed inside me, disconnecting my sense of self. And the constant questions about my ethnic background, often implying exclusion rather than interest, had been both a source of pain and a challenge to my ability to achieve internal wholeness.

Soon after graduation, I got a job teaching English in Japan through a program sponsored by the Japanese government. I spent two years working at the Board of Education in Hokkaido, the northernmost island of Japan. During my first year, I lived in a rural area that had a population of about 10,000. I worked in several different district schools, from primary schools to high schools, from agriculture schools to prep schools. In my second year, I moved to the city and worked with a similar variety of schools. The work was quite redundant and draining. My assignments lasted from one day to a few months at each school.

With each new class I entered, students reacted with surprise, bewilderment, and sometimes disappointment that I did not match their expectation of a blond, blue-eyed American. I would then spend the next fifty minutes describing myself and the diversity that exists in the U.S. Sometimes I left a school feeling satisfied that I had somehow imparted a lasting impression of the U.S. Other times I would feel empty, retreating into apathy from the exhausting redundancy of my presentations.

My time in Japan, however, was a meditative period. The repetitiveness of my countless introductions along with the presence of such diametrically opposite American and Japanese value systems forced me into introspection. It was also my first opportunity to develop friendships with Asian American women: We spent much time commiserating over our similar experiences. I left Japan with many unanswered questions about myself, but, at the same time, filled with optimism. I was there representing the U.S. and the possibilities it held. I felt I had made a lasting impact, however great or small, on the children, students, and adults whom I had encountered. The experience helped to transform my nebulous self into shapes I could begin to grasp and refer to. Leaving Japan, I traveled through several Southeast Asian countries. I could not visit Laos or Vietnam, however, because political tensions still existed between the U.S. and Vietnam.

Before going home to Colorado, I spent six months in France living with my relatives. I took French classes to refresh my skills and stumbled upon Vietnamese history and literature classes, discovering for the first time the depth and richness of Vietnamese civilization. Through my interest in learning more about Vietnam, I connected with one of my aunts, an avid reader and an expressive storyteller. She relished defining words I did not know and enjoyed discussing her views on Vietnam's history and politics. Her best stories, however, were the ones about herself and my mother. This trip to France opened another passage for me to begin reconstructing my identity.

Although I could not articulate the sum of my experiences at the time, I came back to Denver in the spring of 1991 with a stronger sense of direction. I had graduate school in mind and was contemplating a degree in public administration. While I was researching various programs and schools, I decided to volunteer at a refugee service agency in Denver that had helped my family years earlier. Since I spoke Vietnamese on an informal, conversational level, I was limited in my ability to provide translation services for the families that came in. My work was mostly clerical. Several months later, I applied for a case manager position at a another refugee service organization in Denver. It was a Cambodian organization headed by a Caucasian man; ironically, the organization resettled Vietnamese refugees. I was hired for the job, but lacked professional experience in refugee resettlement, as well as the necessary management skills. I supervised three Vietnamese men, all older than me and recent newcomers. The oldest man quit after two months. The other two did their work, but had difficulties accepting my position. I did not address their discomfort because I did not know how.

As I developed an understanding of the services and the political issues involved in local and national refugee resettlement programs, I became increasingly frustrated with not only the politics of service providers, but of the politics within the Vietnamese and Cambodian communities. The struggle for power was over the dollars given to the state; these funds were based on the number of new refugees admitted into the state. Much had changed in the fifteen years since my family and I first came to the U.S. While the resources for resettlement had been drastically decreased, the needs of refugees were greater and more complex. There was little change, however, in the way services were delivered. The "ethnic" staff members were often found in direct services and rarely represented in decision-making positions. In the few community-based agencies headed by refugees, the directors were usually older men who had transplanted patriarchal roles from their homeland.

All the issues I confronted in my work touched upon the feelings of loss, fragmentation, and injustice I had experienced. I began to see my own individual struggles reflected and played out within the larger Vietnamese community. At this point, I also began to understand and articulate the emotional and psychological discomfort I felt about fitting into neither the American mainstream nor the Vietnamese community. Although I lacked a clear idea of how I would expand my community work or manage the difficulties and uncertainties involved, I knew I was on the right course. Eight months after my introduction into the field of refugee services, I was presented with an opportunity to work in Washington, D.C., for a national advocacy organization that addressed the leadership needs of the Southeast Asian community. When the New York Association for New Americans (NYANA), a Jewish refugee and immigrant service organization, sought to replicate a leadership program that I had managed, I accepted a job with them and came to New York City.

Five years after working with Vietnamese refugees in Denver, I find myself broadening my scope to address leadership needs among New York's ethnically diverse immigrant communities. Though I did not pursue graduate studies in public administration, I did receive a Master of Social Work at Yeshiva University, a Jewish institution. NYANA, which serves Jewish and non-Jewish refugees from all over the world, financed 90 percent of my graduate education and has been my primary supporter in developing my career as a community social worker. My work at NYANA is a significant milestone in my life because my family was settled by the Hebrew Immigrant Aid Society (HIAS) when we first arrived in the U.S.; now, here I am working for its affiliate in New York. The generosity that the Jewish institution extended to me also pushed me to further examine the boundaries of my ethnic identity.

My work with diverse immigrant communities and the relationships I have formed with my Asian American contemporaries in New York and other parts of the country in recent years have had a profound impact on my internal efforts to find inner peace. My sense of identity has become more integrated and fluid. I can be Asian American or Vietnamese American, but these labels do not begin to represent me fully. There is an entire generation of young adults and professionals like me, either born in the U.S. or arrived at a young age, who seek a transformed identity—one bonded by shared thoughts, rather than the traditional boundaries of race, language, religion, or gender.

Now, I embrace my Vietnamese heritage, and appreciate having spent the first eleven years of my life in a simple, nonindustrialized country. I hold precious memories of Laos—of living in a stilt house, playing in the yard of a Buddhist temple, watching colorful and festive wedding parades, and many other joyful things that have enriched my life. I am also keenly aware that I would not have had the same educational opportunities and freedom in Laos as I have had in the U.S. I am strongly influenced by the intellectual and social independence of western and American cultures, but my values and belief system are rooted in the collective consciousness of the Vietnamese way of life.

I return to my parents, a quiet, nurturing source, who gave me the freedom to travel the distance I needed to develop as a person. I consider myself quite fortunate because not every little girl who came to this country has received the rich opportunities and the strong support that I did. I know my struggle to come to terms with the internal dissonance of my identity is not unique, but rather is shared by many young people growing up with polarized cultural expectations in an often unkind environment.

While I am still subjected to random caustic racist comments and ignorant questions, they no longer hurl my sense of being into chaos. Any violation against the human spirit causes pain to which no one is immune. But finding peace and internal cohesion has helped me develop compassion for those who would utter such words of hate and ignorance. I know these attacks are not isolated, individual acts, but an infliction against us all, Asian or non-Asian. With this recognition and acceptance of myself, I embark on a new journey to share my hopes with others, and I look forward to many more learning paths laid ahead of me.

Part Four

Living in Two Worlds
A Bicultural Identity

THE FOLLOWING THREE essayists reflect a strong bicultural orientation and identity. Though their high educational levels and successful professional careers indicate that they are well acculturated to American culture, they also exhibit a strong ethnic identity and attachment. All three were able to maintain a strong ethnic attachment partly because their parents have made great efforts to pass on their native cultural traditions.

Sayuri Mori-Quayle's parents made sure she and her sister learned the Japanese language and cultural traditions. They forced their children to speak only Japanese at home and enrolled them in a Saturday Japanese school in New Jersey. During the summers, they sent their daughters to Japan to learn about their culture first-hand. Though Mori-Quayle resisted her parents' efforts to make her appreciate Japanese culture, she gradually accepted it and eventually became highly bicultural. She attended college in Japan and, upon graduating, lived there for three more years.

Monica Jahan Bose immigrated to the U.S. from Bangladesh at the age of ten. Her parents, like Mori-Quayle's, worked hard to teach their children their native language and culture. Bose visited Bangladesh every summer, and stayed in regular contact with her parents' relatives. After graduating from Wesleyan, she spent one year studying painting at a university in India to "remain in touch with [her] roots." Though she has spent most of her life in America, she feels "a strong connection with Bangladesh and the rest of South Asia." Shay Sheth, too, has learned about his Indian roots through his parents and by visits to India. The three trips he made to India as a child created a lasting interest in Indian culture, religion, and history. As an adult, Sheth participated in Indian religions and cultural organizations in this country.

Despite their strong ethnic attachment and identity, Mori-Quayle, Bose, and Sheth felt more comfortable making friends with and dating whites, rather than co-ethnics or other Asians. Bose and Mori-Quayle married non-Indian white partners. Though Sheth married a co-ethnic Indian woman, he dated mostly non-Indians before he married. According to classical assimilation theory, cultural assimilation is a precondition for social assimilation.

However, neither Mori-Quayle nor Bose were forced to relinquish their Asian and ethnic cultures as a precondition for marrying white partners. They married white men who accepted their Asian and ethnic backgrounds. This indicates that in contemporary America, intermarriage and multiculturalism go together.

Finding Myself

WHEN I WAS NINE years old, my parents sent my older sister Mayumi and me to Japan to spend the summer with our relatives. Because we lived in New York City, my parents hoped the summers abroad would help us keep in touch with our cultural roots. My sister and I didn't mind—we loved going to Japan. Our relatives indulged us and we were fascinated by the unusual toys and games that were unavailable back home.

But those summers of fun came with a price. Our parents wanted us to experience a Japanese education, so they enrolled us in a small village school in Kyushu, in southern Japan, where my father grew up. Each year, on the anniversary of the atomic bombing of Hiroshima, the school would show film footage of the unfortunate event. As we sat there in the darkened room, some of the children would always say tauntingly, "Look what your country did."

Those words were not new to me.

As a child growing up in New York, and later in a New Jersey suburb, I was subjected to those very same remarks by my American classmates. I understood that the children—in both the U.S. and Japan—were simply mimicking adults who harbored ill feelings from World War II. But remarks like those showed me that although I embraced both American and Japanese cultures, I was not fully accepted by either.

SENDING MY SISTER and me off to Japan during the summers was just one of the many ways my parents tried to keep us in touch with their native country. They were *Issei,* first-generation Japanese immigrants. My father, a karate master, was sent to America by the Japan Karate Association in 1963 because there was a shortage of instructors in this country. He was first assigned to Hawaii, where Mayumi was born. They eventually returned to Japan, but later my father was reassigned to New York City, where I was born.

Coming to America in their late twenties, my parents firmly held on to their Japanese ties. Throughout our childhood, they enforced a rule that we speak only Japanese to them (although Mayumi and I spoke English to each other). Our family ate mostly Japanese food and always took off our shoes at the apartment foyer. Every Saturday, we were forced to go to Japanese language school. To this day, my parents remain Japanese citizens.

Although my parents encouraged us to learn as much as we could about our Japanese heritage, they also encouraged us to learn as much as we could about America and its customs. They wanted us to retain both Japanese and American citizenship. They encouraged us to socialize with both Japanese and non-Japanese schoolmates. Yoshiko, a Japanese American, and Beth, a Jewish American, were two of my closest childhood friends in New York. After I moved to New Jersey, Jae and Hae Jung, both Korean Americans, and Tina, of Greek, Irish, and Sicilian ancestry, were my best friends.

Our family celebrated both American and Japanese traditions. When we celebrated western holidays such as Christmas, Thanksgiving, or Halloween, my parents often gave them a Japanese flair. Our Christmas trees, for example, were adorned with traditional glass balls and candy canes, and also with origami figures. My parents also taught us about Japanese and Buddhist rituals. They took us to Japanese folk-dancing festivals at New York's Riverside Park in the summers, and to the films of Akira Kurosawa.

Although we adopted American activities, deep down our family structure remained Japanese. My mother was the traditional housewife. She stayed at home, while my father worked and the children attended school. She sewed dresses for my sister and me, and knitted hats, mittens, and ponchos. She would always have an after-school snack ready when we came home. Sometimes it was cookies, sometimes it was a Japanese treat like *kinako dango* (sweet rice balls covered with soybean powder). She took care of everything so my sister and I were freed from the burdens of after-school chores. To my parents, it was more important that we concentrate on our homework and excel at school. Only when I was in middle school did my mother begin to make a life for herself outside the home. She got her driver's license when she was forty-six years old. She was fifty when she got a full-time job as a bookkeeper at a local Japanese school.

Although my father left the role of childrearing to my mother, he remained quite the disciplinarian. Throughout my childhood, he constantly reminded us that we could return to Japan any day; he emphasized that we should act as representatives of Japan while we were here and behave in a proper manner so as not to cause any embarrassment. Perhaps my father's strict philosophy stemmed from his martial arts training, especially the moral codes that are at the core of the discipline.

* * *

LIVING IN A bicultural, bilingual environment was not always easy for me. Though I have no recollection of this incident, my mother told me recently that when I was about eight, I locked myself in my room every day after school for ten days straight. When I finally spoke, it was to ask my mother why I was different, and why I had to go to both Japanese and American schools when all my friends got to watch cartoons and play on Saturdays. Having already gone through this with Mayumi, my mother explained that our family was indeed different, but that this was a good thing, and nothing to be ashamed of.

When I was nine, my family moved from our New York City apartment to a house in a mostly white suburb of New Jersey. Even though the likelihood of our family remaining in America grew greater each day, my father continued to hold on to his dreams of returning to Japan. He tried to persuade both my sister and me to go to college in Japan. Although Mayumi gave the proposal some thought, she eventually decided to go to Yale University. She continued on to medical school, and is now a pediatric ophthalmologist.

My father had better luck convincing me. Even though I had been accepted to a few American universities, I decided to try a Japanese college education. Most of my friends at Saturday Japanese school had already gone or were planning to go to Japan for college. I was curious to find out what it was all about. At the time, I had lofty ambitions of becoming a simultaneous interpreter.

I enrolled at International Christian University in Tokyo, or more simply, I.C.U., a school considered somewhat avant-garde for the country. The school had a mix of Japanese and non-Japanese students. The Japanese students, who constituted about 80 percent of the student body, started school in April since the traditional school year ended in March in Japan. They gained admittance to the university on the basis of their high school grades and their scores on a test. Students such as me, who were graduates of American or foreign high schools, enrolled in September. We were spared a test and were admitted on the basis of the usual admissions criteria, such as SAT scores, high school grades, activities, recommendations, and essays.

In planning my schedule, I tried to balance the number of classes taught in Japanese with those in English. Although the English-language classes were fairly easy, I struggled in the Japanese-only classes. I simply could not write down my notes quickly enough and came home each day with a throbbing headache. After a while, taking notes became easier; soon, it was pretty much effortless. By my junior year, I was taking French interpretation and linguistics classes in Japanese. The professors, most of whom spoke both Japanese and English, were understanding of our special situation and did their best to accommodate the multilingual student body. They allowed us to take the final exam or write the term paper in either language, even if the class was conducted in only one language all semester.

Though I finally got up to speed with my studies, I still had not tackled another challenge: figuring out my identity. As I mentioned earlier, I was always aware of the fact that I was bicultural. But I never had tried to pinpoint exactly what that meant. Now in college, people were constantly asking me if I "was more Japanese or American." Even worse, sometimes they would judge and decide for themselves. I had trouble putting myself in a neat little category back then; I still do. After all, there were times when I felt like an outsider in America as well as in Japan. I also had trouble relating to the term Japanese American because I was never a part of a larger Japanese American community. And I was not what the Japanese call a *kikoku-shijou*—a native-born Japanese who has lived abroad and then returned to Japan for her education.

As far as the existing terminology goes, I have settled on *kibei*—an American-born Japanese who received part of her education in Japan. I would have been just as content not to force myself into any category, but it became very clear to me that being part of a group was of utmost importance to the Japanese. Everybody seemed to be a member of some group and they clung on to that association for their entire lives. I finally understood why the Japanese people have been referred to as *natto,* the fermented soybeans that stick together.

Living in a dormitory placed me in a group. Since on-campus housing was limited, only a small percentage of the student body was admitted into the dorms. Students who lived far from Tokyo had a better chance of getting in. On a campus containing a few thousand students, there were only four dormitories for women and three for men, with each housing about thirty students. No coed dormitories existed. The dorm rooms were cramped, with four girls in one room, or two to a room when you became a junior or a senior. The dorm had strict regulations such as when you could take a bath.

I initially disliked the communal atmosphere of the dorm, but eventually grew to enjoy it. I formed some of my closest friendships there. There was Haruko, a Japanese Canadian girl who was my roommate in my junior year. We had a lot in common, including a passion for care packages that contained Reese's peanut butter cups and cans of corned beef hash. Belinda, an exchange student from Scotland who came to learn Japanese, and Waka, who was born in Japan but raised in Germany, were also good friends of mine.

Many of the people I became close to at I.C.U. had some experience with living abroad and spoke English. With these friends, I spoke three "languages": Japanese, English, and a mixture of the two. The mixed language could be mostly English with a few Japanese words thrown in. The opposite was possible, too. An example would be: "I have to go to the *toshokan* (library) to study for the *kimatsu-shiken* (final exams)." Of course, this mixture is unacceptable in academic circles or in normal social situations. But it did have its place at I.C.U.

Most Japanese, who had no experience with nonnative Japanese, had trouble figuring me out. For some, it was incomprehensible how I could look Japanese but be handicapped in the language (I retained a slight English accent when speaking Japanese); others were befuddled that I could be fluent in a language other than Japanese. For example, Haruko and I were riding the train one night. We were speaking in English, as we always did. Some of the men around us commented that we must be "hostesses" or escorts from Southeast Asia. Another time, Haruko and I were chatting while waiting in line to see a movie. The man behind us told his date that we were probably college students practicing our English.

Of course, not everyone reacted with such naiveté. Many people were sympathetic and eager to teach us if we had trouble expressing some idea or thought. Many remarked how lucky we were to be bilingual and asked how they could educate their children to speak other languages.

Being a native English speaker was definitely an advantage when looking for employment in Japan. But it soon became clear that even though I had a leg up on the competition, not all English speakers were treated equally. I noticed this discrimination when I taught English conversation at a commercial school—one of the many that cropped up in the 1980s to accommodate the burgeoning number of Japanese interested in learning English. Though the Japanese learned the basics of English in school, they often lacked adequate conversational skills.

Because this was a summer job, I was paid on an hourly basis. Although the pay was generous for a college student, I soon discovered I made less than teachers who were Caucasian. I was even paid less than a nonnative English speaker with a thick South American accent. When I complained, it was suggested that I adopt a "western" first name. I guess they figured I would seem more authentic as an English teacher with a western name. My middle name is Theresa and I could have used this easily. But I wasn't about to succumb to the school's policy, and I quit not long afterwards.

Not all of my job experiences were this frustrating. After graduation, when I was unsure of exactly what I wanted to do, I began working at the Tokyo branch of a major U.S. investment firm. I never experienced any discrimination because of my gender at that job; after all, my boss was a woman. The company, in general, was quite liberal compared to most Japanese firms; basically, it was a foreign firm operating in Japan. After about nine months into the job, Haruko introduced me to a producer at N.H.K. (Japan Broadcasting Company) who was looking for people to work at an English-language business program on its satellite channel. It was an opportunity I couldn't pass up. Although it was considered taboo to leave a company after less than a year of employment, my boss and colleagues were extremely understanding and supportive of my decision.

The new job turned out to be the best move I ever made. I worked as an assistant producer for a show called "Japan Business Today" or "J.B.T." (the show has since gone off the air). The production staff included Japanese and non-Japanese members, many of whom had experienced living or working abroad. The executive producers encouraged us to strive beyond our regular job duties. That's why, as an assistant producer, I was allowed to propose story ideas, as well as to arrange and go on shoots.

At this point in my life, I had a job I absolutely loved, my own apartment, many friends, and a long-term boyfriend. But after about a year and a half at "J.B.T.," I decided it was time for me to return to the U.S. I had been in Japan for seven years by then. Although I was quite comfortable, I desperately wanted to live and work in America. Looking back, I must have unconsciously known that if I didn't leave Japan soon, I would become too settled to ever return to America. Ironically, I left not long after finally achieving a certain mastery of language and cultural skills. It was a personal triumph for me when new acquaintances failed to realize that I had grown up outside of Japan. After reaching that goal, I felt satisfied enough to return to the U.S.

IT'S BEEN A few years now since I came back to America. Since then, I have been working as an associate producer at CNBC, a cable TV station in Fort Lee, New Jersey. When I first came back, I experienced a major case of reverse culture shock. It took me a long time to feel comfortable at my job. Back in Tokyo, I was automatically considered a valuable asset because I was bilingual. Without that crutch, I felt totally vulnerable and inadequate. It also took some time to get used to the work environment. For the first time in my professional career, I was clearly a minority.

It was just as difficult to adjust to life outside work. I felt out of touch with American society and was unfamiliar with most of the popular jargon. I felt uncomfortable interacting with people, even those who were my own age. I also missed my friends, and the fast pace of Tokyo. It took some time, but I have eventually settled into my new life. It helped greatly that my family still lived in the area, as did some of my friends from high school. On the flip side, however, I now have few opportunities to speak Japanese or to socialize with Japanese people outside of my family. I still keep in touch with my friends in Japan, but only a few have been able to visit, and I've only been able to go back once.

Still, I'm confident I made the right choice in moving back to the U.S. And I will never regret having gone to Japan. As I feel myself settling deeper and deeper into American society, I realize how fortunate I was to have left when I did. If I had not gone at eighteen, I know I would still have the urge to explore my roots. At a later stage in my life, it probably would have been much more difficult to arrange such a journey.

Recently, I married a white American man. Until a few years ago, my parents had encouraged me to marry a Japanese man. They pointed out the high divorce rate among Americans. They also worried that they would be unable to communicate with grandchildren whose first language was not Japanese. However, I believe my parents were persuaded otherwise by my husband's character and affability (he jokes that they were just desperate to marry off their twenty-eight-year-old daughter). Although we do not share the same ethnic background, we were both raised conservatively and share similar values. I have more in common with him than anyone I have dated.

It's been a little more than twelve years since I boarded the plane for Tokyo. I've undergone many changes since then. But one thing remains unchanged: I am still unable to declare myself either Japanese or American. What I did learn through my years abroad is that I can be comfortable without having a label for myself. It is no longer imperative for me to fit into a neat little category. Perhaps one day I will be able to answer the Big Identity Question. I remain hopeful. But in the meantime, I know that if I do not, it is not the end of the world.

Multiple Identities

ALTHOUGH I HAVE spent most of my life outside Bangladesh, I still feel deeply connected to my homeland. This may sound sentimental, but I feel a swell of emotion whenever I return and the airplane descends upon the green fields and waterlogged rice paddies. Because my parents sought to ensure that I had a strong sense of identity, I have never felt distant from my relatives in Bangladesh or from Bengali* culture. Yet, after twenty years in the United States, I also feel American in many ways. Though there have been difficult periods in my life, overall I firmly believe that growing up between cultures has given me a broader sense of the world and my place within it.

At age eight, I was a budding actress on Bangladesh national television; two years later, I was a Girl Scout selling cookies door-to-door in suburban Maryland. For my senior prom, I wore a purple-and-gold *sari* and ornate gold jewelry and was accompanied by my 6'2" blond date dressed in a tuxedo. While many of my relatives live in mud-floored huts in a remote island in the Bay of Bengal with no running water or electricity, I live in a Manhattan high-rise with a dishwasher and cable TV.

I was born in England in July 1964. My father had received a scholarship to pursue a doctorate in economics at Cambridge University. My father, mother, and brother, who was then seven, moved to England in 1963. Four years later, after my father finished his Ph.D., we moved to Karachi, West Pakistan, where my father had been offered a job. At that time, Bangladesh was not yet an independent nation; it was the state of East Pakistan within the nation of Pakistan.

In Karachi, I attended a nursery school and kindergarten that taught English and Urdu, the official language of West Pakistan. At home, I learned to speak Bengali. This was important to my parents because as students they had

---

* *Bengali* is the Anglicized word for Bangla, the language spoken in the state of West Bengal in India. The word also refers to *Bengalee,* a native of Bangladesh or West Bengal. A new word, *Bangladeshi,* has been coined recently to refer to citizens of Bangladesh.

fought to retain the right to learn Bengali. Pakistan then was controlled by non-Bengalis who wanted to make Urdu the official national language, even for Bengali-speaking East Pakistan, which constituted a majority of the nation's population. Because they were ethnically Bengali, my parents felt like outsiders and were subject to discrimination. Our landlord, for example, treated us badly, falsely claiming that we had never paid rent.

We moved to Dhaka, East Pakistan, in early 1971, just two months before the war that led to the independent nation of Bangladesh broke out. In 1970, the Awami League, a political party based in East Pakistan and led by a Bengali called Sheikh Mujibur Rahman, won a majority of seats in Pakistan's National Assembly. However, the West Pakistan–based government refused to let the Awami League form the new government of Pakistan. In March 1971, East Pakistan declared itself independent, and Sheik Mujibur Rahman raised the new Bangladesh flag.

We lived a few blocks away from Sheikh Mujibur Rahman and, like many of our neighbors, fashioned a homemade Bangladesh flag and flew it on our roof. In response, the Pakistani military came out in force, with tanks and firepower. I vividly remember the sound of gunfire. A military jeep came down our street announcing with a loudspeaker that the Bangladesh flags had to be taken down and replaced with Pakistani flags within the hour, or else we would face dire consequences. I was petrified and remember my mother frantically looking for green-and-white cloth to quickly make a Pakistani flag.

My parents' friends urged my family to leave Dhaka because my father, a Hindu professional sympathetic to the Awami League, was likely to be targeted. In the middle of the night, with the help of a brave friend who volunteered to drive us, we went to find a boat to the countryside. At the port, the Pakistani military was lighting boats on fire. We took an uncovered country boat, so as to look inconspicuous, and slowly made our way to a nearby village where my mother had relatives. We spent the next three months hiding out in several villages in Bangladesh. The Pakistani army engaged in a brutal war, fighting not only the Bengali Freedom Fighters, but also killing Bengali civilians, raping thousands of women, and especially targeting Hindus and intellectuals. Eventually, when the situation looked even worse, we fled to India, and lived for several months as refugees in Calcutta. In early December, India came to Bangladesh's aid, and Pakistan surrendered on December 16, 1971.

In late December 1971, we moved back to Bangladesh. As a child, I felt tremendously proud of my newly independent country and participated in numerous cultural and patriotic events, plays, and children's painting exhibitions. These experiences had a strong impact on my sense of identity. I enrolled in a Bengali-based elementary school and learned to read and write in Bengali.

My family moved to Oxford, England, in early 1974 so my father could spend a year doing research. Even though I was unaccustomed to speaking English, I quickly made several friends at the neighborhood school where I was enrolled. They were eager to meet the new foreigner in class. Because I had studied English in school, I was speaking fluently within a couple of months.

In late 1974, my father received an opportunity to work with the World Bank in Washington, D.C., and we moved to the U.S. I was surprised at how green and wooded the Washington area was. I had imagined the U.S. to be only highways and skyscrapers. My mother started to cry when we first went to a local supermarket. There had been a famine in Bangladesh when we were last there, and she was in shock looking at the packed shelves and the endless varieties of dog food.

We had come to the U.S. with the idea that it would be for only a few years. We did not have immigrant visas, and we considered ourselves expatriates rather than immigrants. My parents maintained close ties with family and friends in Bangladesh, as well as other expatriate Bengalis in the Washington area. Both factors probably resulted in my having stronger connections with Bangladesh.

While my sense of identity has evolved and changed over the years, I have rarely been confused by it. I do not experience culture shock when I go to Bangladesh, or when I return to the U.S. In great part, this is because my parents worked hard to make sure we knew our native language and culture. At the same time, they did not prevent us from venturing outside the Bengali expatriate/immigrant community. For various reasons, including political and economic circumstances in Bangladesh, we never did return to live there. Sheikh Mujibur Rahman, the founder and Prime Minister of Bangladesh, was assassinated in a coup d'état in 1975, and for several years after that the country was ruled by the military.

Because my father was employed by an international organization, we were able to go back to Bangladesh every other summer on home leave. The ability to return there frequently no doubt helped cement my ties with Bangladesh. Compared to some of my friends who emigrated from Asia and were unable to return home, I have found that I have a somewhat different relationship with my native country.

Other than my nuclear family—my mother, father, older brother, and younger sister—all our relatives remained in Bangladesh and India. My mother was born to a Muslim farming family on a small island in the Bay of Bengal. My grandmother was only seven years old when she married my twelve-year-old grandfather. Many of my mother's relatives still live on this island, which to this day does not have electricity or roads. My father's family is Hindu and used to live in what is now Bangladesh, which was once part of Pakistan and, before 1947, part of the state of Bengal in India. They immigrated to India in the 1950s, while my father remained in Pakistan.

When I first moved to the U.S. at age ten, I was shocked when my fellow fifth-graders asked whether I was black or white. I didn't know what to say. I knew that I was neither, and that I was from Bangladesh. (Of course, today I would say that I'm South Asian and that we are one-fifth of the world's population and increasing steadily.) I was surprised at the question, having assumed that the Washington, D.C., area would be very cosmopolitan—surely these children had seen a person of Indian origin before! I had wrongly assumed that the transition from England to the U.S. would be easier than the one from Bangladesh to England the year before. My fellow fifth-graders in my Bethesda, Maryland, elementary school were not only perplexed by my race, they also could not understand my British accent.

Junior high school was a much friendlier environment. By then I was more adjusted to life in the U.S. and had lost my British accent. My parents saw to it that we did not forget Bengali. My mother even organized a Sunday morning Bengali school, in which a dozen or so other Bengali children participated. My younger sister and I would have preferred to watch cartoons on television, but we are now grateful for their decision. If we had not learned Bengali, we would not have been able to communicate with our relatives.

Growing up in suburban Washington, I did not experience much overt discrimination. There were, however, one or two instances where someone called me a "brownie." I found social-science classes particularly trying, because I felt the textbooks portrayed an overly benevolent image of the U.S. and its foreign policy. My opinions were not shared by many others in my classes.

Because my social values were becoming different from those of my parents, adolescence and high school were difficult. I went to Walt Whitman, a large public high school in Bethesda. While the student body was almost all white, there were quite a few international students, including a few from Bangladesh. Of my closest friends in high school, one was a childhood friend from Bangladesh and the rest were white Americans. I was a rather rebellious teenager, and did not want to stay home and study. In fact, my younger sister and I were considered rather wild by the rest of the Bengali community. While my parents were more lenient than the parents of some of my other Asian friends, I still clashed with them when I wanted to go out with friends and stay out late.

The big problem arose when I was a junior in high school and started dating my first boyfriend. There is no concept of dating in Bangladesh. Naturally, my parents were unprepared for their teenager to be spending all her time with a boy. They also feared that I would lose sight of my education and marry this unsuitable boyfriend, who had done poorly in high school and had no interest in going to college. It was a turbulent time, and we were all relieved, I think, when I went away to college.

Compared to high school, Wesleyan University (in Middletown, Connecticut) seemed like a sanctuary. It had a much more open, accepting environment, where many students were genuinely interested in learning and growing, both in and out of the classroom. My left-leaning views were not dismissed out of hand. Indeed, I was exposed to many new ideas and became more involved with progressive politics. I became active with women's organizations on campus and joined the movement to disinvest from South Africa. In my second year, I lived in the Feminist

House, a women's cooperative. Nevertheless, I sometimes had a sense that I did not really belong, that I had a whole history that not many people cared about.

There were few South Asians at Wesleyan, and I did not end up having any close Asian friends. There was an Asian American students organization and I went to one or two meetings. At that time, all the members of the organization were East Asians and East Asian Americans, who for the most part were born in the U.S. I did not feel that I had that much in common with them. I remember not thinking of myself as an Asian American: I was Asian, not American.

I vividly remember a student-run racism workshop conducted in each dorm during my first year of college. At the beginning of the workshop, we were told to write down on an index card "an incidence of black/white racism that you directly experienced." Since I was neither black nor white, I could not have directly experienced black/white racism. I raised my hand to make this point and was simply told, "Well, this workshop focuses on black/white racism." As a result, I felt excluded and was quite upset. I was the only person in the workshop who was neither black nor white. At the end of the workshop, I tried to talk about how I felt and mentioned how ironic it was that I was feeling this way during a workshop on racism. I did not sense a lot of support from the group.

During college, sometimes I had a feeling that people thought of me as "exotic," but did not want to grapple with who I really was. Some of my classmates went through a period of great interest in India, immersing themselves in Buddhism, Hinduism, and Indian music. I felt they were romanticizing India and my culture. Their gushy sentiments would leave me feeling somewhat alienated. At the same time, when I once confided in a close male friend that I sometimes wondered what kind of person I would be if I had never left Bangladesh and whether I would have been better off there or here, he told me I was being ridiculous.

My own perception of who I am, and how I project myself to others, is in part a conscious construction. I have taken some affirmative steps to remain in touch with my roots. After I received my B.A. from Wesleyan, with a double major in art and mathematics, I spent a year studying painting at Visva-Bharati University in Santiniketan, India, near Calcutta, in the state of West Bengal. I went there specifically because I wanted to see what it would be like to live in South Asia, and because I wanted to improve my Bengali.

I also thought it would be useful for me to spend a year painting and thinking about what I wanted to do next: whether to go to law school or to seriously pursue painting. Since childhood, I had been an avid painter. I also liked analyzing and solving problems, which had led to my major in math. My interest in law was sparked by a neighbor in Bethesda who was a lawyer and had studied math as an undergraduate. Law appealed to me because it involved problem-solving and could be a powerful tool for helping people. My mother, a feminist social worker and activist, thought I might make a good lawyer. But my parents did not put any pressure on me one way or the other; they wanted me to decide what to do.

My year in Santiniketan was wonderful. I met several young people from India and Bangladesh with whom I really connected, in terms of our basic values and attitudes toward the world as well as our artistic interests. At that point in my life, most of the South Asians I had met in the U.S. were more socially and politically conservative than I. Many were more interested in making money than in feminism or art; many agreed to marriages arranged by their parents. In Santiniketan, I also met fascinating young people from all over the world—Japan, Kenya, the U.S.S.R., Italy, and the U.S. Interestingly, there was a German Indian woman in the program who had never been to India before and whose father was from India. There was also an Indian American who had returned to India to get to know his relatives and to learn more about India. Over the years, I have remained in close contact with many of the friends I made in Santiniketan.

While in Santiniketan, I made the decision to apply to law school. Although painting was an important part of my life, I wanted to be financially self-reliant and knew that making a living as a painter would be difficult. I also realized that I enjoyed being with people and that painting full-time would be too lonely a profession.

I started Columbia Law School in the fall of 1987. After Wesleyan and art school in India, it was quite a change to be in New York City with a group of rather competitive law students. I was disappointed that so many students had a business-oriented background and did not have much interest in literature, art, or progressive politics. On the other hand, it was a pleasant surprise that one of my professors was a South Asian woman and a feminist. I was even able to take a course on Islamic law at Columbia, and to write several papers on legal issues affecting women in South Asia. There were several South Asians and South Asian Americans in my class, including another woman from Bangladesh with whom I became good friends. I did feel a certain level of comfort in the fact that there were many South Asian and international students at Columbia.

I met my husband, Michael, a Caucasian American, at law school. We were study partners and took most of our classes together. One of the many wonderful things about Michael is that while he respects my culture and loves South Asian food, he is comfortable with his own cultural identity and does not want to appropriate mine. Some white men I've known have lamented that they lack "culture" and traditions and wanted an "in" to another culture—an attitude I always found a bit silly and irritating. My parents were very pleased when I finally married Michael after dating him for many years. They seem to be comfortable with the fact that I did not marry someone from my ethnic background.

Interestingly, although a large proportion of my friends are Bengali and South Asian, I have never had a relationship with a Bengali or South Asian man. Sometimes my mother used to accuse me of having an ethnic inferiority complex, but I always felt she was mistaken. I never had a relationship with a Bengali man mostly because I had not managed to meet anyone I really liked. After all, there were only a few Bengali men I had contact with (all sons of my parents' friends), and a much wider selection of non-Bengali men. For example, there were no Bengali men at Wesleyan or Columbia Law while I was there. Also, even if I had liked someone Bengali, dating would have been impossible because every Bengali in town (or maybe the East Coast) would have known about it and we would have been expected to get married right away. In addition, many of the Bengali men I have met clearly do not share my ideas about dating or about relationships between the sexes. Some have told me that I'm "aggressive" and "very Americanized." Most of the Bengali men with whom I grew up in Bethesda have brought back from Bangladesh more traditional wives chosen by their parents.

Even though I have spent most of my life in the West, I feel a strong connection with Bangladesh and the rest of South Asia—Bhutan, India, Nepal, Pakistan, and Sri Lanka. My Bengali background is important to me, and certainly shapes a large part of my being. I also feel a commonality with other South Asians. There are important cultural and historical links that draw us together. I feel these links especially strongly because I have lived in Bangladesh, Pakistan, and India, the three largest countries of South Asia. Perhaps just as important, I have had the rare opportunity of growing up exposed to both Hinduism and Islam, since my parents are from different religious backgrounds.

Indeed, my Hindu-Muslim background has been an important aspect of my identity. I have learned about the customs and attitudes of both groups, at least in the South Asian context. This has been enormously helpful and interesting, and I believe I have gained a great deal from having both Muslim and Hindu relatives and friends. It has also allowed me to bridge religious differences in my own interactions with people and to better understand my world.

My Hindu-Muslim background has also instilled in me a skepticism of religion, for I have personally experienced the violence and mistrust that religion can cause. Religion is very important in South Asia: Whenever you meet South Asians, they will try to identify your religion. If they cannot tell by your name, they will ask you point-blank. When I was a child in Pakistan and Bangladesh, both Muslim-majority countries, my name identified me as a Hindu, and children in school would ask me what religion I was. I was always confused by this question and would say that I had no religion. This was quite accurate, as my parents did not give us a religious upbringing.

During Bangladesh's war of independence, we had to flee to the villages and then cross the border to India because the Pakistani army was killing Hindus, especially educated ones. I was six years old when we were making our way to the Indian border by foot, ferry, bus, and rickshaw. I remember that a group of Pakistani soldiers boarded our bus and walked up and down the aisle. My mother had instructed me to not tell anyone my father's name because they would know he was a Hindu and we might be killed. She had even memorized a verse from the Koran, so that she could prove she was Muslim. Once we got to India, in order to avoid prejudice against Muslims and mixed marriages, my mother went by the name *Jaya* instead of her real name, *Noorjahan,* a Persian name that would have identified her as a Muslim. These childhood experiences, as well as others when I was older, were important events that showed me that religion could be divisive and hateful.

My sense of my own identity is clear, but it is not easy to define on paper. As a child in the years following Bangladesh's independence, I saw myself as a Bengali and citizen of Bangladesh. Living in the U.S., I developed a broader South Asian identity. In the last few years, especially after becoming a U.S. citizen, I have finally begun to also see myself as an American. Although earlier I had thought that I might not want to become a U.S. citizen, I later changed my mind. It became clear that I would spend most of my life in the U.S., and I felt it was time for me to become a citizen and to really become a part of this country. The fact that the U.S. and Bangladesh recognize dual citizenship also made the decision easier.

I realize that people do not necessarily see or understand the different parts of my identity. A couple of years ago, I was shocked when a high school friend, a Caucasian, told me he thought of me as "white." I was extremely offended and asked him how he could possibly think that. He explained that it was because I did not speak with an accent and seemed totally assimilated. On the other hand, some of my South Asian friends have commented that I seem so South Asian that they cannot understand how I married outside the culture.

I now make sure to let people know a little about my background. Although I have a Bengali name, it does not sound "ethnic" to most Americans. Recently, someone at work asked me how I got such an Anglo name. *Bose* is a common Hindu Bengali surname. *Monica* is also a Bengali name and means "small gem." My parents purposefully chose international-sounding Bengali first names for me and my sister, Anita. While this was a great advantage growing up in the U.S., I now sometimes wish my name did not seem Anglo to some people. A few years ago, my sister and I took on Jahan as our middle name so that our names included our mother, Noorjahan, and not just our father. Many of the women in our family have Jahan, a Persian word meaning "the Universe," somewhere in their names. For me, Jahan also indicates my partly Muslim roots.

My connection with Bangladesh and South Asia is something I have consciously maintained. I try to find time to read books in Bengali. In my adult life, I have also purposefully spent some time in South Asia. In addition to the year I spent studying art in India, I worked for a public interest law firm in Bombay and drafted a legal handbook on domestic violence during one of my summers in law school. I still try to visit Bangladesh every couple of years.

During the last several years, I have been active with a few South Asian women's organizations in the U.S. I have spent many hours volunteering with Sakhi for South Asian Women, a New York–based organization striving to improve the condition of women in the immigrant community. Through Sakhi, I have met many South Asian women from different walks of life, and have learned a great deal from sharing our experiences of being women, immigrants, and South Asians. It has been wonderful to belong to such a sisterhood.

I recently returned to New York after spending two years in Tokyo. We went to Japan because Michael wanted to work at his law firm's Tokyo office. I found an adjunct teaching position at Temple Law School's Tokyo program, and taught international environmental law to visiting U.S. law students. I also held a full-time position at a U.S. consulting firm, where I worked on international tax and other legal issues.

Strangely, in Japan I found myself identifying as an American more than I had done before. In the intensive Japanese class in which I enrolled within days of my arrival, one of the first lessons included the question, "Where do you come from?" The teacher asked me the question and I had to pick a country quickly. It was easier to say "America" than "Bangladesh"; after all, I had literally just arrived from the U.S. For the first time in my life I heard myself say, "From America." There was no one else in the class from the U.S., so I became the sole American.

There were other reasons for my stronger American identity in Japan. I had become a U.S. citizen just before moving to Japan. I was living away from my South Asian parents and my many South Asian friends. Probably most important, I was away from the U.S., which had been my home for twenty years. Though I had never called myself "American" while living in the U.S., in Tokyo I found myself in situations where I was bonding with Americans, reminiscing about "home" and discussing the experience of living in Japan. Americans, like other nationals, tend to socialize together while living in a foreign country. I met only a few people of South Asian origin in Japan, so I seldom had the opportunity to connect with people from that part of the world.

The Japanese, on the other hand, were probably not identifying me as an American, at least not just by looking at me. Often, while sightseeing or visiting a small shop or restaurant, I would be asked where I was from. There was a look of almost disappointment if I simply said "from America," as if they wanted to know where I'm "really from." When I said "from Bangladesh," the response was much more enthusiastic: "Ah!!! Bangladesh!" This was probably because they had never met someone from Bangladesh before and because it fit their expectation that I was from that region. The Japanese friends I made had a fuller sense of my background and were interested in learning about both the U.S. and Bangladesh. But the idea of bi- or multiculturalism is almost absent in Japan, and I have wondered about my Japanese friends' perceptions of who I am.

I have honestly encountered little racism in my six years of law practice. I was the only lawyer of color at Berle, Kass & Case, a small New York City firm that specialized in environmental and land-use law. While there were times I would notice that I was the only person of color and only foreign-born person in a conference room, it was never something that got in the way. In fact, many of my colleagues were interested in my background, and I would always have to provide detailed accounts of my visits to Bangladesh.

I recently started working at the New York office of Arnold & Porter, where I practice environmental law and general commercial litigation. I was surprised to find at the firm two other South Asian lawyers, one of whom is a partner. There are also several other foreign-born people in the office. Even though it does not make a difference in a tangible way, I definitely enjoy being in a work setting that is more diverse and where there are more people from my background.

While I have not encountered racism at work, I have been frustrated that at times I am not taken seriously. I feel that my gender, race, and size all play a role in this. Like many Asian women, I am small in stature compared to most Caucasians, and people sometimes assume I am younger than I am. Recently, during a deposition the court reporter asked me if I was an attorney. When I answered that I was, she said, "Oh, I wasn't sure because you look like a little girl!" I do not find such comments flattering.

I do not know how my bicultural background will play out in the future. When I was younger, I sometimes thought I might return to Bangladesh for some portion of my life. That seems unlikely now. However, my parents are now retired and spend winters in Bangladesh. They are in the process of purchasing an apartment there. I am pleased that they are doing this, both for them and for myself. My mother wants to be back in Bangladesh to work on women's issues and to spend time with her family. Having my parents there part-time will make it easier for me to visit Bangladesh and to maintain my links with the country. If Michael and I have children, I would certainly want them to know Bangladesh and feel a connection to that part of the world.

As for myself, I still occasionally wonder what I would be doing now if we had not left Bangladesh in 1974. As a child in Bangladesh, I enjoyed acting and had performed in several plays and children's television shows. I also loved to write poetry and songs. I never did any acting after leaving Bangladesh, probably because I was not as confident in English. If I had stayed in Bangladesh, it is possible that I would have pursued theater as a profession and been active in the arts. I certainly would have been more literate in Bengali. Of course, I would likely have had a rather staid life as a woman in Bangladesh and had significantly less personal freedom. I would have rarely, if ever, touched alcohol, and would have had much less money than I do now.

I am very happy with the life that I have and would not want to change anything. But I still don't dismiss the possibility that I might have had a totally different, and perhaps equally happy life, in Bangladesh.

An Indian Boy in American Clothes

FIVE PAIRS OF eyes stared at me from around the dining room table. "How should I eat this?" I asked, nervously eyeing the yellow, conical object steaming in my hands. I finally bit into it as if it were a hot dog, then froze with embarrassment when my teeth hit an impenetrable core. It was the summer of 1967. I was five years old, and living in York, a small, rural town in central Pennsylvania. Patsy, a white girl who lived on my street, had invited me to her house for dinner. It was one of the first times I had ever ventured anywhere unfamiliar without my parents; but here was another first that I hadn't anticipated: eating an ear of corn!

"No, no, not like that," Patsy's mother said, jumping in. She demonstrated the "correct" way, holding the ear between her hands. As she gnawed the cob, she stretched back her lips, exposing her teeth to the gums. I caught on quickly and was soon enough eating corn like a Midwestern farm boy.

Though I was born in the United States and grew up playing baseball and eating apple pie, I've never felt completely at home in this country. My parents came to the U.S. from India as graduate students thirty-seven years ago and "fitting in"—whether five or thirty-five, as I am now—has often been a challenge. In unfamiliar social situations, I have found myself wondering whether I was talking, dressing, or acting in a socially acceptable manner. I have been uncertain whether an act of mine would provoke embarrassment or applause. And if it should be embarrassment, I have scrambled furiously to regain my composure. When an unfamiliar subject arises, I often find myself questioning whether my ignorance is due to cultural differences or personal reasons.

While serving as a resident after medical school, I worked for a month on a Navajo reservation in Chinle, Arizona. Many of the elderly Native Americans didn't speak English and didn't trust or even accept western medical practices. Even the younger ones preferred the ritualistic approach, calling upon shamen to do ceremonial dances to cure their illnesses. It was a revelation to discover such a vastly different culture existing within this country. I identified with them. Though Indians and Native Americans have cultural heritages spanning thousands of years, both have been marginalized and treated as members of a cultural minority in the United States. Under such conditions, it is a constant struggle to maintain one's ethnic pride.

As I have grown older, I have steadily grown more interested in my Indian heritage. Whether or not I realized it, Indian culture has always exerted a strong influence in my life. Now that I practice Jainism—an ascetic religion of India also followed by my parents—the connection is even stronger. Jainism, founded in the sixth century B.C., teaches the immortality and transfiguration of the soul and denies the existence of a perfect supreme being. The more I learn about Indian culture, the more I value it. I can't and won't abandon it.

Despite the existential questions involving my cultural identity that have dogged my life, my professional and academic careers have developed unhindered by such dilemmas. I graduated from Rutgers Medical School in 1987 and have worked in a number of different communities across the country. Currently, I practice internal medicine at a large nonprofit staff-model HMO in the Washington, D.C. metropolitan area.

My decision to become a physician was influenced greatly by my childhood visits to India. I first visited my parents' homeland when I was ten. It was the summer of 1972 and the war that led to the formation of Bangladesh was ending. In India, I spent many afternoons in the cinema, watching mass-produced Indian movies. With television just being introduced, the cinema was still the most popular source of entertainment, as in America in the late 1940s. For just a few rupees (then about fifty cents), you could escape into a three-hour movie packed with romance, drama, and conflict, as well as songs, fights, and a tidy resolution. But as soon as you stepped outside the theater, you were besieged by a constant parade of beggars. The dozens of starving, emaciated, and diseased individuals who accosted me every day on the streets of Bombay (now called by its original, pre-British name, Mumbai) made me keenly aware of how vulnerable peoples' bodies are to the ravages of poverty and illness. America, of course, has its fair share of the incapacitated and its growing number of the homeless, as my parents have always reminded me, but my memories of what I encountered in India were probably the single greatest factor motivating me to choose my current profession.

I AM AN only child and was born in Hahnemann Hospital in downtown Philadelphia in February 1962. My parents, both natives of the state of Gujarat, had come to the United States as graduate students in 1959. They both had already received two degrees each from Bombay University. They got married immediately after receiving their degrees, then worked and saved money for three years, selling even their own precious jewelry, to buy passage on a boat to America.

My parents intended to return to India after completing their graduate degrees, but ended up settling in this country. My mother received her Ph.D. and has worked as a sociology professor in New Jersey since 1967. My father obtained his Ph.D. in biochemistry, and has worked as a research scientist for several university hospitals and medical organizations in the Delaware Valley.

During their graduate student days, life was often lean. My mother held manual and clerical jobs to support the family. Though money was tight, they provided me with a sheltered upbringing that has engendered many pleasant memories. As best they could, they tried to give me a balanced view of both cultures. My mother taught me Gujarati, one of India's fourteen official languages, vegetarian Indian and American cooking, and the history and culture of India. My father, meanwhile, nurtured my interest in science and medicine. Today I continue to use many of the rudimentary principles he taught me. They were my role models for valuing an education and practicing good moral habits.

Until I was eight, we resided mostly in the Delaware Valley. In the mid-1960s, we lived in a two-bedroom apartment in a high-rise housing project in Philadelphia. There was a mix of ethnicities: blacks, some Asians, even other Indians. I don't recall any Latinos, but some of the neighborhood stores and businesses, as well as the ice cream trucks trolling in the summer, were operated by Italian Americans. My two closest friends were Greg and Joseph, two black boys my age who lived down the hall. Growing up at the Creswell Street projects was interesting because of the mix of people—from the perpetual dwellers to the temporary ones such as medical students attending the nearby medical school.

Since my parents were busy at work or classes during the day, I was often entrusted to the care of Mrs. Furr, a tall, lean, mild-mannered black woman, who seemed to treat me better than she did her own four children. My parents were gratified to have found such a gentle baby-sitter who provided me with personal attention. Mrs. Furr lived in a two-story row house in a predominantly black neighborhood down the hill from our high-rise project. When I visited the house two years ago, it seemed small, but my memories recall it as being spacious, unlike the constricted high-rise where we lived. I vividly remember learning how to throw and catch a baseball in her backyard.

Due to my parents' study and work requirements, we moved around to several different cities. When I was five, we lived in York, Pennsylvania. The following year, we moved to Camden, New Jersey, and remained there for five years. Despite the omnipresent American culture, our home always retained an Indian flavor. My parents often issued simple commands to me in Gujarati. We almost always ate Indian food at mealtimes, and played Indian classical and popular music at home. We were always in touch with other Indians—some who lived a stone's throw away, others who were accessible only by car. We did not have any relatives living in America, but my grandmother once came for a visit from Bombay.

For most of my childhood, I never felt as if I fit in among my predominantly white peers. I was often the only Indian and my classmates were so ignorant that they mistook me for a Native American. They accused me of doing "rain dances" and said "how" to me, lifting up their hands. Kids also ridiculed me as a "teacher's pet" just because I loved doing my schoolwork. I regularly was taunted for wearing "floods"—pants exposing one's ankles—and for not owning a pair of Converse All-Stars, the reigning sneaker of choice. I even endured physical violence. One time, several kids decided to gang up on me for no apparent reason.

Despite these difficulties, I have fond memories of Camden. School proceeded smoothly, nurturing my self-esteem. I skipped the first grade after two weeks of classes, and maintained a virtually A average straight through school. I won all the spelling bees in the fourth grade, served as an announcer at school assemblies during the fifth grade, and also began learning to play the violin. Later, I joined the Boy Scouts and enjoyed my first week-long camping trip to the Adirondack mountains.

My closest friends, Brian and James, were white. Brian played the drums and performed stupefying magic tricks. James was more mischievous; he tried unsuccessfully to teach me how to steal and educated me on the rudimentary principles of sex. In Camden, I also spent many pleasurable hours by myself, watching TV series such as "Ultra-Man," "Spider Man," and "Speed Racer." My father spent as much time with me as he could. He bought me a bicycle when I was six, and taught me to ride it along the nearby Schulkyll River. He was patient and energetic as a teacher. We also traveled occasionally—family road trips to the New York's World Fair when I was five and to Niagara Falls when I was eight.

But perhaps some of my happiest memories are of the Greek American family who moved in next door to us a year after we arrived. The Sousounis were immigrants like my parents, and the fond memories I have of their three daughters transcended any hardships I suffered in Camden. The girls were about my age, and we became friends immediately. We spent a great deal of time together, playing hide-and-seek, riding our bikes, and reading aloud our comic books. Our families often spent time together. Despite the language and cultural differences, our parents got along well. We seemed to share similar values. It was a rare experience of fitting in. The girls also helped me to understand gender differences that I never knew existed.

One of my biggest regrets, though, was letting them know about a crush I had developed on a girl named Amanda in the fourth grade. With long brown hair and freckles, she knocked me out with her charm and grace. I felt like the luckiest fellow on earth when our teacher designated us as dance partners and I spun her around the room to the tune "Somewhere Over the Rainbow." But I was mortified when she accosted me in the playground one afternoon, and asked, "Someone told me you like me. Is that true?" "N-no," I stammered. "Who ever told you that?" Though I felt betrayed then, I later realized that the girls were just playing Cupid and trying to encourage a romance.

When I was almost twelve, my family decided to move because of the area's rising crime rates and the crummy middle schools. I was mugged outside of our apartment building; thieves burglarized our home. The local middle school, meanwhile, was terrible. Teachers wasted half a class disciplining students. When students misbehaved during a teacher's absence, I freely informed the teacher upon her return, thereby earning the wrath of my fellow students. They called me a "ratter" and physically threatened me. Typing was about the only useful skill I learned there.

We moved to Woodbury, a predominantly white, working-class community in South Jersey. It was here that I spent that difficult period of adolescence. I greatly appreciated the change. The schools were better, and I encountered less discrimination among my peers. I immediately became friends with Jon and Al, two guys my age who lived in the neighborhood. But Jon left six months later, and Steve, my childhood nemesis, moved into his house.

Steve was the most manipulative and negative individual I had ever met. He was white, and a blatant racist. He despised non-whites and ridiculed the importance of an education. He constantly used derogatory, insulting names. Strangely, my need for peer acceptance made me tolerate his attacks on my heritage and family. I accepted his twisted values, almost always doing what he asked. I felt brainwashed, as if I were his slave. Now it seems astonishing that I even listened to him carry on about how he wanted his father and mine to arm wrestle. It's pathetic what he hoped that would prove. Our relationship also caused me physical injuries. Once, when we were riding his motorcycle, he drove me into the fence of a yard with a ferocious dog. The dog bit me in the back and I had to go to the emergency room. Another time, he hurled a heavy spitball the size of a billiard ball at my nose. It hurt for several days. I endured both incidents without letting anyone, not even his mother, know that he had caused them. Since Al passively sided with Steve in all his racist diatribes, I found it hard to consider him a close friend.

Fortunately, my school performance never suffered. I remained focused on going to college. I also tried to broaden myself by getting a job at a nearby Burger King and making new friends. I became friends with Robert, a good kid with intellectual leanings. I spent hours playing pinochle with him and his family. Robert, his sister, and I also made drawings and sketches that their mother would examine. These activities were a welcome change from the times spent with Steve. Robert's parents liked me and always made me feel welcome. I still stay in touch with Robert, who has become a successful computer systems analyst, and have visited him a few times in Florida.

As a teenager, I had a number of hobbies. I collected baseball cards and old comic books; the latter would become a lifelong passion. I listened to Top 40 pop music and rode around on a moped that my parents bought me. I was disdainful of dating, but also afraid of facing rejection, I think. I skipped homecoming dances and the prom, and never experimented with alcohol or illicit drugs.

In my senior year of high school, my attitudes began to shift. Steve had moved away and I no longer felt such a strong need to prove myself to anybody. High school had outlived its usefulness. Up to that point, I had often been the only Indian or Asian at my school. I was restless for a change and hoped that college would provide it. Most of the kids I knew never even considered going to college.

I decided to attend Rutgers College in New Jersey. It was close to home, had a strong pre-med program, and a relatively low tuition. The student body was diverse, and many of the students were open to becoming friends—quite a change from the well-established cliques of high school. I spent much of my first year adjusting to my new lifestyle and forging a new identity for myself. I felt as if my identity had been repressed throughout much of high school. I began listening to more classic rock, and attended a fair number of dormitory and fraternity parties. It was the golden age of college partying and we drank unhampered by the fact that we were below the legal drinking age. I was initially carefree with my newfound freedom and didn't take studying very seriously. But by the second semester, I cracked down and started getting better grades. I received many academic honors and scholarships. In my third year, I declared myself a chemistry major. I began doing research on ozone kinetics, and published two articles in peer-reviewed journals. I pursued new hobbies such as tennis and cooking, and also participated in a service fraternity called Alpha Phi Omega.

During college, I dated a few women; none were Indian, although one was Korean. I also formed some of my closest relationships. One of my best friends even today is Nat, an African American with whom I endured many late nights studying for exams. He went on to Columbia Medical School, where he did his residency in internal medicine and radiology. He now lives in southern New Jersey, with his Filipino wife, also a physician.

When deciding which medical school to attend, I narrowed down my choices to about twenty schools on the East Coast. I was accepted by four and decided to enroll at Robert Wood Johnson (then called Rutgers Medical School). I was attracted to its solid curriculum, its proximity to home, and its reasonable tuition. Medical school went reasonably smoothly. Much of my time, especially the first two years, was spent studying. One of my roommates, Ramesh, whom I knew from college, was also Indian. We shared similar interests and often went out together for a late-night snack after an evening of intense studying. My third roommate, Aalok, a longtime friend of Ramesh's who was also Indian, taught me how to cook Indian dishes, especially curries and vegetarian dishes.

One of the rare, carefree moments I can recall was a successful party that my two roommates and I threw during our second year of medical school. I also enjoyed performing in the follies, the annual show mounted by the medical students. A guitar-playing friend and I called ourselves "Nexus" and sang a few songs. I played the bass. The audience loved us.

Just before the start of my third year, I had to take the National Boards, a series of three standardized medical tests required for graduation. It was an ordeal having to relearn anatomy, embryology, biochemistry, physiology, and a host of other subjects, but I survived. In my third year, I held a medical clerkship at Cooper Hospital in Camden. I performed six-to-twelve-week rotations through different wards of the hospital. It was the beginning of a long alliance. The clinical years were very enjoyable, and even today I still use many of the elementary things I learned there, such as how to listen to patients and record notes. By the beginning of my fourth year, it was time to decide where I would spend my residency. I was interested in staying at Cooper and eventually got matched with their internal medicine department. The three-year residency was highly gratifying. I was able to apply directly all the knowledge that I had acquired.

Though my medical studies consumed my life, I occasionally rewarded myself with vacations. I greatly enjoyed traveling. When I finished medical school, Nat, Ramesh, Jerry (another medical school buddy), and I went backpacking through England. Ramesh then headed off to India to get married, while Nat, Jerry, and I continued on to France, Italy, and Greece. That trip still provides some of my happiest memories. I was far, far away from home and among good friends. The trip proceeded smoothly except for a terrifying incident at a Paris train station. Two security officers wielding machine guns suspected us of being Lebanese terrorists, and we had to empty our bags to prove our innocence. They backed off as soon as they realized we were doctors: *"Etes-vous médecins?"* they asked. That experience certainly validated my career choice.

Near the end of my residency, I spent a month working on a Navajo reservation. My residency director knew the medical director of the reservation, and thought I would be challenged by the work. The Navajo suffered common problems such as tuberculosis, alcoholism, and sexually transmitted diseases, but they could also be stricken by unusual illnesses like the bubonic plague, which is transmitted by prairie dogs. More recently in the news, one reservation suffered an outbreak of hantavirus, which is transmitted by aerolized rodent excreta. As I mentioned previously, many Navajo were skeptical of western medicine. I recall one case in which the parents wanted their baby who had been diagnosed with meningitis to be treated by a medicine man, rather than admitted into the hospital to receive fluids and antibiotics. The medical staff compromised by alternating doses of antibiotics with ceremonial dances. I felt well received at the reservation; it helped, I think, that I didn't look Caucasian. During my stay, I became a collector of Native American art. I was dazzled by their handwoven rugs, sandpaintings, and wooden Kachina dolls.

As I neared the end of my residency, I realized I didn't want to immediately get attached to one place. I wanted to explore my possibilities and decided to participate *in locum tenens*—i.e., filling in for vacationing or absent doctors across the country. I was lucky enough to start off in Hawaii, where I was stationed on the island of Kauai. Though I had to study for the internal medicine boards while I was there, I made the best of it, trying to take in many of the island's delights. I enjoyed the blue waters, the unsoiled beaches, and the free mangoes that could be plucked off trees or picked off the roads.

After completing the boards, I worked in a number of different communities—with impoverished Appalachians in West Virginia, senior citizens in Tampa, Florida, and loggers in Oregon. Next to Hawaii, Oregon was the most enjoyable place to live. With my abode only a block from the beach, I was back in paradise. The only problem was the constant rain, which many blamed for the area's high suicide rate. All in all, the year of *locums* was a welcome and refreshing change after the rigors of medical school. But since each assignment lasted only one to two months, it often meant packing up just as I was settling in. Any friends I made, I soon abandoned. At the end of the year, however, I still didn't feel ready to set up a practice. Such an endeavor was a major undertaking, and required a careful consideration of many different factors: choosing a location, establishing a referral network, hiring a staff, determining benefits.

So when Cooper Hospital asked me to become chief resident in internal medicine, I accepted gladly. It was an honor to be asked to return and it also allowed me to take it easy for a while longer. I pursued some research, studying the significance of staphylococcus bacteria in urine, and scouted around for a good practice. The downside of working as a chief resident was that it was an extremely demanding job. I had to supervise fifty-two interns! Overseeing them was a formidable task. I even had to question a particularly hairy intern about his bathing habits after a nurse complained about his persistent body odor.

After a year at Cooper, I felt the need to get away again and signed up for another assignment in Native America, this time at the Standing Rock reservation, which straddles North and South Dakota. The reservation was exclusively Sioux, with the Lakotas and Dakotas being the two dominant tribes. I was as mesmerized by the Sioux as I was by the Navajo. At Standing Rock, I befriended a stray puppy, a shepherd-labrador mutt I named "Tomahawk" or "Tommie." When I brought her home, my parents were initially upset because Jainism shuns the practice of keeping animals in captivity. But they grew as attached to her as I. Though we eventually ended up giving her away to another family because she was too rambunctious for us, she left a strong impression on us all. She made me appreciate animals more and also influenced my later decision to become a vegetarian.

My first real practice was in New Jersey, at a community health center in a downtown metropolitan area. This clinic served a population that was about 40 percent black and 40 percent Hispanic. Many lacked insurance and a handful were illegal aliens. I liked the ethnic and cultural mix, and also appreciated the opportunity to learn Spanish. But the center was poorly managed and had serious problems. I stayed for two years, but decided to leave when I became convinced that nothing would change. Though the overall practice had increased nearly two-fold since I started, the same problems were raised at each staff meeting, to no avail. My next job involved working once again with Native Americans, this time in an Oklahoma suburb. There was a mix of different tribes in the community—Chickasaw, Choctaw, Cherokee, and some Seminole. It was a transitional job that lasted a month. In December 1994, I started my current job.

As I review my medical career, it seems evident that I have achieved professional success with relative smoothness (notwithstanding, of course, the requisite hard work and long hours). My parents, however, seem to have encountered anti-Asian or anti-Indian sentiments in the course of their careers. Some of my mother's colleagues have said that they believe her ethnicity has hindered her career. She has played an active leadership role in professional organizations, and advocated fearlessly for the recruitment and promotion of ethnic and racial minorities. My father, meanwhile, often failed to get promoted even though he published scientific articles and won several competitive federal grants. Often his superiors received recognition and credit for his work. Younger, less qualified colleagues were promoted ahead of him. My father's immigrant and minority status, the vagueness of intellectual property rights in this country, and the predominantly white bosses in the workplace were all factors against him. My lack of an accent and the fact that I am more assimilated into American culture may account for the different reception I have received.

My career has been fulfilling on several different levels. My profession has given me the opportunity to travel and live in different parts of the country. I've been challenged and fulfilled by working with disadvantaged populations. I enjoy my current position and the salary is gratifying. But the future is cloudy with the rapid growth of managed care. Managed care, as well as the current legal system, has hindered my ability to practice "raw" medicine, that is, what the competent patient wants and what the doctor thinks is best. Further down the road, I may decide that it would be better to work in a rural community.

Right now, however, my more immediate concerns involve more personal goals. When I was an undergraduate, a Korean graduate student named Lee who worked in the lab with me gave me some advice that I've always taken to heart: "Finish all your education, and don't let a woman interfere in the process," he told me." "OK, what else?" I asked. "Every ten years or so, your philosophy and outlook on life changes. Always remember that."

I do. With my professional career in bloom, I began focusing more on personal goals, such as getting married and setting roots. I have learned more about India's history, culture, and religions, and hope to visit the country more regularly.

So far, my perceptions of Indian culture have been formed by three visits to India and my association with religious and cultural groups here in the U.S. My first trip, when I was ten, was a majestic interlude from our suburban life in Camden. The 747 jumbo jet, introduced only two years before, was just the first thrill of a magical journey. The pilot allowed me inside the cockpit once we reached cruising level. I remember the stewardesses as being beautiful and the in-flight Indian meals as being delicious.

It was hot and muggy when we landed in Bombay. At least a dozen family members, including my maternal grandmother and paternal grandfather, greeted us at the airport. They draped our necks with sandlewood leis that overwhelmed me with their fragrance. I noticed immediately that life in India was much simpler than in the U.S. The buildings were drab and the roads, dusty and bumpy, though paved in the city. No one was in much of a hurry and two-hour naps in the afternoons were common in the summer. All the banks and stores shut down from 2 to 4 P.M. to accomodate the nappers. During that first trip, I spent a lot of time with my younger cousin, Nilesh (actually, he was the son of my father's uncle). We enjoyed each other's company and spent countless hours playing together. I also traveled within India, visiting stunningly beautiful buildings and temples, including the Taj Mahal. We visited Kashmir, the cooler northern area that now is accessible only at great risk because of the violence ravaging the region. We rode horseback over steep mountains. The vistas were spectacular. I visited India two more times, at the ages of fifteen and eighteen. Back then, I had only a passing interest in Indian culture, history, or religion. Now, I have a hunger for such knowledge. I'd like to go back and stay for longer than six weeks. I want to learn and absorb as much as I can about the country of my ancestry. And now that I've developed a keen interest in photography, I'd like to use my camera to capture India's majestic beauty.

In the U.S., I have learned about my Indian roots by attending several religious and cultural programs. Over a year ago, I attended a Jain conference in Chicago that drew 5,000 participants from as far away as India. It gave me the opportunity to learn more about the religion of my parents. The message of Lord Mahavir, the twenty-fourth and last lordmaker of Jainism, is contained in five basic principles: nonviolence (which extends to animals and insects and includes vegetarianism); the constant pursuit of the truth (including knowledge and education); celibacy; nonstealing; and nonmaterialism. I occasionally attend Hindu and Jain temples near my home and try to observe secular and nonsecular Indian holidays.

As far as relationships, I am now married. After a long search, I have finally found a woman who has a rare combination of beauty, grace, and education. In the past, most of the eligible women I've met were either too western or not western enough for me. To make matters worse, the young women's parents have often been in a rush for an immediate decision. Although I met my wife through an arranged introduction, the decision to marry her was entirely mine and supported by my parents. My wife, who was born in India and immigrated to the U.S. at the age of three, is also a doctor.

In closing, I want to say that I am happy for the opportunity to have grown up in America. Though there have been obstacles along the way, as there would be for anyone, none have been insurmountable and I am optimistic about the future.

Part Five

Blending In
Weak Attachments to the Ethnic Group

ERIBERTO LOZADA, Joel de la Fuente, and Jean Hotta are all of Filipino descent. They also share a weak attachment to their ethnic group in comparison with the other essayists. Although it is difficult to generalize from these three cases, it may not be accidental that these essayists, who are the most assimilated into the mainstream culture and the most weakly attached to their ethnic groups, are Filipino.

Lozada says his parents, both physicians, focused on their own careers and their children's future careers, and did not educate their children about their ethnic heritage. Fully supported by his parents, Lozada never stopped his quest for assimilation, even in college. To escape the stereotype of being an "Asian American geek" and to prove his "successful assimilation into American society," he played varsity sports and even became an officer in the U.S. Marine Corps. Lozada grew more aware of his ethnic background during his military deployment in the Philippines, and later in the course of seeking a Ph.D. in cultural anthropology. He still remains highly assimilated to the mainstream and weakly attached to his ethnic group, culturally, socially, and psychologically. His ex-wife and current spouse are white, and he has never dated a Filipina.

Joel de la Fuente's parents, like Lozada's, were medical doctors. They, too, placed a high priority on having their children assimilate into American society. De la Fuente says his parents wanted him and his brother "to assimilate as fully as possible." His parents honored his brother's request to use only English in front of his Caucasian friends, and never attempted to teach them their native language or customs. In predominately white schools, de la Fuente rarely had the opportunity to think about his Filipino heritage. He later developed an Asian American identity at Brown after meeting many other Asian American students. His Asian American identity has been strengthened by the discrimination he has encountered as an Asian American actor. He says movies and television perpetuate racist stereotypes and that Asian American actors have moral obligations to humanize Asian American characters. Throughout his essay, de la Fuente uses the terms "Asian Americans" or "Asian American identity" without once saying "Filipino Americans" and

"Filipino American identity." Thus, he has a strong pan-Asian identity but maintains a weak ethnic identity and a weak attachment to his ethnic culture.

Emigrating from the Philippines at age twelve, Jean Hotta is fluent in Tagalog and familiar with Filipino customs. Her decision to work as a counselor for foreign students at UCLA was closely related to the difficulties she faced as a new immigrant. Nevertheless, there is no indication in her essay that she is strongly attached to the Filipino group culturally, socially, or psychologically. Nor does her essay suggest that her parents, like those of other non-Filipino essayists, made great efforts to teach their children the ethnic language and culture.

NARRATIVE TEN / **Eriberto P. Lozada, Jr.**

What Being Filipino American Means to Someone Called Fuji

SEATTLE, WASHINGTON, 1996. I took my six-year-old son Patrick to a matinee of *Heart of the Son* because children were admitted for free in the afternoons. A Pinoy (Filipino American) student group had e-mailed me an announcement about the play and I was intrigued by the prospect of a musical based on the early Filipino struggles for independence. There was just a handful of us in the audience, but the enthusiasm of the musicians, dancers, and actors was undampened. I knew the story of the Filipino patriots Rizal and Aguinaldo, yet the play made me feel out of place. This feeling was foreshadowed early in the play when Aguinaldo was repeatedly asked *"sino ikaw?"* (who are you?) during his initiation into the revolutionary movement. The play, written and performed by members of the Filipino diasporic community, sought to galvanize Pinoy identity by showing how Filipino Americans could be proud of what they were.[1] It ended by asserting a clear vision of Filipino identity, a strong and determined self rising out of the ashes of postcoloniality.

Diasporic identity, a social category that includes Filipino Americans, is often portrayed as fractured, dislocated by spatial and temporal rifts. As an anthropologist, I am well acquainted with the trendy literature on "identity," and how one of the characteristics of postmodernity[2] is the fragmentation of identities that occurs as metanarratives—ideas that ground everyday life, like Christianity, science, or capitalism[3]—are delegitimized. But I have always felt uncomfortable seeing people—let alone myself—as fragmented, surface areas of superficiality playing out the machinations of late capitalism. In the offices, streets, and shopping malls, people at any given moment generally don't walk around with identity-angst, though they may be tired, overworked, or in foul moods. The portrayal of fragmented identities, moreover, is often an attempt to displace one metanarrative with yet another—for better or worse—such as the Filipino nationalism promoted by some Pinoy activist groups. There are times and situations, as the character of Aguinaldo experienced in the play, when the fictions of everyday social life that we take as fact become exposed as made-up, and another set of fictions

143

takes its place as social truth. Using my own life story, I will describe some of the situations that have shaped my own Pinoy identity.

One of the reasons that I wanted to see *Heart of the Son* was to expose my son to Filipino history and tradition. I myself had received little formal instruction on such matters. My parents, both physicians, emigrated from the Philippines in the early 1960s as part of the "brain-drain" of professionals from third-world countries like the Philippines and India; they were too busy establishing their own careers and ensuring that their children were prepared for successful careers of their own to educate us about our ethnic heritage. Growing up in New York City and various Long Island suburbs, I was socialized more into Jewish American culture than Filipino culture. We lacked access to social mechanisms, such as a social network centered around kin relations, to solidify my sense of being Filipino. With my grandparents and most of my cousins still in the Philippines, I was different from my childhood friends. During quintessential family holidays like Thanksgiving or Christmas/Hanukkah, I remember visiting "relatives" in Long Island or New Jersey. Even today, I'm not sure how I'm related to the people I called *tito* (uncle) and *tita* (aunt). Growing up, Filipino culture was not manifest in either everyday or ritualized experiences.

As a child, food was the one thing that helped identify my family as Filipino American. We ate *pansit lug-lug* (noodle dish) and my father put *patis* (salty fish sauce) on everything. Food is one of the most salient markers of cultural traditions; entire cultures have become objectified and made tangible in terms of food and dietary habits.[4] However, even this connection lessened as I grew older. As my parents became more acculturated, we ate less typically Filipino food. I remember eating *balut* (boiled fertilized egg) and *dinuguan* (blood stew) as a young child, but these dishes were served less frequently as I grew older. As the eldest of four sons, with thirteen years separating me from the youngest, I'm probably the only one who has eaten and enjoyed *balut*. When I was twelve, my mother took cooking classes, and learned to make French and Italian dishes. She, in turn, taught them to our nanny. In high school, we ate chicken marsala and shrimp fra diablo more often than Filipino dishes like *okoi*.

After years of graduate school in anthropology, I can see other markers of Pinoy identity. For example, we always ate rice at dinnertime, even with noodle dishes like *pansit lug-lug* or spaghetti and meatballs. We also ate canned meats like Spam. In my own anthropological study of dietary habits, I have discovered that a pantry full of canned meats is common among Asian Americans, especially in Filipino, Vietnamese, or Korean households. To this day, my wife (a "real" American from Kansas) cringes at the mere thought of buying canned meats. Perhaps this consumption of canned meats comes out of third-world experiences—for my parents growing up in the war-torn Philippines, canned meats were a costly treat. I find it ironic today that Spam continues to be included in gift baskets in first-world nations like Japan.

Growing up in New York, my Pinoy identity was challenged most when it was subsumed by others into the more generic category of Asian American, or Oriental, as was commonly said back then.[5] In the 1970s, most New Yorkers culturally categorized Asians as either Chinese or Japanese—remember the children's rhyme, "Chinese, Japanese, dirty knees, look at these..." Filipinos were an unmarked category. No one ever called me a "flip," but I remember hearing "chink" or "jap" a couple of times. In addition, no one could ever pronounce my first name. Since we moved from place to place when I was growing up (from the Bronx, to Manhattan, to various towns in Long Island), I would pick up a nickname in one place then acquire another one when we moved someplace new.

When I was in junior high school, we moved to Roslyn, where my parents still live today. I used to wrestle back then, and picked the nickname "Fuji." In the 1970s, Fuji was a popular wrestler featured in Championship Wrestling—you know, the fake, staged stuff. Fuji was Japanese and his shtick involved throwing "Fuji dust" into his opponents' eyes; as they staggered about, blinded by the "dust," he proceeded to pummel them. Nearly everybody, including my wife, my parents, and my brothers, still calls me Fuji today. In this time of greater ethnic awareness, people get confused when they hear the nickname and think I'm Japanese. My acceptance, even propagation, of this nickname could be seen as an internalization of childhood categories.[6] I prefer to regard it as a usurpation of categories, much as the Quakers turned the once-pejorative slang term *Quakers* into something positive. In high school, I carried the nickname, and then set about trying to show others that I was fully American, maybe even more American than they.

The students at my high school were predominantly Jewish. They were from middle- to upper-middle-class families, and the student parking lot was filled with BMWs, Porsches, and other expensive cars. There were also many Catholic kids of Irish and Italian descent, some African Americans, and some Asians. I don't remember anyone who was white, Anglo Saxon, Protestant, the group that I had heard composed most of the United States. My community tended to be stratified along these ethnic lines: the "cool" kids who went to Studio 54 and other New York City hot spots of the late 1970s were mostly Jewish kids from affluent families who had parents who were doctors, lawyers, and corporate executives; the "smart" kids who aspired to attend Ivy League or other prestigious colleges were mostly from well-to-do Jewish or Asian families; and the "tough" kids who attended local colleges like Hofstra or Adelphi, or colleges with "real" football teams—college teams whose games were broadcast on TV—were mostly African American or of Irish or Italian descent, and from lower-middle- to middle-class families. Since I didn't fit into any of these groups, my goal in high school was to show how American I could be by socially navigating among all of them.

I performed well in my classes, especially in the sciences, and participated in a science research program organized by a teacher to whom I'm deeply indebted. The program placed high school students in various university or professional research laboratories, sent them to summer programs funded by the National Science Foundation, and helped them prepare for Westinghouse and other science competitions. But I didn't want to appear like an Asian geek, and gave up playing the violin, a sacrifice I regret today. I became a three-season varsity athlete, since athletics and Asians were seen as incompatible. In the fall, I played football, and made up for my height (5'8") with speed, smarts, and recklessness; by my senior year, I was a co-captain and starting both ways. In the winter, I was on the riflery team. In the spring, I played lacrosse, a sport I continued in college. I also made it a point to take auto mechanics, a class shunned by those who wanted to get into an Ivy League school; it's a decision I'm glad I made, even today. I also held several offices in student government. In trying to be well rounded, I had a thoroughly wonderful high school experience. I didn't worry about trying to figure out who I was or why I didn't quite fit in—I was having too much fun! I had friends and girlfriends, did well in athletic and science competitions, and enjoyed partying with my friends.

Fuji could do these things, because he, like many a Vietnam-era cabinet member, decided that reform was possible only from within. As I had in football, I took who I was and who people thought I was and made the best of it. Anthropologists would say I made instrumental use of my ethnic category;[7] political activists might say I was a collaborator. It was easy to be Fuji because I didn't have to contend with social pressure from a Filipino American community. Instead, my family fully supported my quest to assimilate.

When I attended college at Harvard, it was even easier to be more American since I was separated from my family, my one solid link to being Pinoy. Back in the mid-1980s, ethnic identity wasn't the hot social issue it is today. I did little that reminded me of being Pinoy, except regularly attend Mass at the local Catholic church. I again tried to balance academic success without appearing like an Asian geek, but it was a lot harder at Harvard. I majored in chemistry and physics, but graduated without honors, unlike about 75 percent of my fellow seniors. Back then, I attributed my less-than-stellar academic achievements to my pursuit of being "well rounded," that is, more American. I wanted to continue being an athlete, so I played lacrosse. I earned a varsity letter, but quit in my junior year after realizing my limits. I discovered that I couldn't play lacrosse, pass my classes, and have fun like I did in high school. The Marine Corps had given me a four-year scholarship to college, and after my sophomore year I was committed to continuing my service in the Naval Reserve Officers' Training Corps (NROTC). Even without playing a varsity sport, what could better prove my successful assimilation into American society than serving as a Marine Corps officer?

It was in the Marine Corps that being Pinoy became more obvious; at the same time, ethnic identities were becoming more of a social issue. In college, I had active-duty stints during summers and drill time during the academic year. From 1986 to 1989, I served as an infantry officer. Before I continue, I want to say that

I think the Marine Corps, as an organization, is structurally less biased, in terms of race or ethnicity, than most American organizations. A person's race or ethnic background is irrelevant, since it will all be stripped down and rebuilt into "Marine Green." In its education and training, the Marine Corps consistently emphasized racial and ethnic tolerance and imposed severe penalties for those who transgressed such policies. But, ultimately, the U.S. Marine Corps was made up of people from different backgrounds and experiences, and non–Marine Corps attitudes would surface occasionally. As opposed to the safe havens of home and college, I stuck out as a Filipino American in "the real world" of the Marine Corps. Filipinos, especially for American military personnel and expatriates with experience overseas, were often stereotyped as cooks, musicians, and prostitutes. Several incidents during my Marine Corps experiences forced me to be aware of being Pinoy.

It started almost immediately at the Marine Corps Officers' Candidate School (OCS) in Virginia. As part of our training, Marine-option midshipmen—college students preselected to receive a Marine Corps officers' commission—attended a six-week version of hell; actually, it was more like a purgatory in which the Marine Corps tested the mental and physical toughness of its officer candidates. OCS was a daily rigor of harassment: the stuff you see in movies, you know, like no use of personal pronouns. "You?! You?! Ewe is a female sheep!" you would hear a drill instructor screaming to one officer candidate, while in the background you would hear a hoarse but hardy officer candidate yelling "Right eye! Left eye!" as he stood in the middle of the courtyard pointing to his own eyes—we learned quickly not to say "I" or "you." These were tricks of the trade, as the Marine Corps sought to desocialize college kids and remake them in its own image.[8]

There were very few Asian American officer candidates in my class; in my platoon of about forty, I think I was the only one. After a few weeks of wear and tear, I was approached by a drill instructor who remarked "Lozada, huh? That's a Filipino name—why aren't you in the Navy as a cook or something?" "This officer candidate doesn't know how to cook, sergeant instructor," I remember yelling back, trying to be a smart-ass without earning his wrath. I'm sure the drill sergeant wasn't trying to be racist toward Filipinos but just trying to find a way to get under my skin. I remember thinking nothing of the remark, or maybe something along the lines of "Is this the best you can do?" At least he knew what a Filipino was, I thought. However, about a year after I graduated, an Asian American officer candidate filed suit against the Marine Corps, charging that racial discrimination was a source of undue harassment that had led to his being dropped from the program. I don't remember the details of the case, but I do remember thinking back then, "What a wimp, looking for an easy way out." Many years later he won the case against the Marine Corps, and received a commission of captain—the rank he would have attained if he had not been dropped. Looking back, I can better understand what motivated him to file this suit; today, I am less hasty in passing judgment.

But it was another incident, much more innocuous on the surface, that sharpened my awareness of being Pinoy. My parents had come to Virginia for my graduation. That last week of OCS was the most strenuous. It was not physically taxing, for we had finished our last field exercises the week before, but it was mentally draining to wait around and do nothing but practice marching and filling out paperwork. Looking back, maybe this was the Marines' true test of mental toughness. Anyway, after the parade, I met my parents underneath a tent filled with refreshments and high-ranking officers. I introduced them to some friends. Suddenly, my mother zeroed in on a particular major and said, "Look, a Pinoy officer." Dragging me along, she ran over to him and chatted with him like she would with her *barkada,* gang of friends. I was so embarrassed. I didn't want to talk to anyone, especially a major who, according to his badge, worked for the Joint Chief of Staff. I just wanted to change into my civilian clothes and get off base. After my mother had exhausted her repertoire of personal, probing questions that would embarrass most non-Filipinos or non–New Yorkers, the major looked at me and said, "You're the forty-second Pinoy to be commissioned as an officer in the USMC." My first thought was, well, wow, not that many of us, huh? But then I started thinking, how does he know? Why would anyone bother to keep track of something like that? What did it mean for me? Do I have to do something special now, like eat *balut* in the officers' club? I never did check up on his remark, to see if it were true. Sometimes I still wonder about it even today.

Being a Pinoy Marine Corps officer didn't matter much in Camp Lejeune, North Carolina, but it was much more significant when my unit was deployed to the Philippines in 1988. I had visited the Philippines once as a young child in 1971, but didn't remember much besides the sweltering heat and the annoying bugs. I do remember coming back to the United States so fluent in Tagalog that my third-grade teachers put me in a speech class to work on my English. My parents spoke Tagalog at home and in public when they didn't want people to know what they were saying. Like many first-generation children, I could understand "kitchen Tagalog," and answer back in English. Anyway, after a few months in the Philippines, my Tagalog improved to the point where I could get by in the streets and watch a Filipino movie. Although my Tagalog improved, my awareness of being Pinoy was jarred by my intense exposure to Filipinos. I visited my relatives around Manila and in Cavite and the stark difference in attitudes between my mother's and father's relatives was immediately obvious. My mother's side of the family was well-to-do and showed me what it meant to live the good life in the Philippines. My uncles took me to various tourist areas like Tagaytay and resorts in the Philippines,[9] and we talked about doing business in the U.S. Nearly half of my mother's siblings lived in California. Being Pinoy, and America in general, were recognized social goods.

With my father's side of the family, however, the situation was very different. Most of my father's family had remained in the Philippines and I got a chance to meet many of my cousins. Those who were close to me in age often asked me to explain my presence in the Philippines—not as a Pinoy visiting relatives in the Philippines, but as a U.S. Marine Corps officer stationed in Subic Bay. At that time, there had been an attempted coup against the Aquino government. The political turmoil and attacks upon American military personnel were among the reasons why my unit had been deployed to Subic. My cousins questioned me about my feelings on participating in encroachments on Filipino sovereignty. I was surprised by their strong, nationalist feeling,[10] but should have realized that they would have such attitudes when I noticed earlier that some relatives were running for local office under Aquino's party. I defended the American military presence back then, but looking back, I also felt like some kind of collaborator in some postcolonial hegemony—not at all like a proper Pinoy.

My sense of being Pinoy was heightened as I learned how non-Filipinos developed their stereotypes about Filipinos. During that Pacific deployment, I saw and met many Filipinos who served as domestic workers, prostitutes, and musicians in Hong Kong, Okinawa, and the areas surrounding American military bases in the Philippines. Throughout East Asia, bars that catered to U.S. military personnel and businessmen were primarily staffed by Filipinas who would "entertain" lonely men by listening to their chatter, dancing with them, or sleeping with them. Around the U.S. bases, many were professionals who were quick to separate a man from his money, for in order to get the attention of these women you would have to buy them a ten-dollar glass of soda, and refresh them periodically to keep them by your side. In the Officers' Club on base, there were more Filipinas—for conversation or dancing, not sex. In talking with them, I would listen to their stories about how they were earning lots of money to support their families in other provinces, or saving money for school or for their children. Many dreamed about marrying a U.S. serviceman who would bring them to the States. They would mask the business aspect of entertaining in the bars by talking about the relationships as romantic affairs.

There were similar bars in Hong Kong, but most Filipinas worked as domestic workers. On Sunday afternoons after morning Mass, crowds of them would gather in the squares and streets of Hong Kong Island, picnicking and gossiping with one other, buying and selling things to one other. On the other six days of the week, Cantonese or English was the language you heard on the streets, but on Sunday the air would be filled with Tagalog. During my first visit in 1988, it was a bit disconcerting to see so many Filipinas—I wondered where they all hid during the week. Thumbing through the Hong Kong papers later in 1994–1995, I read various solutions to the "Filipino problem"—about shelters for abused domestic workers, crime among Hong Kong Filipinos, and other issues that Hong Kong residents—which meant Chinese or British, I guess—sought to remedy. In 1988, however, I was embarrassed to be Filipino, believing that I came from a people that were best suited to serve as prostitutes, domestic workers, and entertainers. We weren't strong enough to compete with the Chinese, British, Americans, or Japanese in the world arena, and there was something in our culture that made us Filipinos submissive and ignorant, resigned to our dependent position in the world, I thought.[11] Filipino poverty and underdevelopment served as proof of the inadequacy of Filipinos and Filipino culture, especially when compared to the economic success of Hong Kong.

What I perceived as the strength and vibrancy of Chinese culture, as seen in Hong Kong, ultimately lured me into anthropology. Like the majority of Filipinos, I am Roman Catholic. I regularly attended Sunday Mass while overseas. In Hong Kong, I was struck by the mixture of familiarity and otherness of the Masses. The order of the Mass was the same, but it was conducted in Cantonese. Instead of shaking hands as a sign of peace, the Chinese would bow to one another. There were always many Filipinos attending Mass, and I would hear patches of Tagalog floating in the murmur of Cantonese. After six years of graduate school, this phenomenon of globalism[12] ultimately became my dissertation topic: an examination of how transnational organizations,[13] like the Roman Catholic Church, influence local social relations and cultural identity. As a Pinoy, I shared something with the Filipino prostitutes, domestic workers, and other residents of Hong Kong, but I also had something in common with the Chinese Catholics. Yet I was also an outsider as an American, belonging more fully to the community back in the United States. Social anthropology would help me understand the processes involved in my own personal feelings of familiarity and strangeness.

Returning to Harvard for graduate school meant a dramatic change in my own identity. I had no background in either Chinese studies or anthropology, and went from being an infantry officer to a house-husband and graduate student. Patrick was born just before I left the Marine Corps, and my first wife, who had gotten an M.B.A. while I was in the service, returned to work, leaving me to become the primary care provider. Taking care of an infant was one of the hardest challenges in my life. Again I was a social oddity—not as a Pinoy, but as a male who stayed home to care for a child while his wife supported the family. As a house-husband attending "mothers' groups," and arranging childcare as my son got older, the fact that I was male was much more salient than being Pinoy. As happens to other primary care providers, my child became the major part of my identity. Patrick's own identity, in fact, is a statement of my own experiences of being more American than other Americans. Even though my parents flew into Kennedy Airport in the early 1960s, their first grandchild, my son, was a Son of the American Revolution through his mother, herself a Daughter of the American Revolution. How American can you get?

Speaking of romance, I have never dated a Pinoy woman. In high school, all my girlfriends were Jewish; in college, I began dating those white, Anglo-Saxon, Protestants that I had heard of but never met. My first wife, whom I met at Harvard, was white, from rural South Carolina. My second wife, whom I met in graduate school, is a fourth-generation German American from rural Kansas. Also an anthropologist, she often has remarked that my attraction to mostly white women says something about my attitudes towards my Pinoy ethnicity.[14] Am I attracted to white women because of some desire to be white, some self-hate of my Pinoy identity? I don't think so, but others may suggest it. Am I attracted to white women because they are the standard of beauty pushed by the media, and I want to prove to other white Americans that I can attract white women? Maybe closer to the truth, but I also think that my choice of partners reflects the fact that there have been many more white women in my social domains, particularly at Harvard, the community I have been with most of my adult life.

I never thought of my wife and myself as a multiethnic couple until we bumped into another couple, an African American man and a white woman, in a bridal shop. While our fiancées were taking care of business, he questioned me about Seattle, asking, "How do they treat multiethnic couples like yourselves out there?" It's been a long time since *Guess Who's Coming to Dinner* and unfortunately, I'm no Sidney Poitier. Having always thought of myself more as American than Filipino American, I had never noticed that my wife and I were multiethnic. In the early 1980s, when I did most of my dating, being a hyphenated American wasn't on everyone's mind.

But when I attended graduate school in the 1990s, ethnic politics had drifted into the American social and political spotlight and it was cool to be a hyphenated American. As novice anthropology graduate students, we read—digested may be more accurate—ethnography after ethnography about "others," also called primitive, premodern, underdeveloped, or whichever politically correct term was in use when the ethnography was written. I learned how unfamiliarity and a feeling of disorientedness were standard operating procedure for fieldworkers, and key tools for anthropologists. Social anthropologists play a tight game, for their principle instrument of observation is the anthropologist himself. As fieldworker, the anthropologist must assume that she has some basic element of humanness that is shared with the people at the fieldsite, but the people must also be different enough from the anthropologist to highlight certain social or cultural facets of humanity in general.[15] In other words, disorientation, achieved through being embedded in unfamiliar social relations or immersed in strange cultural patterns, is where the anthropologist begins to analyze people. Perhaps this is why anthropology is a staple discipline for ethnic studies; hyphenated Americans, in one way or another, are living out the anthropological fieldwork experience.

As an anthropologist, I do not study "my own" cultural area, but not out of any intent for "objectivity." My Pinoy experience is different enough to make the Philippines as "other" to me as it would be to any non-Filipino. This became readily apparent after my experience in a particular seminar. Each week, we were expected to read one or two ethnographies and be prepared to summarize and critique the material if chosen by the professor at the beginning of class. Somehow,

I was picked to comment on Michelle Rosaldo's *Knowledge and Passion: Ilongot Notions of Self and Social Life,* an ethnography about a tribe of headhunters in the Philippines. I presented what I felt was a mechanical summary of Rosaldo's methodology, key ethnographic detail, and theoretical points, drawing largely on my previous anthropological coursework and my own experiences in the Philippines, primarily my military deployment to Subic Bay. For comparison with the Ilongot, I could only draw similarities arising from my own negotiation with the Negritos who lived in the training areas, where, in retrospect, I had played a tidy part as an American imperialist demanding to make payment to the "chief" without any regard for the intricacies of Negrito social organization.

During my fieldwork in China, people often asked why I was not studying the Philippines. In China, when people ask "where are you from?" the answer they expect is not where you live, or where you were born, but where your parents and your parents' parents are from. Implicit in their reckoning of identity is the idea of descent, a primordialist perspective on who a person is. In other words, I'm Filipino because my ancestors come from the Philippines; likewise, a fourth-generation Chinese American is still Chinese. People in the rural area of south China where I worked, as in Beijing, where I have also conducted fieldwork, would chat with me about the Philippines, even though they knew that I held an American passport. As a result, I often talked about the Philippines during my fieldwork, highlighting similarities and differences between Chinese, American, and Filipino cultural traditions. In the Chinese Catholic village where I did my fieldwork, the men and women were well aware of the Philippines, since it is the only Asian country where Christianity is the dominant religious tradition. In my role as an anthropologist studying China, then, my Filipino American identity still remains salient in who I am and what I do.

The major point that I have tried to convey through my various experiences as a "Filipino American professional" is to show how the balance between primordialist and instrumentalist attributes of ethnicity shifts depending upon context. Many immigrants, and children of immigrants, enter the United States with the goal of assimilating, or as I have described it, of becoming more American than most Americans. As you can see from my own reflections on my Pinoy identity, I have more or less thought of myself as American as apple pie, and sometimes as American as *leche flan,* a Filipino/Spanish dessert. My Pinoy identity enters the picture largely as a result of others who attribute a sense of "other" to me—not just white Americans, but also people in the Philippines, Hong Kong, and China. In my social relations, I cannot ignore how other people classify me. My Pinoy identity is unshakable; I cannot discard who I am, what I look like, who my parents are. My Pinoy identity is permanent, in that my kinship group is who it is. Moreover, the subdued sense of being Filipino comes from the hopes and dreams of my parents, whose primary focus was for us to succeed in the land to which they had immigrated. When I was growing up, we did not have access to a *patrimoine*[16] (material objects and ideas that represent a cultural heritage, like the play I described in the beginning), nor a kinship group/community that reinforced my Pinoy identity.

My Pinoy identity has been instrumental, in that I have largely not used my ethnicity as a resource in my professional pursuits. I didn't turn off being Pinoy; it just never mattered much in what I did. However, as the social context has shifted, with an emphasis on the ethnic variety of 1990s America, my Pinoy identity has become more salient, more a factor in what I do. After all, I'm writing this essay as a Pinoy professional. And with the establishment of more active Pinoy networks and social groups, I am learning more and more about what it means to be a part of a Pinoy community.

But most importantly, I am a father who seeks to guide his son in growing up. I have retained principle custody of Patrick, and would like to teach him what it means to be Pinoy, especially since ethnic heritage, the *patrimoine* of the diverse ethnic groups that comprise the United States, has become an important part of 1990s elementary school curricula. I don't know much about Filipino ritual markers that are used to mobilize feelings of ethnic solidarity, like Kwanzaa for African Americans. But I do know something about *halo-halo* (Filipino dessert), *sukis* (stores that are regularly patronized), and *barkadas*. I know something about the social and historical experiences of Filipinos, as was depicted in the play I took my son to see. In our postmodern world, national boundaries have become more fluid as people cross borders more readily and transnational organizations become more prevalent. A people's awareness of their diasporic identity has become more salient in who we are, what we do, and how we do it. As my parents did for me, I hope to prepare my son for success in his life. This includes teaching him, as well as myself, what it means to be Filipino American today, and what it has meant for me and other Pinoys in the past. Hopefully, this will provide him with the resources to find out what it will mean for him in the future.

ENDNOTES

1. *Heart of the Son* brochure, distributed by *Sining KilUSAn,* March 1996. To avoid lengthy theoretical discussions, I will not cite, review, and critique relevant literature, but will instead add footnotes giving references to works that interested readers can later examine.

2. For theoretical works on postmodernity, see Jean-François Lyotard, *The Postmodern Condition: A Report on Knowledge* (Minneapolis: University of Minnesota Press, 1984); Fredric Jameson, *Postmodernism or, the Cultural Logic of Late Capitalism* (Durham, NC: Duke University Press, 1991); and David Harvey, *The Condition of Postmodernity* (Cambridge, MA: Blackwell Publishers, 1990). For ethnographic treatments of postmodern identities, see John D. Dorst, *The Written Suburb: An American Site, An Ethnographic Dilemma* (Philadelphia: University of Pennsylvania Press, 1989) and Dorinne Kondo, *Crafting Selves:*

Power, Gender, and Discourses of Identity in a Japanese Workplace (Chicago: University of Chicago Press, 1990).

3. Metanarratives are "large-scale theoretical interpretations purportedly of universal application" (Harvey 1990:9).

4. See Jack Goody, *Cooking, Cuisine, and Class: A Study in Comparative Sociology* (Cambridge, England: Cambridge University Press, 1982); Arjun Appadurai, "How to Make a National Cuisine: Cookbooks in Contemporary India," *Comparative Studies in Society and History,* vol. 30, no. 1 (1988), pp. 3–24; and James L. Watson, *Golden Arches East* (Stanford, CA: Stanford University Press, 1997).

5. For discussion on the social uses of such categories, see Michel Foucault, *The Order of Things: An Archaeology of the Human Sciences* (New York: Vintage Books, 1971); Edward Said, *Orientalism* (New York: Vintage Books, 1978); Johannes Fabian, *Time and the Other: How Anthropology Makes Its Object* (New York: Columbia University Press, 1983).

6. Some cultural critiques have described this phenomena as an internalization of self-hate; see Garrett Hongo, *Under Western Eyes: Personal Essays from Asian America* (New York: Anchor Books, 1995). For a discussion of the social importance of names, see Rubie Watson, "The Named and the Nameless: Gender and Person in Chinese Society," *American Ethnologist,* vol. 13, no. 4 (1986), pp. 619–631.

7. For a discussion of primordialist and instrumentalist perspectives on ethnicity, see Abner Cohen, *Custom and Politics in Urban Africa* (Berkeley: University of California Press, 1969); Charles Keyes, *Ethnic Change* (Seattle: University of Washington Press, 1981); and Stanley J. Tambiah, *The Nation State in Crisis and the Rise of Ethnonationalism* (Punitham Tiruchelvam Memorial Lecture, 1992).

8. See Marcel Mauss, "The Notion of Body Techniques," in *Sociology and Psychology: Essays* (London: Routledge and Kegan Paul, 1979), pp. 97–123 (especially for a discussion of military training), and Pierre Bourdieu, *Outline of a Theory of Practice* (Cambridge, England: Cambridge University Press, 1977), for a discussion of *habitus,* the socialization that the Marine Corps sought to displace.

9. See Ulf Hannerz, *Cultural Complexity: Studies in the Social Organization of Meaning* (New York: Columbia University Press, 1992), for a discussion of "cosmopolitans" as a theoretical category in describing issues of globalism and nationalism. My relatives on my mother's side of the family fit Hannerz's description of cosmopolitans.

10. See Benedict Anderson, *Imagined Communities: Reflections on the Origin and Spread of Nationalism* (New York: Verso, 1983), for a discussion of nationalism.

11. See Andre G. Frank, "The Development of Underdevelopment," in *Latin America: Underdevelopment or Revolution* (New York: Monthly Review Press, 1969), pp. 3–17; Arturo Escobar, *Encountering Development: The Making and Unmaking of the Third World* (Princeton: Princeton University Press, 1995); Mark Hobart, *An Anthropological Critique of Development* (London: Routledge, 1993), for discussions of dependency theory and development. See Michael Taussig, *The Devil and Commodity Fetishism in South America* (Raleigh: University of North Carolina Press, 1980); June Nash, *We Eat the Mines and the Mines Eat Us: Dependency and Exploitation in Bolivian Tin Mines* (New York: Columbia University Press, 1979); and Aihwa Ong, *Spirits of Resistance and Capitalist Discipline: Factory Women in Malaysia* (Albany: SUNY Press, 1987), for a discussion of the effect of world capitalism on social relations and cultural traditions of third-world countries.

12. For an anthropological analysis of local/global issues, see Mike Featherstone, *Global Culture: Nationalism, Globalization, and Modernity* (New York: Sage, 1990); Marilyn Strathern, *Shifting Contexts: Transformations in Anthropological Knowledge* (New York: Routledge, 1995); Arjun Appadurai, "The Production of Locality," in *Counterworks: Managing the Diversity of Knowledge,* edited by Richard Fardon (New York: Routledge, 1995), pp. 204–225; and Sally Falk Moore, "The Ethnography of the Present and the Analysis of Process," in *Assessing Cultural Anthropology,* edited by Robert Borofsky (New York: McGraw-Hill, 1994), pp. 362–374.

13. For studies on transnationalism, see works by Joseph Nye and Robert Keoehane, *Transnational Relations and World Politics* (Cambridge, MA: Harvard University Press, 1972); Samuel Huntington, "Transnational Organizations in World Politics," *World Politics,* vol. 25 (1973), pp. 333–368; and Akhil Gupta, "Song of the Nonaligned World: Transnational Identities and the Reinscription of Space in Late Captialism," *Cultural Anthropology,* vol. 7, no. 1 (1992), pp. 63–79. For a discussion of transnational ethnicity in particular, see Linda Basch, Nina Glick Schiller, and Cristina Szanton-Blanc, *Nations Unbound: Transnational Projects, Postcolonial Predicaments, and Deterritorialized Nation-states* (Amsterdam: Gordon and Breach, 1994).

14. For sociological analyses of desire, see Ann Stoler, "Making Empire Respectable: The Politics of Race and Sexual Morality in 20th-Century Colonial Cultures," *American Ethnologist,* vol. 16, no. 4 (1989), pp. 634–660; Robert C. Young, *Colonial Desire: Hybridity in Theory, Culture, and Race* (London: Routledge, 1995); and Parveen Adams, "Representations and Sexuality," *m/f,* vol. 1 (1978).

15. For those interested in a description of anthropological epistemology in action, see Claude Levi-Strauss's *Tristes Tropique* (New York: Criterion Books, 1961).

16. See Richard Handler, *Nationalism and the Politics of Culture in Quebec* (Madison: University of Wisconsin Press, 1988), for the relation of ethnic markers in the construction of identity.

An (Asian American) Actor's Life

THE LAST TIME I was in the unemployment line, I was struck by how my life seemed to fit so easily onto a generic government form. It seemed insultingly reductive, yet strangely accurate. Under "Race/Ethnicity," I had checked the box next to "Asian American/Pacific Islander." On the dotted line, I had signed my name, testifying that I was a U.S. citizen. And, finally, under "Occupation," I had written "Actor." Asian. American. Actor. Like a factual haiku, here was my portrait in three words. My sense of identity resides strongly in those three words because only a few people are likely to use them in describing themselves. Men, after all, constitute less than half of the American population; Asian Americans comprise less than 4 percent of the population; and full-time actors are an even more minuscule percentage.

For much of my life, I believed that I could keep separate these various aspects of my identity. Growing up, I considered myself an "American" and unconsciously avoided all things "Asian." Later in college, I explored and grew proud of my Asian American identity. Throughout my acting career, I have wanted only to be given the same consideration as any other actor; as I grow older, I am realizing that it is impossible to isolate these different aspects of myself. My life as a professional actor is inescapably influenced by all three words: I am an Asian American actor. Despite my wishes, I cannot make career choices based simply on my identity as an actor. To be an actor who is Asian American means continually walking the line between artistic merit and political consciousness.

Several years ago, when I was a student at Brown University in Providence, Rhode Island, I attended a forum on Asian American men in the media. The audience was composed of about thirty Asian American men. We were asked to name our Asian American role models. One by one, we went around the room. When we were done, the vast majority of us had responded either "my dad" or "Michael Chang," the professional tennis player. For an evening that was supposed to deal with Asian American men in the media, this was a striking, even disturbing revelation. Other than a sports star, who were they? Why didn't they come readily to mind? Why weren't they emulated? There was some sheepish laughter. We all looked at one another, many of us complete strangers to one another. It was a little awkward. In fact, just being in a room full of Asian men was unusual. But to be there, with the purpose of talking about oneself and one's feelings of being Asian American, was even stranger.

I GREW UP in Chicago's North Shore, and attended a small private school in the predominantly white, upper-middle-class suburb of Winnetka, Illinois. The school taught students from kindergarten through twelfth grade, and had a total enrollment of about 450. There were only forty-one kids in my graduating high school class. I cannot recollect any other Asian male in the Upper School, which covered grades nine to twelve, except for Shaio Xiao Feng, an exchange student from China.

Because of its small student body and its relatively abundant resources, the North Shore Country Day School encouraged its students to participate in as many aspects of extracurricular life as possible. The school's motto was "Live and Serve." This philosophy fostered an environment of inclusiveness, manifesting itself in several ways. First, students were encouraged to participate in any group in which they had an interest. So if you wanted to be on the football team, you just had to show up at practices. Depending on your ability, you might not play much, but you always had the experience of being on a team. Another way the school promoted inclusiveness was to discourage competition between the students. While North Shore prided itself on having high academic standards, individuals were never awarded for receiving the highest grades. The message was that one's effort was as important as the results. The memories I have of my time at North Shore are almost all fond ones. The school offered many opportunities that I probably would not have had at other schools, including perhaps my involvement in the theater.

Though the student body included people of different races and ethnicities, the administration never really made an attempt to discover the cultural differences among us. In its attempt to include everyone, differences were often ignored or overlooked. Consequently, North Shore never made me feel that my Asian heritage was something to be discussed or explored. Brown University, however, was different. It had a population that was ten times my prep school, and infinitely more diverse. For the first time, I was in an environment where a significant number of people looked like me. Still, many of the Asian men on campus, like myself, came from affluent, predominantly WASPy high schools.

When I first started college, I jokingly referred to myself and other Asian Americans as "vampires." In Anne Rice's novel, *Interview with the Vampire,* the vampire lives a solitary, secretive existence. He lives among an unsuspecting human population, looking enough like the people around him to walk down the street, but different enough to remain perpetually on the outside. Believing that he is the only creature of his kind, he relies upon humans to offer him spiritual and psychological sustenance. His perceived isolation is an existential dilemma.

Parallel that thought with this image: two groups of freshmen coming together during the first week of college, each group a hastily put-together bunch of young men, all of whom are eager to make friends, to bond over similarities. Every man is white, save a single Asian American on each side. Who notices? No one but us Asians. Who better to sniff out the secret identity of a vampire than another? We put our hands in our pockets and shuffle our feet awkwardly. Never looking directly at the other, there is a strange, silent communication taking place: *Don't blow my cover.*

Reflecting on that reaction today, it seems silly—yet also entirely under-standable. For years, we had to make do with being different—like myself, virtually the only Asian at North Shore. It's a quandary I never figured out how to articulate fully in high school—that I could have the same sensibility, the same sense of humor, the same interests as my friends, and yet somehow feel inescapably different. At some point, that difference became a badge of individual identity for me. Neither the quarterback nor the funny guy, I was the actor with black hair and almond-shaped eyes. But then suddenly at Brown, being Asian was not so unique. My iden-tity needed to be revised. It was unsettling, but it was also about time. Brown, with its multicultural community and its Asian American Studies department, gave me the awareness and resources to discover a whole side of myself that had long been ignored. I found myself in an environment that celebrated differences and encouraged strong opinions. All around me were hundreds of Asian men and women from across the country looking to understand their place in America as people of Asian descent.

I was a vampire no longer.

I ENTERED THE North Shore Country Day School in the fifth grade. For the next eight years, my social circle consisted, more or less, of the same small group of stu-dents. We were all very familiar with one another, and I never questioned my place among them. The displacement I felt was kept to myself. Who among my friends could I talk to about such things? There was no one else who seemed to share my specific dilemma, certainly no one else who was Asian American. It never occurred to me to broach the subject with my family.

My parents immigrated to the United States a year before I was born. My older brother was born in the Philippines and spoke Tagalog fluently by the age of two. But soon after my family arrived in America, my brother asked my par-ents to address him only in English in front of his Caucasian friends. I think my parents were shocked by his request, but they decided to honor his wishes. They wanted us to assimilate as fully as possible. Consequently, I never learned to speak Tagalog, although I have heard it my entire life.

My best friend growing up was an African American named Fred. We were inseparable. When I was in the seventh or eighth grade, a little boy, who was about five or six, asked me, "Why are your eyes like this?" He pulled his eyes sideways. I was dumbstruck, speechless. I stuttered, stumbling for an answer, then finally dismissed the child with a rude retort. The boy was scared and rightfully upset. Fred later put his hand on my shoulder, and calmly said, "It's okay, Joel. He didn't mean to hurt your feelings. He really wanted to know." I already felt bad, but it made me feel even worse to realize that I had allowed my feelings to be hurt by an honest question. My anger came from a place of confusion and embarrassment. My ethnicity as a Filipino American, it seemed to me, was a big secret.

My major passion growing up was the theater. North Shore had a wonderful 400-seat proscenium stage where we attended all-school assemblies three times a week. On that stage, we also saw professional artists who came to perform at our school. The high school produced several different plays during the year; the lower and middle schools, only a few. The entire student body, as well as many alumni, attended most of these performances.

A big theater holds a tremendous amount of mystery and power. The whole process of collaborating to tell a story just amazed me. I wanted to be a part of the process, so from the fifth to the eighth grade I worked on the stage crew despite my abysmal relationship with power tools and stage design. Near the end of my freshman year in high school, however, teachers in the theater department began pushing me to audition for the student-directed, one-act play festival. They told me that acting was a fundamental component in the storytelling process that I needed to experience, that only then would I complete my exposure to the theater.

I was terrified by the prospect. Getting up on the stage involved people watching me portray a character, and deep down I feared that no one would ever believe me as someone else. After all, who had I seen onstage in my young lifetime? Only white people, white people playing white characters. In the script, one did not see "white" attached to character descriptions, but the implication was obvious in all of these western comedies and dramas: An American character was a white character. I feared there was no place for me. I would be setting myself up for rejection in front of a community that I had grown up with. For an audience to reject me onstage would essentially mean rejecting me in my real life. If people did not accept me as an American character, didn't that mean that they also rejected me as an American in my daily life?

As it turned out, I was cast in a two-character, one-act play called *A Storm Is Breaking,* by Jim Damico. The experience of acting was intoxicating. Being inside the theater, collaborating with others, attempting to serve a story, trying to create a character—so many aspects of the process enthralled me. I had found something I truly loved to do. And those around me reacted positively. My teachers were encouraging, my friends were complimentary, and my parents, very supportive. At this point, I had not come to the belief that one of art's major responsibilities was to reflect the community around it, that in a community as diverse as the United States we must all be represented. I just felt grateful to have been accepted. Back then, it was much simpler. It was about acting and nothing else.

The rest of my time in high school involved a lot of theater. I had the opportunity to play a variety of roles, ranging from various characters in the Neil Simon comedy *The Good Doctor,* to Antonio Salieri in Pushkin's one-act *Mozart & Salieri.* I played Macbeth in Shakespeare's *Macbeth,* and, finally, Henry Higgins in George Bernard Shaw's *Pygmalion.* In this small community, my race was not an issue. I was expected to perform in a diverse variety of roles. This insularity proved very helpful in my development as an actor. For at least four years, I felt completely entitled to play an Italian, a Scot, a Brit. Acting was not only fun, it bolstered my self-confidence. Within the small, exclusive environment of North Shore, my love of acting was allowed to flourish and was not limited in any way because of my race.

A HOBBY IS an entirely different thing from a profession.

After graduating from high school, my parents began subtly and not-so-subtly pressuring me to pay less attention to acting. My father made me feel that acting was better suited to being an avocation; that it was now time to put the pursuit into perspective now that I was entering college; that I should begin to focus on education and establish a career. Both my parents were medical doctors, as was my maternal grandfather. When my older brother enrolled in law school, the collective eyes of the family turned toward me. Dutifully, I enrolled in a neurology course during my first semester at Brown; it was the first and only time that I nearly failed a class.

It was a confusing time, especially since I agreed with my father. What was I going to do with my life, I wondered. Though I was becoming very active in the theater department at Brown, the idea of being a professional actor seemed to be remote, just a fantasy. Becoming a professional actor did not seem to be a viable option for an Asian American man. Nonetheless, I continued to throw myself into acting simply because I loved it. And despite my father's occasional query into my studies, both my parents would fly in from Chicago to see as many of my shows as possible.

One of the major turning points in my decision to pursue acting occurred in a dentist's chair back home in Evanston. As the dental hygienist cleaned my teeth, she told me about the various plays I'd done, including a season of summer work in Providence, my first professional acting job. "How do you know about all this?" I asked, surprised at the extent of her knowledge. "You father," she said, "He's your biggest fan." Until this point, I had never thought he believed in my abilities as an actor. At most, I thought he was marginally supportive. To hear his praise for me coming from a stranger was shocking and very moving.

When I asked my mother what she thought about the possibility of me trying to act professionally, she said without a pause, "No matter what you choose to do with your life, your father and I will support you. Be the best actor you can be." The support of my family gave me the additional strength I needed to seriously pursue acting as a professional career. Without their support, I don't think I would have been able to take the risk.

Let's return to that forum on Asian American men in the media. Our limited response when asked to name Asian male role models was so telling. Those who named their fathers acknowledged the strong influence their fathers had made in their lives, but also admitted that they could not think of anyone else. Meanwhile, most of us who named Michael Chang knew little about him other than that he was an Asian tennis player. None of us had watched his matches with any regularity; in fact, some had never even seen him play. The lack of positive Asian male role models seemed obvious in our limited and tentative response.

Most of the images we Americans see are created by the entertainment industry. The influence the industry wields over our most basic perceptions about ourselves is powerful. For decades, John Wayne was the embodiment of American heroism and know-how. Jennifer Aniston cut her hair on the TV show "Friends," and millions of American women and teenagers followed. As I write this, I turn on the TV and sportscasters are yelling, "Show me the money," the popular refrain to last year's Tom Cruise movie, *Jerry McGuire*. What starts out on the screen permeates into our daily lives.

And how has popular culture portrayed Asian Americans? The first answer would have to be, "Hardly at all." The overwhelming absence of Asian American performers not only made it difficult for those of us in the workshop to cite role models, it also sent the unspoken message that Asian Americans were not a part of popular American culture.

Significant exceptions to this rule exist, of course. To cite a few, Sessue Hayakawa was a matinee idol in the 1920s; Maki assembled a fine body of work, namely his Oscar-nominated performance in the 1966 film, *The Sand Pebbles*; George Takei brought Lieutenant Sulu into millions of American homes in the TV show "Star Trek"; Bruce Lee became a cultural phenomenon, first as Kato in the TV show "The Green Hornet" and later in his film career; and Pat Morita played in ABC's number-one rated show, "Happy Days."

As a young boy growing up in Evanston, seeing Pat Morita every Tuesday night and George Takei every afternoon was a secret thrill. Like the rest of the country, I loved "Happy Days." To me, the Fonz was the coolest character in America and the Cunninghams were a great family. But whenever they went to Arnold's, there was Mr. Morita, as Arnold himself, just another member of the "Happy Days" world, and his very presence on my television set made me inexplicably happy. The same was true with George Takei. Sure, everyone loved Kirk, Spock, and McCoy, just as I did; but I was always scanning the screen for a glimpse of Mr. Sulu. On a certain level, these characters were telling me that I had a right to be here, too. I was just as American as someone who was white.

Though the aforementioned actors made significant contributions, they were the exception. More often, movies and TV have provided less than flattering images of Asians and Asian Americans. There has been a terrible perpetuation of racist stereotypes. The list of negative images is long and comprehensive. They are of a mix-and-match variety, these wily, inscrutable men of the Orient. There is the bow-legged Chinese waiter; the buck-toothed Japanese soldier of World War II propaganda; the quiet, effeminate houseman; the bullying, misogynistic father; the abusive, adulterous husband; the stoic businessman; the camera-laden tourist. These are just a few of the many images that come to mind when I think of Asian American men in the media.

To me, no character stands out as much as Gedde Watanabe's portrayal of Long Duk Dong in John Hughes's *Sixteen Candles*. Long (his last name?) is the diminutive, highly sexed exchange student who spends much of the movie looking for a "new-style American guhlfriend." After numerous jokes on his generally bizarre behavior, he mistakes the movie's leading man for a woman near the end of the movie, grabs his crotch, and ends up getting beaten up. The movie came out when I was in the seventh grade, and with its arrival, John Hughes was hailed as the master of the teenage film. Everyone, including myself, wanted to go see it. I remember sitting in a packed theater listening to everyone laugh uproariously at Long's antics. People laughed because he was exaggeratedly different. Anthony Michael Hall, another actor in the movie, was also playing a misfit, but he was considered a hero of sorts. The major difference between his character and Long's was that Long was different from the outside in: His Asian appearance was used as a key for the viewers to understand how different he was on the inside. So while people laughed *with* the trials and tribulations of Hall, they laughed *at* Long. I tried to laugh with the rest of the crowd, but could not help feeling that the audience was laughing at me, too. I left with my ears red, feeling very empty and vulnerable. When asked about the movie, though, I recommended it enthusiastically. Since I had already seen so many variations of Long in the media, I took the film's portrayal to be my problem. To a certain degree, I thought I should feel comfortable with that kind of humor.

The other, more subtle message these images sent was that Asians in this country are all from Asia or lack a familiarity with American customs and language. In the examples listed above, only Takei and Morita played people who seemed to be American. Sessue Hayakawa was Japanese, Bruce Lee originally hailed from Hong Kong, and Mako, by and large, played mostly "foreigners." Popular culture was telling me that there was no one with my experience, no one who was "Asian American." Growing up in the environment I have described, I did not readily identify with characters who were from Asia. And the negativity normally ascribed to these images made me hate them. I hated seeing Asians on the screen because I hated how they were portrayed; consequently, I was learning to reject a large part of who I was.

In this discussion, it is so easy to overlook or ignore the abilities of these actors. Since Asian Americans have made so few appearances onstage or onscreen, I have the tendency to judge them with different, more critical standards. It becomes terribly easy to focus on them as political representations and to dismiss their work as performers. For example, when I think today about Long Duk Dong in *Sixteen Candles,* it affects me differently. In the seventh grade, I saw Watanabe's representation of an Asian man as a horrific piece of work that was damaging to the self-esteem. As a real-life Asian American boy in the Chicago area watching a fictional Asian boy in the same city, the racist overtones of the movie hit close to home. Obviously, the character of Long would have had a different effect if he were not Asian. His ethnicity sent a clear message to me. He told me that Asians were exotic, strange, ridiculous people, and for that, I judged myself, and later him, accordingly.

Today, I also consider Watanabe's performance from the perspective of a fellow actor. In this regard, he is very successful. Watanabe is startlingly original, has great timing, and is very funny. In the privacy of my thoughts or among close friends, I have been able to laugh at his risks, the audacity of his acting choices. Perhaps this is because I've had more of an opportunity to identify with what it is to be an Asian American man. Stereotypes bother me less than they used to. I am a little more sure of my place in the world, and I've learned that it helps to have a sense of humor. I also know that Asian actors do not have an abundance of acting opportunities. I understand the difficulties of having to make a living. As a fellow actor, I feel compassion for Watanabe and a respect for his exceptional abilities.

In fifty years, Asian Americans hopefully will have appeared in a greater variety of roles than they have thus far. Perhaps then Watanabe's performance will be watched and enjoyed with a new level of collective understanding. Hopefully, racial politics will not even be an issue in onscreen representation. Until then, however, an Asian American actor, whether he likes it or not, bears not just an artistic responsibility, but a social one as well, in the roles he plays. Brilliant or not, working or not working, we actors must accept that we serve as Asian American ambassadors to the rest of America and the world.

FOR A YEAR and a half, or twenty-two episodes, I played a character named Lieutenant Paul Wang on "Space: Above & Beyond," a science-fiction television show produced by Fox Television in 1996. Throughout my involvement with the show, I struggled with issues of social responsibility, especially in relation to the craft of acting and the process of telling a story.

The show revolved around a Marine Corps squadron in the year 2063 A.D. and followed them through a war between the earth and an alien civilization.

Originally, Wang was one of two supporting characters created to complement the three leading characters. One of the executive producers later told me that both supporting characters, Wang and an African American woman named Vanessa Damphousse, were almost an afterthought, following the realization that they would need additional characters to play around with later in the series. Thus, Wang and Damphousse had virtually nothing to do in the pilot show and no character backstory to speak of. Wang was described simply as an Asian man, and Damphousse as an African American woman.

Wang's big moment in the pilot comes in basic training when he is terrorized by a drill sergeant. He hates to be yelled at, so being in boot camp is just about the worst possible situation for him. Of course, he becomes the target of an enormous screaming incident—his fear is a moment of humor in the episode. I was extremely conflicted over the storyline. Clearly, Wang was being used as a comic element in the show; yet I felt that the laughs were at his expense. Because the writers defined the two supporting characters only by their non-white status, I was dubious about their intentions. How did they think that race informed character? How did they plan to develop Wang and Damphousse? Already it seemed as if Wang was an Asian coward who would barely be seen. If this was the case, I did not want to be involved with the show.

One of the executive producers assured me that the character of Paul Wang would evolve if the show went to series. At the time, the success of the pilot show would determine the show's future. After a successful airing in front of network executives, "Space" began its first and only season of shooting. Sure enough, true to the producer's word, Wang reappeared in sharper focus in the first few episodes, gradually having more to do with the story points of the show. The original idea of Wang as a timid youngster, afraid of aggressive behavior, was replaced with several characteristics that had been patterned after casual conversations between myself and the writers. Wang was still an unsure and untested individual. However, Wang, like me, was now from Chicago. They took my enthusiasm for professional sports teams and raised it to an exaggerated, at times comic, level. His sense of humor and world view became the source of what made him funny, not merely what happened to him. Suddenly, I could identify with the person I was playing. He did not seem to be a simple stereotype.

Still, my frustrations continued. Over the course of the season, I discovered it was impossible for me to keep my artistic process separate from my ethnic identity. I was constantly finding myself in situations where my "acting" side was in potential conflict with my "Asian American" side. In what turned out to be the main throughline for my character, Wang is imprisoned at one point during the war and tortured. Eventually he breaks down, claiming responsibility for war crimes, becoming a pawn for enemy propaganda. Although he is later rescued and rejoins the battle, he is wracked with guilt at his failure to resist the enemy. In one episode, his shameful secret results in Wang betraying the group for his own potential absolution; in the final episode before cancellation, it works its way to its conclusion, with Wang sacrificing his life for the good of the group.

Dramatically, it was strong stuff. The human conflict was palpable, and the acting work should have been a pleasure. For much of the process, however, I was frustrated and anxiety ridden. No one knew how the storylines would work themselves out, not even the writers. I found myself more and more preoccupied with the political implications of my character's actions. In one episode, for example, Wang betrays the group to protect the secret of his torture-induced confession. His actions compromise the safety of the squadron and involve treasonous activity punishable by court martial and even execution. In the context of the show, no other character had ever behaved with such blatant disloyalty. That Wang did it purely for self-serving reasons made him completely unsympathetic, I thought. His personal weakness drives him to knowingly jeopardize the lives of his fellow soldiers, and, in the end, he is dependent on their forgiveness.

Whenever I see Asians in military uniform, I cannot help but recall common images of Asians that stem from the Vietnam War and World War II. In both cases, Asians were the enemy. They were "yellow-bellied cowards" who took the lives of loyal Americans. They were treacherous and crafty, impossible to gauge. These images of Asians have spanned more than fifty years, over the course of two major U.S. wars—three, including the Korean War. Wang could be seen as all of these stereotypes, I thought. Was he not cowardly? Was he not deceptive and disloyal? To top it off, he wasn't even successful in his deceits. His insubordination was thwarted and his redemption was dependent upon the benevolent forgiveness bestowed upon him by his comrades. To see an Asian, albeit an Asian American, causing harm to American forces exacerbated an already negative image, I thought.

This was an incredibly frustrating time for me. I felt so powerless. I received the script less than sixteen hours before we were to begin shooting, and felt profoundly disappointed by the producers. There was no time for adequate dialogue. What were they thinking when they created this storyline? Did my ethnicity influence their writing? Were they subject to the very stereotypes that I was so intent upon avoiding?

I'm sure the producers were equally exasperated with me. From their perspective, it was one of the few scripts that dealt primarily with Wang. I believe they made a concerted effort to create a dramatic situation that would be challenging for me. To hear my heated criticism of the script must have been a surprise. It certainly underscored our differences. Ultimately, my concerns about Wang were not resolved to my satisfaction. The producers were trying to navigate a path for the entire show, and my concerns about Wang were not foremost in their minds. To their credit, they always took the time to hear what I had to say; although there might have been a limit to our understanding of one another, the opportunity was at least there.

The social responsibility I felt was overwhelming and completely over-shadowed the acting. I feared portraying negative characteristics and worried about sending out a racist message. I would become paralyzed with anxiety. I also feared that I was not committing to the work and worried about doing a poor job. It seemed completely absurd to play characters who were without negative traits. My desire to be socially responsible was sterilizing my acting.

In drama school, whenever students would struggle over some esoteric ele-ment of acting, my acting teacher would always say: "Acting is your job. Do your job." Ultimately that's what I tried to do. I focused on the basics. I tried to make clear, strong choices and to be truthful. I stopped worrying about creating a posi-tive image. I began to trust the idea that people would empathize with Wang, no matter what situation he found himself in, if I could make him a real person with his own sense of dignity and truth. With this approach, I felt more in control. I had been trained to do this as an actor, and I felt capable of taking the risk.

Working on "Space," I learned how difficult it is to walk the line of social responsibility. There were two separate things to be responsible for: the work as an actor and the potential message or messages sent by the Asian image onstage or onscreen. By allowing the latter concern to preoccupy me, I was sometimes over-whelmed by the seeming immensity of it all, and paralyzed with indecision. Only by focusing on the act itself was I able to feel as if I were contributing anything at all. Do the work and the rest will follow, I told myself. In most circumstances, cre-ating a strong, vibrant character serves both responsibilities beautifully. But it was not so simple in my case.

My experience of working on "Space" convinced me that the actor alone could not be responsible for creating positive images of Asian Americans. There needed to be writers who were interested in focusing on or including Asian Amer-icans; producers and directors who felt a commitment to tell their stories. There needed to be a concerned effort from every department employed in the story-telling process.

The longer I am in the acting profession, the more I realize how depen-dent I am on so many other aspects of the business—particularly writing and pro-ducing. I hope to become more active in these areas in the future so I can exert more creative control and introduce stories with greater ethnic diversity.

TO A CERTAIN degree, I still feel at times as if I'm living a double life. I spend most of my time with my friends and colleagues in the entertainment industry, a mostly white field without an abundance of Asian Americans. It's sometimes dif-ficult to articulate my thoughts on the subject to my peers, to my employers, to you, but I'm learning that I can only do the best I can.

Unlike that forum I attended years ago, I now know of many more Asian Americans in the public eye. It seems as if the number of Asian American actors is increasing and that we are appearing in a variety of different contexts. There are more and more Asian Americans interested in telling their own stories in dramatic writing. It is time we contribute more of ourselves to American popular culture, be it through a celebration of our differences as people of Asian heritage, or as another texture to the beauty of being American. The more our stories become accepted as American tales, the more we will be able to welcome all representations, positive or negative.

I look forward to the day when Asian vampires travel in packs; when Long Duk Dong plays a friendly game of tennis with Michael Chang. I will laugh with delight when the boy next door is an Asian American who speaks with a southern twang, and the new Fonz's parents are from Korea. I want to sit with all my friends and guffaw at the Chinese waiter and marvel at the epic Japanese gang war. We are Asian Americans, and we are all of these things.

Let us tell all our stories.

My Own "Family"

DEAR MICHELLE AND JOEY,
We all get so busy, caught up in the everyday rituals of going to work, or going to school, or simply just going. It's often difficult to make the time to just talk. And that is why I have begun this letter. I want you to know about your mama and how she came to settle in this new country all those years before you were born.

I was born in Manila, a city as big and sprawling as your native Los Angeles. Our family moved often, usually from one suburb of Manila to another, because of my father's work as a banker. Though I say our family, I mean only my father, my younger brother, my older sister, and myself. I am not including my mother. She left the Philippines for the United States when I was just three, and remained absent for much of my childhood, aside from occasional visits once a year. When I was twelve, my family made the biggest move of all, coming to San Francisco to be reunited with her. That didn't quite happen, but I'll explain more about that later.

Moving so often was difficult. People often say that young children—infants and toddlers—don't feel the impact of moving from one place to another, that they're too young to understand what's happening, but I disagree. Each time I hated leaving. I missed places, relatives, and friends. Even now I hate good-byes. Writing letters was a way of maintaining ties to people and places I've left.

My love for writing letters began when I was very young. Often late at night, my father, your Lolo (Grandfather) Pepe, would take out his portable manual typewriter and compose letters to my mother, your Lola (Grandmother) Remy. He disliked his penmanship so all his letters were typed, even brief notes and greeting cards. My father, brother, sister, and I, as well as a maid, slept together in one room to save on air-conditioning costs, so we always knew when he was writing her.

My father was very lonely and writing to her was a way of staying in touch. One night, I asked if I could also write her. He was delighted by my request and enclosed my letter with his own. Often when I wrote, I felt as if I were addressing Santa Claus, asking for a new Barbie doll, chocolates, or whatever else I craved. We would all get so excited when the post office telephoned to let us know that another package had arrived. She often sent *padala*—care packages filled with toys, chocolates, hard candies, and clothes. At other times, however, I didn't have the heart to ask for anything. I sounded like your Lolo, plaintively asking her when she would return home to the Philippines.

My memories of my parents from that time are vague, so I have pieced together those years by talking with my aunts, Tita Nena, Tita Birut, and Tita Luz, sisters of your Lolo Pepe. My parents first came to the United States in 1969. My father worked for a large bank in Angeles City, Pampanga, and was sent by his company to attend international banking seminars in New York City. My mother accompanied him and fell head-over-heels in love with the city. She was delighted by the city's fast pace. Manhattan—so unlike Manila—was modern and bustling with life. She decided she had discovered her element.

One morning as she was walking down 14th Street, she saw a line of people standing outside a building. They appeared to be as foreign as she. When she found out they were signing up to gain legal entry into the United States, she joined the queue. Weeks later, she was interviewed and granted permanent resident status. When the seminars ended six months later, my father returned to the Philippines alone.

For the next nine years, she was absent from our lives except for brief trips once a year. This was not a "normal" family situation. No one I knew was in a similar situation. My mother's decision created a bit of controversy on my father's side of the family. Though they tried to shelter my siblings and me from their opinions, I heard my aunts and even some of the servants discussing our family situation. What could possess a mother to leave her three young children—ages two, three, and four—with their father and relatives, they asked. A better life? That's the reason we were always given growing up, but I've come to think that it's not true. Or at least, that it's not the only reason.

Yet I still don't have a clue to what the real reason was. Recently, I asked your Lola why we lived in Manila and she, in New York. She told me she didn't want our family to struggle as much as some of the working couples she'd met. Many parents with young children, Lola said, appeared to have great difficulties in making ends meet and finding trustworthy baby-sitters. She didn't offer to elaborate any further, and I didn't pursue the topic. Whenever I do think of raising the issue, my mother's voice echoes inside me like a ghost from the past: *"Anak lang kita,"* literally meaning "you're *only* my child." She would often say this to me during big arguments. It was painful to hear her say that; she might as well have just driven a stake through my heart. A part of me still fears that she will say it again, especially if I should question her decisions or motives. To this day, I dare not ask her why she left our family.

As a child, though, I didn't really question her absence. My siblings and I were so blinded by all the *pasalubong* (gifts sent from abroad) she sent us. I thought then that she was in New York just so she could get us the neatest toys and clothes; that was often a good enough reason for me. But at other times, I would miss her terribly and resent her absence.

We were finally reunited as a family when I was twelve. It was a cataclysmic change. We left Pasig the summer after I graduated from the seventh grade. After nine years of separation, I was so excited at the prospect of our reunification. I was also eager to live in the United States—to experience four seasons, to touch snow, to finally see the land of the world's greatest toys. Our father had suits custom-tailored for my sister, my brother, and me. You should have seen us. We looked like miniature corporate executives. We didn't know what to expect from this country. Was it true that people wore their shoes inside their homes instead of wearing house slippers or going barefoot as they did in the Philippines, we wondered. Would we still be able to eat *lumpias* (Filipino eggrolls) and *kare-kare* (Filipino beef-and-vegetable stew)? "When you come back you won't be able to understand Tagalog anymore," warned an uncle as we prepared to leave for the airport to catch our flight to California. I vowed to prove him wrong.

We joined our mother, who was now living in San Francisco. More than a year earlier, she had left Manhattan after being diagnosed with a serious heart condition. The doctors recommended open-heart surgery if she expected to continue her fast-paced lifestyle, but she decided against the operation. She quit her job as an intravenous therapist at Lawrence Hospital in Manhattan and returned to the Philippines to rest. After a ten-month stay, she returned to the U.S. to maintain her permanent resident status. At that time, the U.S. immigration laws required resident aliens not to be absent from the country for more than twelve months at a time. She had relocated in San Francisco because she had an uncle and a brother who lived there. She found work as a private, live-in nurse.

One of my first and lasting impressions of San Francisco was of loping hills dotted with pastel-colored houses stacked tightly together. For the first time, I experienced dense fog; I thought it was a prelude to snow. There were many changes. Our house now had wall-to-wall carpeting instead of hardwood floors. No more *banigs* (woven straw mats used for sleeping on wooden floors); sofa beds and sleeping bags instead. I was surprised to find fresh vegetables and fruits being sold inside a grocery store, instead of in an open-air market. I had to learn how to open a carton of milk and a carton of orange juice. I discovered the magic of plastic wrap!

In my mind, I had envisioned our family's reunion a thousand times, yet it did not unfold in the picture-perfect manner I had imagined. Instead of working as a doctor, as in the Philippines, Lola worked as a private, live-in nurse for a Jewish Russian widow. Lola lived with her patient seven days a week and came home rarely, only if it was necessary and on the condition that she found someone, usually one of her aunts, to take her place. The widow's niece who hired my mother was very demanding and wanted my mother to be with her aunt constantly. When she did visit us, she could stay for only a few hours, or else she would bring her patient with her.

My father, meanwhile, had a very difficult time finding a job. It was virtually impossible to get a position as a high-level bank executive in San Francisco with only a bachelor's degree. Friends advised him to look for a job in Los Angeles. It was a much bigger city, abundant with opportunities and Filipinos, he was told. In L.A., he eventually found a job as a vice president for an international bank owned by a group of Asian and American investors. He usually stayed in Los Angeles and only flew up to San Francisco on weekends when my mother would not be working. He didn't regularly spend weekends with us. He often complained about San Francisco's chilly climate, saying that it induced him to sleep all day. Sunny, smoggy Los Angeles reminded him more of the Philippines and made him feel less homesick. My siblings and I stayed in my mother's house in San Francisco, usually with other relatives since she was rarely there.

For the first few days, it felt strange that she was in the same country, let alone the same city, yet not in the same house with us. But after a while, it was just like living in the Philippines. We had plenty of surrogate moms and dads. There was Lola Aning and Lola Dianang, my mother's aunts. We also had our cousin, *Kuya* (big brother) Alex, and *Ate* (big sister) Dolly, a friend of our Tita Luz, one of my father's sisters. Though we had come halfway around the world, things didn't seem so different. Our mother was still not home. Only now, neither was our father.

Since we were usually home alone, my siblings and I learned to be self-reliant. Gone were the maids to handle the household chores. My mother showed us how to wash the dishes. My siblings and I even worked out a dishwashing schedule for ourselves—my brother was responsible for doing the dishes on Mondays, Tuesdays, and Sundays (breakfast); I, on Wednesdays, Thursdays, and Sundays (lunch); my sister, on Fridays, Saturdays, and Sundays (dinner). Although most of the cooking was done by our great-aunts, we slowly learned to cook for ourselves by watching them prepare our meals and experimenting with a variety of cookbooks. I did the laundry; my sister folded, ironed, and put the clothes away. We also did our schoolwork by ourselves. We didn't really play with other kids our age. I always thought living in the U.S. would be like living on Sesame Street, where you knew your neighbors and played with other children on the block. But that didn't happen. We had no friends from school; we only had each other. My sister and I relied on each other to solve any problems we encountered in our studies. Just as in the Philippines, we remained mostly indoors, pursuing our studies and letting television, books, and records serve as our baby-sitters.

Having graduated from the seventh grade in the Philippines, I had expected to enter high school like my classmates in Manila. However, my mother enrolled my older sister and me in an eighth-grade class at a Catholic parochial school that was next door to the apartment complex where she worked. Our brother was enrolled in the sixth grade at the same school. At first I thought she had made a mistake, or that American high schools started with the eighth grade.

Actually, she deliberately placed my sister and me into the eighth grade, thinking that would make it easier for us to adjust to the U.S. school system.

After having attended an all-girl Catholic elementary school for eight years, I had a difficult time adjusting to a coeducational, parochial school. There were about twenty-five students in the entire eighth grade and we were all in one class. In Manila, there were at least eight separate classes in each grade, with an average of thirty-five to forty students per class. Most of my classmates were Caucasian. There was one African American girl and five Asian American girls, my sister and I being the two newest additions.

I'd always enjoyed attending school, but for the first time I didn't. Most of the kids already had well-established friends and didn't really try to get to know my sister and me. I was also shocked by how they didn't seem to respect the teacher, especially challenging her authority when she tried to discipline them. I was surprised that we were still studying spelling in the eighth grade! My sister and I often excelled in the class, outperforming all the other kids. Sometimes we even found ourselves correcting the teacher's spelling or explanation, more to our surprise than the teacher's. This would never have happened in Manila! The only extracurricular activity in which I participated was singing Latin hymns for Sunday Mass. Much against my outgoing nature, I had become a recluse.

After a grueling, tortuous ten months, I welcomed the changes that high school brought. I was back at an all-girl Catholic school. It was much easier making friends since everyone was in the same boat, entering as freshmen. Mercy High was a much bigger school, with more than 100 students in the freshman class. The classes were more diverse, with whites, African Americans, Asians, and Latinas. There were male and female teachers, as well as nuns. Mercy High initially felt strange, but I grew more comfortable as I made new friends. I felt as if I had found my niche and actually began looking forward to school again.

Unfortunately, this feeling didn't last very long. At the end of my sophomore year, my parents announced that we were moving to Los Angeles. For three years, my father had been flying in and out of our lives, from L.A. to San Francisco. He finally had enough and said that he wanted my mother and us to join him in Los Angeles. I didn't want to go. I had just gotten acclimated to San Francisco and really liked the new friends I had made at school. I resented having to adjust to another strange place. The only positive aspect about the move was that our family would finally all be together. It would be one more attempt to become a family.

We moved to a house in Woodland Hills, a predominantly white residential neighborhood in the San Fernando Valley, just northwest of Los Angeles. We were the only Filipino family on the block. My father had carefully researched the area, and already decided where we would attend school. He had also scoped out the nearest church and grocery stores. So there I was. Sixteen years old, and for the first time our entire family was together. Or were we? It depended on what time of day it was. My father worked in a bank in downtown Los Angeles, with typical business hours of 9 A.M. to 5 P.M. My mother, on the other hand, worked as a lab technician and plebotomist at various hospitals in the valley, usually during the graveyard shifts—from 3 P.M. to 10 P.M. or from 11 P.M. to 7 A.M., including weekends. We rarely got the chance to do what other "normal" families did. It was rare for us to eat a meal together. We did not take vacations or go to church as a family. We were often not even together on holidays.

I was back at another all-girl Catholic high school that was about a fifteen-minute drive from our home. The class composition—predominantly white and upper-middle-class—was reminiscent of the eighth grade. Unlike Mercy High, the girls sported designer clothes. My sister and I wore our off-the-rack, on-sale outfits. My sister and I were among four Filipinos in the entire school. We were also the only Asians. Entering this school as a junior was just as difficult as starting the eighth grade. Everyone had established her own circle of friends and was unreceptive to newcomers, especially to non-white strangers. Luckily, I had my sister, and she had me. I managed to join the sign language club and also participated in fund-raising activities and outings that the club organized. Other than that, I studied at home. Though I was sociable by nature, I didn't feel welcome at this school. Fortunately, my junior and senior years passed quickly.

Just as it was a natural transition for me to go from elementary to high school, so it was from high school to college. I didn't even consider any other options. I was actually looking forward to college, thinking that anything would be an improvement over high school. I wanted to start fresh, to meet other people, to make new friends. L.A. couldn't be this homogenous, I thought. I applied and got accepted to the University of California at Los Angeles, in 1983.

As I prepared to enter college, I didn't have any clear career goals for myself. I knew I liked working with people. I also liked math, Spanish, and the sciences. My tendency was to dabble in several different areas, not excelling or concentrating in any. Though I was undecided about my future, my father had very definite plans. He wanted me to study accounting or commerce, just as he and all his siblings had. It was the most practical thing to do, he told me, and with his connections, a job was practically guaranteed upon graduation. However, he couldn't persuade me. I couldn't narrow my choices and entered college as an undeclared major. My father hoped that I would eventually decide on some business-related major, but I eventually chose to study linguistics, much to his chagrin. "What are you going to do with that after you graduate? What is linguistics anyway?" he would always ask. Even I didn't really know. I only knew that I didn't want to work as an accountant or banker. I wanted to study something I enjoyed for the pure satisfaction of learning, not because it was practical or profitable. My sister, on the other hand, was accepted into UCLA as a biology major. A medical career in the making, much to my father's delight.

Despite the battle of wills over my major with my father, and my own agony over my indecisiveness, I thoroughly enjoyed my college years. The first two years were uneventful. I simply went to class, then headed straight home, a twenty-mile commute that took about forty-five minutes on the freeway. I didn't have much of a social life outside of the classroom because I was slowly adjusting to the ten-week quarter system, a change from the high school semester system. UCLA was enormous, with roughly 32,000 students from diverse ethnic and economic backgrounds. I sought out different student groups, trying to find my own "home" or group. It was a huge campus and easy to feel disconnected.

Although there was a well-established Filipino club on campus, I didn't join. I didn't identify with the other Filipinos in the club, most of whom were either born in the U.S. or had immigrated at a very young age. There were a few Filipinos who arrived in their early teens like I did, as well as a few that came on a student visa, but I didn't feel as if I fit in with them either. Although I spoke Tagalog, ate Filipino food at home, and practiced certain Filipino customs, a part of me just didn't feel Filipino. Unlike most of the members of the Filipino club, I lacked a "real" family, that is, a close-knit nuclear family. Nor did I have an extended family consisting of relatives and friends.

During my third year in college, I began working as a volunteer at the campus's Office of International Students and Scholars (OISS). Working with people from different countries was exciting and invigorating. Through the experiences of these foreigners, I saw myself. I was reminded of my initial arrival in the U.S. and all the difficulties I had faced in adjusting to an unfamiliar country. I empathized especially with those who came without any friends or relatives in the U.S. Though both my parents were in this country, I often felt very much alone because of how fragmented our family had been. I sought friendships with these foreigners, eventually "adopting" some as my big or little sister or brother. I think I was trying to create a family of my own to dispel the loneliness that had always haunted me.

It was through my work there that I eventually met your papa. He, too, volunteered at the office. As an international student from Japan, he also empathized with the international students and their needs. He later introduced me to the International Students Association (ISA), a student group he belonged to that promoted increased interaction among international students. I felt as if I had found the perfect club. It was an extension of the volunteer work that I loved and, at the same time, the best avenue for me to meet even more people at UCLA. I was finally achieving a balance of academics and fun in college!

With your papa's guidance and encouragement, I became the editor of the "International Quarterly," a newsletter put out by the ISA. I also cohosted "International Coffeebreak," a weekly program that gave international students a chance to gather informally at the campus coffeehouse. Because of my involvement in OISS and ISA activities, my college experience turned into some of the best years of my life. To this day, a lot of the students I assisted as a volunteer have kept in touch with me, either through letters or e-mail. Some live in Los Angeles, while others have returned to their home countries several thousands of miles away. I felt a wonderful, exhilarating sense of accomplishment at having finally established a place for myself and a network of friends. I finally felt at home. And, of course, having met your papa, I no longer felt alone.

Though my parents did not openly object to my marrying a non-Filipino, during the first few months of our relationship my father always referred to your papa as *yung Hapon,* meaning "that Japanese" in Tagalog. Oh, I got so annoyed when he did that. Then he would repeat his stories about how he and other members of his family had hidden from Japanese soldiers in abandoned buildings and in rice fields during World War II. Your Great-Grandma Nanay would even recite some of the Japanese words she still remembered from overhearing their conversations. Even today, my Filipino relatives lament how they were forced to learn Japanese during the wartime occupation. To prove their point, they would begin counting in Japanese: *"Ichi, ni, san, shi, go . . ."*

I was always nervous when your papa visited our house. I was unsure how your Lolo Pepe would react. I was never told by either my parents or relatives how courtship was to be conducted—whether it was the Filipino style or the American style or a little of both. I couldn't even model myself after my parents, since I had hardly observed them interacting with one another. Most of my college friends didn't have boyfriends yet or were not actively dating, so I couldn't talk to them about it either.

It's not difficult to recall those initial months of dating your papa. I invited him to our house and we would have dinner, watch TV, or just hang out. Often your Lolo Pepe would use these visits as opportunities to have your papa run errands for the family, like running out to the market to pick up some groceries. Once your Lolo discovered how handy your papa was with a hammer and other tools, he started asking him to do minor repairs around the house. Your Lolo Pepe, a wanna-be carpenter, was quickly impressed by your papa's resourcefulness and diligence. As time went on, my parents grew to accept your father.

Your *Bachan* (Japanese grandmother) and *Jichan* (Japanese grandfather), meanwhile, were also disturbed by our cultural differences. They worried that your father and I would fight constantly because of our cultural differences. But, over time, they've learned first-hand that our different nationalities do not create a problem. In fact, they often tend to forget that I'm not Japanese because I blend in so well. But whether they realize it or not, I'm just being myself, and your father and I are not as different as some people may think. Soon after I graduated from college, we got married in a Catholic church. Both of our parents attended the wedding.

In discussing my marriage, I cannot help but recall the day that I changed my name from Jean S— D— to Jean A. Hotta. I recall it vividly, as if it were yesterday. I immediately signed up for a new social security card, a new American passport, and a new driver's license. Names have a particular significance for me, perhaps because of all the considerations that went into deciding my present one. My middle name at birth, S—, you see, was given to me because it was my mother's maiden name. After I married into the Hotta family, my name should have changed to Jean S— D— Hotta, with D— as my new middle name. But rather than adopting the name of Jean D— Hotta, I decided to use "Angela," my baptismal name, as my middle name.

I had two reasons. First, I wanted to correct a misunderstanding that had plagued me ever since I arrived in America. When I applied for my social security card, I had been asked what my middle name was. I answered "S—," since that was my mother's maiden name. I didn't realize at the time that in America a middle name is a second name given to you when you are born. I later realized why my classmates had always wondered why my sister and I had the same middle names. I wanted to correct this misunderstanding. I also wanted to establish myself fully as Jean, a Filipino now married to a Japanese man. Jean, now a member of the Hotta family. Relinquishing my maiden name did not mean I was giving up being Filipino. I just wanted to de-emphasize the part of me that belonged to the D— family.

I had always resented my family for not conforming to the traditional housewife-and-breadwinner model. They didn't seem like a "real" family, at least not my ideal sense of family. When I assumed your father's name, I was keenly aware of how my life was changing in a fundamental way. It was the beginning of a new me. Almost as if I were being given a second chance. Now I could create my own family, the way I had always wanted one. I was now the wife, your papa, the husband, and together we would live under one roof.

For the first three years of our marriage, we lived with your America-Bachan (Japanese great-grandmother) and America-Jichan (Japanese great-grandfather) because we didn't have enough money to afford our own place. Your father had been living with them before our marriage, so it wasn't such an adjustment for him. But I was nervous. Bachan, fortunately, reminded me of my own grandmother, with whom I'd lived for many years in the Philippines. So though Bachan spoke mostly Japanese, I felt an immediate closeness to her.

Since it was her house, Bachan was in charge of most of the household chores. She cooked every meal while I did the dishes. She did the dusting while I vacuumed. I took it upon myself to be responsible for taking her to the grocery store, doctor appointments, *hakamairi* (visiting the cemetery), and a host of other errands. Since your papa's parents lived in Japan, Bachan and Jichan were more like my parents-in-law than grandparents-in-law. We spent a lot of time together, especially since your father traveled often in the first few years of our marriage. Bachan praised me as a good wife since I stayed home with them instead of going out with friends while your papa was away. In fact, when Bachan and I ran into any of her friends in the grocery market, she would introduce me as her daughter-in-law, then laugh and correct herself and reintroduce me as her grandson's wife. As I observed how she tended your Jichan, I learned much about how to behave as a Japanese wife.

What does it mean to be a Japanese wife? It means that I always fill your Papa's *chawan* (rice bowl) first when serving *gohan* (rice). It means that I stay at the dinner table until he leaves the table. It means letting him lead or begin a conversation and only entering the conversation afterwards. These are just a few of the things I've learned from observing both your American and Japanese Bachans. I'm not so sure what it means to be a Filipino wife, though. Since your Lola was away most of the time when I was growing up, she only taught me what it was like to be a dedicated working woman.

After living with Jichan and Bachan for three years, we managed to save enough money to buy a small two-bedroom house in Gardena, about thirty miles southwest of my parents' house. My parents were excited for us, yet at the same time they often commented that we were only playing *bahay-bahayan* (playing house) because we didn't have any children. Soon after settling into our new home, we decided to start a family. It was the start of another chapter in our marriage. A year later, Michelle, you came along. Then three-and-a-half years later, Joey, you joined us.

I hope this letter has helped you both understand me a little bit better. It was difficult—at times painful—to consider the past and to write it down here. When I abandoned my family name, I thought it would distance me from the pain I experienced growing up in my family. But it hasn't. Of course, not everything in my past has been negative. In fact, there are certain aspects of me and my Filipino heritage that I would like for you to uphold as well. For instance, I have tried to impart upon you the value of respecting your elders—the custom of *mano*, placing the back of the palm of the elder's right hand to your forehead, and the use of the words *ate* or *kuya* when addressing older female or male relatives. I do not want to abandon these traditions because they are a part of who I am, just as I hope they remain a part of you.

Though my parents were often separated, living in different cities or countries, they always loved each other and are still happily married today. Although they were often absent when I was growing up, it will never be that way for you. We will always remain one family, no matter where our work or life takes us. Having absent parents for most of my life was often very painful. I've denied it for so long, because I was trained not to question my parents' choices. I was to accept things blindly and to feel grateful for whatever I had. The Catholic in me sometimes makes me feel guilty for questioning their decision. But whatever reasons my parents had for separating our family, I think it was a mistake. I don't want to deny my feelings anymore.

In my present job as an immigration counselor to foreign students, I am often reminded of what a disorienting experience it was for me when I arrived in this country. I work at OISS, which is where I met your father and first felt a sense of community. Though my job technically involves advising students on current immigration regulations and how they will be affected, the job covers so much more. I organize and coordinate a variety of activities to assist foreign students, and try to build bridges between them and the domestic students.

I enjoy my job because I get to meet people from all over the world, and because I like to be in a position to help others, especially those who have never been to America before. It's part of my being Filipino—welcoming people warmly and trying to serve their needs. Currently, I am planning to pursue a graduate degree in education. I am interested in pursuing an administrative career in higher education and want to expand on my work with foreign students. Though I recall feeling excluded while working as a secretary at a predominantly white, all-male engineering firm, my ethnicity has been an advantage in my current job. My own experiences make me particularly adept at dealing with foreign students. In fact, within the university, I do not feel that my ethnicity has been an issue.

Some of my colleagues tell me that I'm "too nice" to the students because some of them abuse my generosity and barge unannounced into my office. But I look at it differently. I feel that they are my clients and that they have every right to demand my services. Also, I often feel as if I'm looking into a mirror when I'm dealing with them. I understand their sense of displacement. If I can make them feel more at home in an unfamiliar and sometimes cold place, I also benefit. They energize me, making me feel less alone and more connected. In a way, it's my attempt at continuing to build my own family. By adopting friends here and there, I realize that I am slowly filling that vast void I felt in my earlier days, attempting to re-create the family I never had as a child.

Part Six

A New World
The First-Generation Experience

IT IS LOGICAL to group together the essays written by the three first-generation immigrant women—Lakshmi Malroutu, Margaret Yah-Min Kan, and Hoang Hau. Their essays indicate that as Asian immigrant women they have encountered more discrimination in their careers than the 1.5- and second-generation essayists, but they did not suffer the identity crisis experienced by the younger-generation essayists. Further, all three women are highly critical of patriarchal customs practiced in their home country and in their own marriages.

While none of the 1.5- and second-generation essayists mention specific experiences with discrimination in their career mobility, two of the three immigrant essayists, Hau and Malroutu, discuss experiences with discrimination in the workplace. Hau says she was unfairly passed over for a promotion to vice president while Malroutu points out the disadvantages of a white, male-oriented academia. Though both emphasize their non-white and gender categories as the basis of discrimination, their imperfect English pronunciations and the lack of job information networks associated with their immigrant backgrounds seem to contribute significantly to their experiences with unfair treatment at work.

While the 1.5- and second-generation essayists devote much space to discussing their quests to define their ethnic and racial identities, none of the three immigrant essayists make any reference to struggling over their ethnic and racial identities. The three immigrant women have not undergone the inner conflict over their ethnic identity because, unlike the 1.5- and second-generation essayists, they had already completed the major stages of their personality development in a society where they were accepted.

Though almost all the female contributors are critical of the patriarchal customs practiced in their home countries and in their families, the three immigrant essayists have more to say about sexual double standards and gender-role division associated with Asian patriarchal practices. They are more critical of and concerned with Asian patriarchal practices because these practices played such a powerful role in restricting their careers and shaping their domestic lives. Kan, for example, feels that she "reached the glass ceiling . . . at home." Because her husband considered tending the home and the family to be the wife's primary responsibility, he discouraged her ambitions to go to law school. Hau describes herself as being competitive in the workplace, but laments her victimization by the Vietnamese patriarchal tradition at home that always puts the needs of the family ahead of her own.

The Balancing Act

I REMEMBER GETTING dressed for a Halloween party when I was in graduate school in Corvallis, Oregon, in 1988. My eighteen-month-old nephew, who had seen me disappear into the bedroom, shrieked in terror and scampered away when I later reappeared as a chameleon. Although I tried to reassure him that it was me, just his aunt, beneath the brilliantly striped costume, he remained unconvinced and refused to approach me. Reflecting on that incident today, it seems emblematic of my life. Having lived for long stretches of time in several countries, I feel quite comfortable donning the mantles of different cultures. For me, such transformations don't feel like the schizophrenic mutation of a Dr. Jekyll to a Mr. Hyde; yet, perhaps for others, my mutability is disconcerting, even frightening, as it was for my nephew on that Halloween.

Currently, I am a professor of consumer studies and personal finance at Queens College in New York City. I am single, and much of my life revolves around my job—this makes me an oddity among most Indians. Even back in Corvallis, a small university town of about 40,000 people, I stood out because I lived alone in my own apartment, even though my brother and his wife had a house in the same town. My sister-in-law told me that Indians often commented on my "situation."

Though most Indians will not say outright that I have chosen to live an uncensured life by remaining single well into my mid-thirties, they say as much through their gestures and indirect comments. In Indian society, a woman is admired and considered virtuous if she is gracious, soft-spoken, and well versed in the domestic arts. Getting married is a key event and provides a woman with respectability and a sense of decorum. A married woman is not gawked at when she steps out in public, nor is she subject to probing, indelicate questions about her personal life. She possesses a label that provides her with a social identity and self-esteem.

The fact of my life is that as a single, working woman I command more awe than understanding, more questions than solutions, more isolation than inclusion. It is not just a social divide that I experience; it is an emotional one as well because most Indians have yet to accept or even understand the possibility of someone, especially a woman, being both single and content.

BOTH MY PARENTS were from the southern state of Andhra Pradesh. Shortly after their marriage, they moved to Calcutta because my father got a job as a paint technologist with a British company. Unlike many other Indians who lived together as an extended family, ours was a nuclear one since our relatives were at least a thousand miles away. I was the youngest child, with two brothers and a sister. Our household also included a cook, four maids, and a chauffeur. We lived on the third floor of a huge house that was almost a hundred years old. It was lovely, with open verandas and balconies and a rooftop garden that was exclusively our family's.

When I was a child, my father was rarely home because of his job. He would leave the house at 7 A.M. to make the one-and-a half hour commute to work, and not return home until late in the evenings. Though he would spend some time with us during dinner, he was not an integral part of our lives. He was someone we respected and obeyed from a distance; he was our role model for how to be sensitive, hard-working, and upright. My mother, on the other hand, was a much more immediate presence—she was our confidant, friend, and disciplinarian.

My mother didn't work outside the home, so she was always there for us when we returned from school in the late afternoons. She would spend at least an hour or more with us each evening, discussing philosophy, religion, or fashion, or simply listening to what had happened to each of us during the day. She was a charming, gracious person with a wonderful sense of humor. She always supported our endeavors and made each one of us feel special. She effectively held the reins in the household. Truly, the home was her domain and homemaking her joy. Though she listened to whatever my father had to say, in the end she made sure that he agreed to whatever she wanted, winning him over with her charms. With the children, she was friendly but firm, quickly withdrawing our privileges if we didn't abide by the household rules.

Calcutta didn't have a television broadcasting station until the mid-1970s, so I was unaware of the "idiot box" for much of my childhood. My siblings and I played with our friends in the neighborhood and chatted with them over the phone. My parents didn't overemphasize the importance of an education; it was just assumed that we would do well and enter college. Reading and daydreaming were two of my favorite activities. The books of A. J. Cronin made me fantasize about becoming a doctor, while the books of Erie Stanley Gardner made me want to be a lawyer. But even then, it was apparent that I was meant to be a teacher. My friends would teasingly call me "Teeeeeach" because I was always trying to instruct them about this or that.

Since my sister was nearly ten years older, I rarely played with her. I spent more time with my brothers and a boy who lived next door, and as a result grew into quite a tomboy. I scorned dolls and always preferred climbing trees to playing house. I wore my hair short and donned dresses only when my mother forced me to. In general, I sought to disassociate myself from any pursuit that could be considered remotely feminine. At times, my mother would urge me to learn to cook or crochet, but I never felt the need. Such activities seemed frivolous and a waste of time. It didn't help that I never saw my mother cooking in the kitchen.

During my teenage years, I became more feminine. When the disco dance craze hit India in the 1970s, just as it did in Europe and America, my friends and I dressed in bell-bottom pants, platform shoes, and tie-dye t-shirts adorned with peace symbols. The discotheque was the height of pop culture and my friends and I would spend hours dancing to the music of the Beatles, the Rolling Stones, and Led Zeppelin.

Though my siblings and I emulated western culture, our parents made it clear that they expected us to uphold our family traditions and values. Though my parents were not devout Hindus, our entire family worshipped together each week. Sitting cross-legged on the floor before a shrine, we would chant Sanskrit prayers and sing hymns. Our dietary habits were also relaxed. We were permitted to eat pork and beef dishes in restaurants, but never in our home. Our cook had worked in the homes of British expatriates and knew how to prepare many delicious non-Indian dishes. Both my parents were proud of how my siblings and I blended Indian and western cultures.

When I was fifteen, my mother died after a year-long struggle with heart and kidney failure. She was a pivotal figure in all our lives, and my siblings and I suffered a deep sense of loss and helplessness at her death. The task of raising and disciplining the children fell on the shoulders of my father and he assumed the role with great fervor. He spent more time with us, helping us with our schoolwork and participating in our other activities. He also became much more protective, questioning us about our friends and our plans. My father never remarried because he thought we were old enough not to need a maternal figure; but these days I often wish that he had found another partner to ease his loneliness and to provide him with companionship in his old age.

Though my mother was irreplaceable, my sister, family friends, and neighbors were willing to assume the role of surrogate mother whenever necessary. Our cook, an elderly woman who lived with us, made sure that I was always chaperoned whenever my brothers' friends were visiting. Even if I wasn't with them, she would wander into the living room just to let them know that she was in the house. I would be so embarrassed when she would start questioning them about their families and personal life; often the boys would grow so uncomfortable that they would finally leave. Whether I wanted or not, she was always searching for a "nice" husband for me.

When I was eighteen and enrolled in college, my sister got married. Suddenly, it fell upon me to manage the household. I was responsible for planning meals, entertaining guests, and managing the household staff. The maids and cook, all of whom had been with us for many years, were not too happy about answering to me since I was completely unprepared for the task. It was not a happy situation. One day our cook complained that I didn't "chat" with her as my mother and sister had. She accused me of not confiding in her and said that I didn't make her feel as if she were a part of my life. From that day on, I made a point of sitting with her each evening, engaging in gossip, even though I didn't see the point. It took me a year and countless blunders before I began to understand how to effectively manage others.

When I felt overwhelmed by the situation—which was often—I would retreat into my bedroom and read novels to escape. My brothers, on the other hand, had it easy. They were granted a lot of freedom and took advantage of the situation. I resented how our cook permitted them to go out with their friends in the evenings, but always required me to stay at home. Though our cook was technically an employee in our household, she had been with us so long that she was like a member of the family. I lacked the courage to disobey her, and my father always deferred to her wishes. Sometimes I would vent my frustrations against my brothers by yelling at them, or else I would complain bitterly to my sister or father about how inconsiderate they were. Though it was the adults who were controlling my life, I vented my anger against my brothers because it was unacceptable to challenge my elders. My father and sister would urge us to get along better and we would try, but it was often an uneasy truce that lasted for only a day or two. I missed my mother. I thought she would have been able to manage the situation better and I also loathed the household duties that I had assumed.

When I was twenty-one, my father announced that he had accepted an overseas assignment in Jamaica from the parent company of his employer. At first, I didn't pay much attention to the news, assuming that he would go alone; then, a few days later, he invited me to accompany him. I originally thought it was the dumbest idea. I enjoyed attending college and had a network of friends with whom I socialized on the weekends. Why would I want to venture onto some completely foreign territory, I thought. But my father had made up his mind. My older brother was completing his M.B.A. at the University of Utah in Salt Lake City, my sister had her own family to take care of, and my other brother was about to enter an M.B.A. residential program in a management institution in Calcutta. In his mind, my father felt he had no choice but to take me with him: He considered it inappropriate for a young woman to live alone. He knew that forcing me to go would be disastrous, so he gently prodded me, pointing out that I would learn much from the experience (which I didn't believe for a second) and saying that I could come home if I was unhappy (later he told me that he had no intention of sending me home).

So began my travels. The first three months in Kingston went by quickly—lazy days filled with swimming and sunbathing, and long, leisurely dinners at the hotel where we were staying. I quickly shed my inhibitions about talking to strangers. The staff and guests at the cottage-style hotel were always introducing themselves and most of the Jamaicans I encountered were extremely friendly. But the warm, comfortable glow that infused my first three months faded abruptly when my father and I moved into our own apartment in a quiet, residential neighborhood. Though a maid cleaned our house twice a week, I was totally unprepared for the challenges of everyday life. I didn't know how to cook, clean, or even shop for groceries. In India, these tasks had been handled by our household staff. My father patiently endured the burnt food, the half-cooked rice, and the mushy curries that I prepared.

To ease the boredom that set in, I began working as a high school teacher at a private Catholic high school in Kingston four months after our arrival. The job exposed me to youngsters who were dealing with pregnancies, broken homes, child abuse, and other problems that I had only read about in books and magazines. The students came from all walks of life and it was a shock to learn what they endured in their homes. I realized how sheltered and fortunate my own life had been. I no longer took my life for granted.

The Jamaican wife of one of my father's colleagues acted as a surrogate mom and became one of my dearest friends. She took me under her wing and showed me about the island. We had a great deal of fun, visiting farmers' markets, going to the beach, attending parties. Other than her, I had a few other Jamaican friends through my job and the neighborhood.

My father and I also befriended a few Indian families. Nearly 25 percent of Jamaica's population was comprised of Carribeans of Indian descent, many of whom perpetuated familiar traditions and customs. Since there was no Hindu temple in Kingston, about sixty of us would assemble each month in the auditorium of a local university or in one of our homes. While Indians who had recently come to the islands worshiped with those born in Jamaica, the two groups rarely socialized beyond that. The Caribbean Indians had acculturated to the West Indian way of life. They ignored traditional dietary laws by eating beef and pork, and the women wore dresses instead of *saris*. The Indians who had moved to Jamaica in recent years were appalled by these differences.

In Jamaica, I was struck by how many of the households were headed by mothers or grandmothers. Though men lived in the house, they were common-law husbands and never officially married. It was a striking contrast to my own grandmother. Though she had been the matriarch of the family, her status was connected directly to her husband and family.

After living in Jamaica for two years, I decided to move to Corvallis, Oregon, where my brother lived with his wife and young daughter. At this time, I was planning to marry an older, Indian man whom I had met during a brief trip to

India. He had lived in the United States for at least six years and we wanted to be closer together. Though I had known him for a few years, I had never met his family. As soon as I did, I knew that the marriage was doomed. It would never be a private union between a man and a woman, but rather my injection into a rigid and hierarchical family structure in which I was expected to serve and obey. Even though some of his relatives had lived in the United States for at least twenty years, they still expected us to adhere to the same customs that prevailed in India. They wanted to control our lives, to make all of our decisions. If I ever expected the marriage to be harmonious, I would have to accept these conditions. Being independent and emancipated, I was unable to acquiesce. I backed out of the relationship. His family, who had always regarded me as too westernized and something of a misfit, was just as happy to see me go.

The concept of marrying for love is still foreign to most Indians. Most of my friends in India, including my sister, had arranged marriages. Relatives or friends would suggest a suitable match or a man's family would inquire about a young woman after spotting her at a social function. Eventually, the man and his family would visit the woman's house for a preliminary get-together. A few of my friends selected their own spouses, but they usually chose someone who was from the same caste and socioeconomic background, out of deference to their parents' wishes and social pressures. Another determining factor in choosing a mate is the color of one's skin. It is an amusing but enlightening experience to read matrimonial advertisement columns in Indian newspapers. In the ads, the gradations of color quoted include "white," "very fair," "wheat," and "dark wheat." My mother transcended these narrow prejudices that shackle so many Indians, and I remember her always cautioning us to judge a person not by their color, looks, or money, but by their industry and human nature. She was an exception compared to most Indians.

For women, the search for a spouse is further complicated by the importance of preserving one's chastity. When one of my friends began regularly dating one fellow, her parents pressured them to marry hastily because they didn't want her to develop a "bad" reputation. My sister had three dates with her future husband before being rushed to make a decision. Not much by American standards, but a lot more than what my parents had. When my mother and father got married, they were virtual strangers, having exchanged only a few words with one another. Although my parents never displayed any outward signs of intimacy (I never saw my father kiss my mother in front of others, for example), my siblings and I always felt that they shared a deep bond and similar interests. My mother always told us that love, respect, and friendship did not occur overnight, but rather developed over years of careful nurturing.

I worried about whether I would tarnish my father's reputation in India by breaking off the engagement and shared my doubts with him. He told me not to worry about the opinions of others and said I should only be concerned about my own happiness. Contrary to his peers, my father was unusually liberal and progressive; perhaps it was the result of having lived in the United States during the late 1940s. My father attended Brooklyn Polytechnic as a graduate student in chemical engineering and worked for the U.S. Department of Agriculture for a year and a half after receiving his degree. His views may have also been more lax since my older sister and brother were already married. If I had been the eldest, my life might have taken a different turn. My brother, to whom I also turned for support, was very understanding as well. His wife was Caucasian, and he knew that love and understanding were more important in a marriage than common traditions and customs.

After the dissolution of my marriage plans, I didn't feel able to face my friends and family in India. I felt as if I had somehow disappointed myself and my family. But I found the strength and courage to go on. I decided to remain in Corvallis and to pursue a master's degree in consumer economics at Oregon State University. The entire engagement experience had been very stressful. The small-town atmosphere of Corvallis calmed my frayed nerves. I looked forward to the challenges of graduate school and regarded it as an outlet for my pent-up energy.

I began my graduate program in February 1987. International students, particularly from China, Korea, Indonesia, and India, constituted at least 10 percent of the entire student body. The faculty made us feel welcome and provided us with a friendly, nurturing environment. Professors and students alike enjoyed learning about India and comparing it to life in America and other countries; I especially spent many hours discussing the similarities and differences between women's lives in India and here. The discussions made me more conscious of the historical and social significance of gender.

Most of the international students tended to associate with members of their own ethnic groups. There were clubs for each nationality and it was common for students to room with someone from the same country. I wanted to be different and deliberately shunned the Indian community. I picked a Caucasian roommate and attended parties given by my American friends and other international students not from India. I felt I had developed a veneer of western culture. Though I was active in the International Students Association and became friends with students from all over the world, I kept my contact with other Indians to a minimum. After a year, I began to feel as if a part of me were frozen. I realized that I had dropped a protective curtain over painful memories associated with my broken engagement. I decided to stop dwelling on the past and to look toward the future. That year, I ran for an office in the Indian Students Association and won by a substantial margin. I finally felt accepted by other Indians.

Oregon State operated on a quarter system and the academic year just seemed to race by. The competition was fierce, and some professors seemed to scrutinize the work of foreign students more closely. Since my academic training in India had been so exacting, I was able to meet the heavy demands that my research and coursework made on my time and intellect. But it was difficult to relax when classes were in session.

Since I had been awarded a research assistantship and a tuition waiver, as well as a monthly stipend, I was able to live on my own and to graduate without acquiring a huge debt. However, life was not always easy. I constantly had to prove myself. I remember one classroom assignment in which a partner and I had to redesign a client's kitchen and bathroom. The client ignored me and paid attention only to my white partner, until she realized my designs were better. Some of the town residents and professors from other departments were unaware that I was a straight-A student and seemed to regard me as a dilettante only interested in having fun. Over time, they realized that I was highly motivated and willing to make personal sacrifices to excel in the program.

There were about twenty-five families of Indian origin living in Corvallis and getting to know them posed a bigger challenge than adjusting to mainstream American society or graduate school. As I mentioned earlier, I was not a typical Indian female. I felt uneasy about being single and disliked disclosing this fact. I often sensed that people were gossiping about me. In addition, I was unaccustomed to the aggressive and fragmented nature of Indian subcultures after having grown up in a busy metropolis. Religious, state, and caste stratification played an important and decisive role even among the small group of Indians in Corvallis, especially among families with teenage daughters. These parents would invite into their homes young Indian men who were from the same state and caste. Each family zealously guarded its turf and was quick to voice its displeasure whenever any single women intruded. Just the tone of their voices would clearly convey their displeasure and hostility. In India, the voice is a dominant force in articulating messages regarding color, race, caste, and gender. It is not the words, but the tone in which they are uttered that indicate if you are welcome or not.

As I neared the end of my Ph.D. program, I applied for a teaching position at Queens College and was selected out of about five candidates. I completed and defended my dissertation three months after I was offered the job. During graduate school, I wanted to work for the United Nations. These days, when I stand in front of one of my classes where at least fifteen or twenty countries are represented, I often think that it's even more exciting than standing before the United Nation's General Assembly. Queens College is one of the most ethnically diverse colleges in the world and has allowed me to meet and learn from students from dozens of different countries.

I HAVE VIVID memories of visiting my grandmother's house in the town of Vijaywada as a young girl. It was a large, ranch-style house with a big courtyard filled with mango, berry, and banana trees. The kitchen was filled with huge pots and pans, and the preparation of everyday meals seemed to promise a feast. My grandfather had died before my mother married, so my grandmother was the grand matriarch, responsible for managing the estate and other land holdings. Her life was bound to the house and its courtyard. She would spend her mornings in prayer in her bedroom, and then tend to the family for the rest of the day. She was *amma* (mother) to many. It was a role she cherished and took great pride in. We had a large network of immediate and extended family who lived in the house. Visitors freely wandered in and out of the house. There was no doorbell and the main gate was not closed until late at night. Sometimes the house would be filled with people and noise, making it impossible for anyone to find any privacy. Sometimes arguments would erupt between family members, but my grandmother made sure that any disagreements were contained within the family walls.

When I compare my life to those memories, I miss the spontaneity, generosity, and gaiety of my grandmother's house. My life follows a routine that revolves around patterns of work, not of family. Its pattern is mechanical and saturated with technology—television, computers, and other machines. Except at work, I am isolated from the human touch. When my doorbell rings, it is almost always an expected visitor.

Change is neither easy nor simple. I have broken free of the confined and sheltered life common for women in India by making work the center of my life; but now I find myself in a male-dominated, diverse, highly competitive world in the U.S. I have discarded the rigid caste, religious, and social hierarchies that existed in India, only to encounter prejudices among different ethnic groups here. I have a love-hate relationship with New York City. I enjoy its vibrancy and vitality, but I'm also overwhelmed by its insensitivity, indifference, and intolerance. I take great pride in my job and the fact that I am supporting myself. I have a career, independence, and above all my own name. I am not identified as merely someone's daughter, sister, or wife.

However, I still face discrimination, both at work and in the community. Academia today is primarily a white, male-oriented arena, and women are still viewed as sideliners. Adjusting the curriculum to reflect gender, racial, and ethnic differences may serve as a timely topic for panel discussions within the university, but it remains unattained in reality. I must work doubly hard to prove myself to others, as well as to myself.

Affirmative action has dealt an injustice to bright, young, minority professionals by making others think they are beneficiaries of a system not based on merit. This sentiment was brought home when a former colleague cruelly quipped that I was offered the job at Queens College because I was a member of a minority group. No, it is because I am smart, articulate, and hard-working, I wanted to respond. But I didn't, because that person had already made up her own mind.

To find the balance between Indian traditionalism and western realism has always been one of my goals. In America, I feel more Indian than I did in my native land. There, I was a face among 900 million—my identity was never questioned and my heritage, taken for granted. Now that I am a proponent of my native culture and country, I find myself eager to learn more about its people, rituals, religions, and cuisine. This interest has led me to my current area of research: the acculturation problems and service needs of the Indian elderly. I have enjoyed studying and understanding a generation that I had previously overlooked. The elderly often display a fatalistic, Hindu attitude that their lives are predestined by their karma as a result of their previous lives. But they have also given me great insights into human endurance, courage, and dignity.

On a recent visit to India, I felt like an outsider looking in. But even though I no longer felt as if I belonged there, I realized that my Indian core remained intact and untouched. I have a great empathy for the people, and a bond that cannot be easily broken. I have changed, but so has India. It is a country with more consumer durables such as cars and electrical appliances. It has a burgeoning middle-class eager to adopt western culture, technology, and individualism. There are more two-income families, unlike when I was growing up. Within certain limits, women in India have realized their potential and are striving to achieve it. I do get nostalgic for my native land, but I would never relinquish what I have now. Sometimes I wonder what happened to all that sadness I felt when I reluctantly left India with a fistful of dirt to remember my country. And I wonder if I would have left in the first place if I had known it would be a bon voyage for such a long, long time.

Reaching the Glass Ceiling . . . at Home

EXHAUSTED FROM A long day at the office after having recently returned from a trip to Australia, I was gladly attending to the mindless task of washing the dinner dishes. Unfortunately, my mind kept drifting to the reasons for my trip. My sister-in-law, at the prime of her life and of her career as a pathologist, had died recently from cancer. My father, meanwhile, had just been admitted to a nursing home, unable to see, speak, stand, or walk. There was no logic in who gets to live and who gets to die, I thought.

As my brother and I were returning home after visiting our father in the nursing home, he said that it was probably best that his wife, such an active and independent person, had died relatively young. Fresh with the memories of the elderly patients we had left in the nursing home, he said that his wife would probably have had a difficult time dealing with old age, being confined in a nursing home, and relying on others to perform her essential daily activities. She was able to come to terms with her imminent death, telling her family that she had lived a full and meaningful life. She had died without regrets, he said.

Tears rolled down my face as I listened. I felt sad for my brother. I also admired my sister-in-law's courage. If I had been in her shoes, I definitely would have had regrets, I thought. The regrets of having lived an unfulfilled life, of having wasted my potential, and of lacking the strength and courage to make a meaningful difference for myself. I had this image of myself as one of those old ladies, sitting in a wheelchair, staring into the garden, regretting, regretting, and regretting.

My parents, in-laws, and Asian friends perceive me as a "capable woman," a "superwoman," some might tease. I manage the nutrition department of a 380-bed hospital in Los Angeles, reporting directly to the hospital's chief operating officer. I live in Cheviot Hills, a nice neighborhood in the west side of Los Angeles that is heavily inhabited by yuppies. I should be content with the golf-course views from the bedrooms, the worldly possessions in the house, and the cars in the driveway, but I would gladly trade away all those creature comforts for a fulfilled life, a life where I might have accomplished something meaningful.

I was born in China, but was raised in Hong Kong. My father came from a highly educated and wealthy family in China. After graduating from the best university in China with a major in foreign literature, my father continued his studies in England. My mother came from a family of landowners, and attended a school run by foreign missionaries in China. My parents were quite westernized. The bookshelves in our home were lined with books written in English. Occasionally, my father would entertain his foreign clients at home. On weekends, we often served afternoon tea with French pastries to visitors.

My father worked for a very well-known British firm, managing the China trading department. My mother was a high school English teacher. There was a maid for each of the three kids when my older brothers and I were quite young, and other helpers to take care of the other chores. Later, a very capable maid took sole responsibility for the house. She preferred to work alone and took excellent care of everything. How I wish I had someone like her working for me these days!

Without any special lectures from my parents, I knew they expected me to get a college education. Like my older brothers, I was to be sent abroad to study after graduating from high school. My parents never had to worry about me. From the seventh to the twelfth grades, I attended a highly competitive Chinese school that had a 50 percent attrition rate. I was an honor student. I was required to take piano lessons, to behave and talk properly like a young lady, and to occasionally serve my male cousin afternoon tea during his visits. I never had to do any housework, not even to hang up the clothes I tried on. I wish I had been taught cooking, especially those delicious Chinese dishes that were made for special occasions or as special treats. These days, I can only think about them and salivate. Even though it is commonly known that boys are held in higher regard than girls in Chinese families, I was unaware of any close friends who were placed in an inferior position because of their gender. I lived a sheltered life that was considered to be appropriate for my upbringing.

ARMED WITH TWO suitcases totaling forty-nine pounds, which was more than half my body weight at the time, I left behind seventeen years of a very sheltered life to pursue a college education in the United States in 1965. My suitcases carried enough personal belongings—from stationery to clothing—to last through my college years. I really had not given much thought to my major after my mother and my grandmother opposed my desire to study law in England. Ever since I was a little girl, I had always wanted to be a judge, a British-trained one, no less. Medicine was immediately ruled out since my oldest brother was finishing medical school in Australia at the time. My mother decided that one doctor in the family was enough, and her favorite son had fulfilled her dream of a lifetime.

I was supposed to major in chemistry, at least that was what my parents coached me to reply as they prepared me for my visa interview at the American consulate. Though I had done well in chemistry at school, it was a subject I disliked.

I arrived in San Francisco before the Labor Day weekend. After a nice, leisurely tour of the Golden Gate Bridge and the San Francisco Bay Area, a distant relative drove me to the junior college in Salinas, also known as the lettuce capital of the world. I was not certain why I was sent from bustling Hong Kong to sleepy Salinas, nor did I have the foggiest idea about how to register for my classes. In Hong Kong, we did not have to register for classes. We just reported to our assigned classroom and took our seat for the year. The teachers would rotate among the classrooms.

When I registered, I decided to check out home economics, a subject that I had absolutely no knowledge of other than a weekly class in the tenth grade. Our very capable and loyal maid, who had taken care of me since preschool, took care of all household chores. Needless to say, my parents were traumatized and disappointed by my decision. "What would you do with a degree in home economics?" they asked, in the first letter I received from home.

I BECAME A Chinese foreign student. I found room-and-board accommodation with an American family. It seemed that I was forever explaining my background—yes, I am Chinese. No, I am not from communist China or Taiwan (or Formosa). I was born in mainland China, but raised in Hong Kong. Yes, it is a British colony. Yes, it is a great place to shop. People were curious and often direct. I have long since left school, but I am still faced with questions about my origin. Except now people might make additional comments, such as "you don't look too Chinese" or "you have a slight accent, but it is not exactly Chinese."

After spending a year in the home economics lab, I realized I was at a disadvantage compared to my American classmates. Until I left home, I had never even cooked an egg, not to mention a whole meal. It was a struggle to find the right equipment, and, more so, to follow a recipe. When I saw something about dietetics in the school catalog, I remembered that the sister of my friend was a dietitian. I told my advisor that I wanted to be in dietetics instead of home economics, without really knowing what the field was. There is a reason why I am so fatalistic . . . for someone who did not like chemistry, I ended up having to take organic chemistry that year, then biochemistry after I transferred to a four-year college. I literally jumped from the frying pan into the fire, from the home economics food lab to the chemistry lab, without even getting to try the products of our experiments!

I graduated from San Jose State University with a degree in home economics with an emphasis in dietetics. I was accepted into a joint master's degree/

internship program at Indiana University. My parents were relieved that I was at least in the medical field and had not wasted four years of college education to become a home economist, or a housewife as they imagined. There were a few Chinese people at the medical center and I found myself explaining my ethnic origin all over again. The other workers were just as curious about my background. I met some very nice people during my internship, for which I was grateful.

Before leaving for Indiana, I became engaged to a Chinese engineer. We had met while attending San Jose State. I must have found his poor family background interesting, for that distinguished him from all the other guys I had dated, all of whom were from wealthy families. He spoke very fondly of his parents and family, making me think that he would be a good family man. My parents were not particularly excited about such a union because of the vast differences in our backgrounds. At Indiana, my husband was accepted to the Ph.D. program in engineering at UCLA. I decided to return to California to get married after I completed the one-year internship. I thought I would finish the master's program later, after we settled down.

Shortly after our move to Los Angeles, I found a full-time position as a clinical dietitian. We lived a rather frugal life. I was a good wife, considerate, hardworking, and supportive. I taught myself to cook and sew. I made my own clothes, which were quite different from the tailor-made clothes to which I was accustomed. I even made clothes for each of my husband's four sisters so we could save money. It was important that my husband concentrate fully on his Ph.D.

After a year and a half, I was promoted to administrative dietitian. I accepted the management position without the slightest idea of what it would entail. I was in charge of the kitchen employees of the hospital's dietary department. Almost all of them were black or Hispanic, and most were old enough to be my parents or grandparents. The last thing they wanted to do was to take orders from a young, petite Asian woman. I did not have much training in personnel management, nor was I familiar with how to handle cross-cultural differences. I also lacked the proper attire of their former bosses—the habit of a Catholic nun. But I was armed with Chinese discipline and expected each person to do their work properly, without exception. Blessed are the foolish and the ignorant, for they shall be oblivious and fearless. In recent years, I was told that some of the employees I disciplined and subsequently terminated were gang members.

After graduating from UCLA, my husband found a job in the Los Angeles area. We bought a house. I was getting tired of my job. Making sure that the positions were filled, that dishes were washed, and that the meals were served on time—it all seemed trivial. I thought it would be a good time for me to return to school to complete my master's degree. But my husband said I would not need an advanced degree now that I had a few years of work experience. He said it was time to start a family since "we all have a responsibility to the human race and our family to procreate." To the contrary, I worried about my ability to be a good parent, especially when I remembered those sick, deformed children I saw during my internship. My in-laws were getting anxious to have grandchildren, though, and the baby came. It was a boy, the first grandson to carry the family name. Two and a half years later, another baby came, another boy. Even in procreation, my husband did the right thing for his family! It was ironic that at the time when I felt the need to get on with my life, my mother-in-law thought I should stop working and stay home to take care of the children. Little did my husband's family know that I was determined never to rely financially on their favorite son.

After being married for about fifteen years, I was feeling desperate about my future. I did not want to be stuck in a job that I did not find intellectually stimulating. I not only wanted to go back to school, I wanted to go to law school. My husband dismissed my desire as unrealistic and decided that I was prematurely going through a mid-life crisis and menopause. He suggested I take some fun classes instead, such as pottery. He also thought I might want to quit working and volunteer at school as a room-mother. Above all, *he hated lawyers.* I was horrified and angered by his suggestion, but, even more so, saddened at his lack of understanding of my desires and needs. I knew I would never have a mentally and intellectually challenging future as long as I remained a "good wife." It was the curse of being a woman in this conservative Chinese family. I also recognized that I was imprisoned by my familial responsibilities. I would have to defer my dreams until the children left home for college, or perhaps even until they graduated from college, because of the expenses involved. I felt completely doomed and trapped. I also felt cheated out of a brighter and more interesting future. I believed I had the potential, but what could I do with a master's degree in another field at my age? To get a job without any previous experience would have been a challenge in itself.

The most miserable part was that I could not even let my parents know about my frustrations and disappointment. Any such admission would have brought unpleasant comments from my mother; my parents would have worried unnecessarily, too. When they received the news of our proposed engagement, my father said only that he wanted me to be happy and well cared for. He did not comment beyond that. As mentioned previously, my mother had great reservations about the match because of the differences in our social, economic, and educational backgrounds.

As hard as I tried to free myself from that sense of feeling doomed, I continued to feel trapped. At times, I exploded uncontrollably. I recognized my own madness and hated myself for it. I hated it even more when others commented on what a great family I had. On the surface, I had the ideal family—a nice, successful husband who was an engineer with a Ph.D., two nice boys, a nice house in a nice neighborhood. Every time I heard about my good fortune, I wanted to scream. I wanted more education. I wanted a more intellectually challenging job. I wanted to be mentally stimulated. I wanted to be emotionally nurtured.

Knowing that it was out of the question to further my education, I decided to make another life for myself. I took tennis and music lessons and classes in calligraphy. I read and drowned myself in classical music. I made new friends and established a new identity separate from my husband. I opened my eyes to the world around me. I reached out. I took time to enjoy what the world had to offer.

At the end of 1993, my husband told me that he was going to apply for an overseas assignment that would require working in Taiwan for approximately three years. He had reached the top of his pay scale and the move was an opportunity for him to move up in his career, he said. He also wanted to explore opportunities in Southeast Asia. He was delighted when he got the position, and left for Taiwan a few months after the Northridge earthquake that severely damaged our house.

I felt a great sense of relief and serenity after his departure. I actually felt calm and happy amidst tons of dirt and dust created by the construction workers in our home. The repairs took over a year and cost about $100,000. My sense of freedom came to an end when his contract was shortened to two years. We have become two people sharing a roof, but living our own separate lives. It is a strange, though relatively peaceful way to coexist.

MY FRIENDS CONSIDER me to be quite westernized. My husband and his family think I'm too westernized. Yet I have never dated any non-Chinese men. In college, the Chinese students were a close-knit group. Most of my classes were held at the home economics building where male students were rare or absent. When I began working, I made friends with people from all different ethnic backgrounds. Nowadays, people I associate and socialize with are mostly non-Chinese. My Asian friends seem too preoccupied with family activities and the kids to do anything beyond getting together for a meal. Even then, the topics of discussion usually center on kids, jobs, and investments. Perhaps I am avoiding them so I will not have to be constantly reminded of my "good fortune."

With my set of friends, I share different activities. I enjoy the opportunity of getting to know people from different backgrounds, and, especially, trying different cuisines. I also appreciate learning about different experiences, sharing information. It really makes no difference to me what a person's skin color is as long as the person is nice. And you can never learn whether another person has that quality unless you reach out to them, with the acceptance that we are all different and yet the same.

Despite my naturalized U.S. citizenship, I have always considered myself Chinese. My husband, however, has always considered me a person without roots, probably because I do not share his passion for Taiwan, where he received his undergraduate education, nor his hatred for communist China. My upbringing in

Hong Kong did not give me a sense of belonging to either Taiwan or Mainland China. I always knew that no matter where I was born or what passport I held, I simply looked Chinese and would always be judged as such. I do not want to do anything that would give anyone the opportunity to denounce the Chinese race, and I try to teach my sons the same.

I have not really given much thought to my hyphenated, Chinese American status. I am not sure at what point of my life I made such a transformation. Unlike some of my contemporaries, I do not get angry or feel discriminated against when my ethnic origin is questioned. In most cases, I truly believe that the question is benign. I myself am curious where people come from, and have started many conversations with this question. It often provides a great opportunity to learn about different cultures.

However, at a conference sponsored by the Chinese Historical Society, I was surprised when some of the participants became very emotional and angry during a discussion of ethnic identity. Since then, I have been hesitant to ask people where they are from. I must admit, I do not have much empathy for those who are so easily offended—they easily can ask the same question in return. I feel that Chinese people in general tend to harbor prejudice. When I was growing up, foreigners were called "foreign ghosts," and here in the United States, they are further divided into "white ghosts" and "black ghosts." Generally, the darker the skin, the lower the status.

Among the Chinese, there are also subdivisions and stereotypes for each subgroup. In the United States, the subgroups—such as those from Hong Kong, Mainland China, Taiwan, or America—tend to socialize with their own kind. Jokes and unkind remarks are still made about other subgroups at social gathering. It is ironic that while we are so keen on our own subethnic origin, we should be offended when non-Chinese question us about our origins. After all, we pose the same questions to our own.

At one of the frequent gatherings of my high school classmates, the topic of interracial dating and marriage came up. One couple—both physicians—was definite in their desire for their children to marry other Chinese. Another classmate who lived with a Jewish person thought that was prejudicial. The couple argued that a relationship where both partners shared the same ethnic background would be easier. Based on my own experiences, I am afraid that the same ethnic background did not help me much.

The one common area we share is food. While I enjoy eating different ethnic foods, I must admit that I prefer Chinese food, especially when I do not feel well. It seems to provide a certain comfort. Some foods, especially those served during special occasions, definitely bring a sense of nostalgia. When I cook, nothing can take the place of the wok, the cleaver, and the chopsticks. It is incredible that Chinese food did not mean much to me when I was young. Now that I am older, it is on my mind more often than necessary.

I am happy that certain Chinese traditional values, such as hard work, humility, perseverance, and respect for elders, are still observed by most of the younger generation. My sons generally hang out with Asian friends, mostly Chinese and Korean American kids. It delights me when my sons' Asian American friends politely greet me or other adults with their titles, a gesture that is often missing from their non-Asian friends. At my older son's high school graduation ceremony, I noticed that the majority of Asian students wore the gold cord of honor. I am certain that basic Asian values have contributed toward their success at an early age, and that those values have also held together quite a few marriages that would otherwise have fallen apart, Unfortunately, some of these basic virtues are disappearing with assimilation. Win some, lose some, I guess.

I wish I had spoke Chinese at home more regularly so that my children would have learned the language. We speak mostly English at home, with occasional Cantonese and Mandarin. The boys attended Chinese school every Saturday morning, but have not learned much. They have a certain degree of comprehension, but can hardly speak Chinese. When it comes to mathematical calculations, I have to think in Chinese to get the answer faster and more accurately. When my husband and I argue, it is always in English. Perhaps because of our upbringing, we do not feel free to swear in our own language.

Being in a profession that is predominantly female, and in a work environment where white people are a minority, I really cannot say that I have been discriminated against. I have climbed up the ladder by working hard and doing a good job. I do not think I got where I am because of my skin color. I was also fortunate in landing a job at a good, stable institution. I was spared the need of having to look for other jobs.

Recently, due to the tremendous changes in health care, my hospital has merged with a large medical group. There is lots of talk and action about standardizing functions and the possibility of expanding the duties of those in management. I may be forced to compete with other food-service directors for the diminishing positions in this shrinking market. The lack of an advanced degree will put me at a definite disadvantage.

As I reach the end of my career path, I really have no one to blame but myself. I did not prepare myself for advancement by pursuing further education. I was too busy meeting others' expectations or needs. I allowed myself to be a victim of my culture.

I reached my glass ceiling at home!

NARRATIVE FIFTEEN / **Hoang Diem Hau**

An Unwilling Refugee

"HOANG, PLEASE COME in my office. I have something very important to tell you," said Ms. Edmund, my boss and owner of Edmund Jewelers in Fresno. It was November 1975, and the dreaded request came on a gloomy, rainy night, the eve of my first Thanksgiving in the United States. As I sat in front of her shiny, mahogany executive desk in the dimly lit office, my thoughts were running wild. I was convinced that my worst fear had finally come true. I was being fired. What had I done wrong, I wondered.

As Mrs. Edmund entered the room, her stern face contrasted sharply with the colorful, beaded diamond earrings and necklace she was wearing. I always wondered if she needed an armored car to transport her around.

"I have asked you here to tell you some good news and some bad news," she said. "The bad news is that you will have to work overtime from Thanksgiving all the way into New Year's. This is our busiest season and we need to stay open late. You'll need to make plans for a baby-sitter for your son. The good news is that I'm giving you twenty-five cents more an hour."

A rapid calculation ran through my mind. That would be an additional net of $2.75 a day, an extra $43 a month. Not bad at all, I thought. My god, this is the best news I've had in months. My heart jumped to my throat, my head started spinning, and my hands got sweaty. That night my husband, my two-year-old son, and I went to Happy Steak restaurant and celebrated. To this day, I recall it as the biggest, juiciest steak I've ever had. Sitting today behind my own shiny, mahogany executive desk, as the financial controller of a small private college, a smile flutters across my face as I reminisce about that day twenty-one years ago.

I immigrated to the United States on the eve of Saigon's fall to the Communists. My husband, my two-year-old son, and I left in such a hurry that we couldn't tell our families we were leaving. My husband got a fellow employee to cash his whole month's paycheck. With only thirty U.S. dollars in hand, we boarded a cargo airplane that was en route to the Philippines. Our personal belongings, our new Volkswagen automobile, our four-bedroom condominium, our clothing—all was left behind. Our closest relatives did not learn the reason for our "disappearance" until almost a year and a half later.

At an American airbase in the Philippines, my husband, son, and I learned of the defeat of the South Vietnamese government and the North Vietnamese Liberation Army's take-over of the presidential palace. We thought we would be gone only temporarily, just until things calmed down, but April 30, 1975 was the last day we ever saw our mother country.

BORN AND RAISED in Saigon, I was the eldest of nine children, five girls and four boys. My parents both belonged to the upper class. My mother was a direct descendant of the royal family of Emperor Bao Dai in Hue, Central of Vietnam, and my father's father was the most prominent vice minister of interior under Emperor Minh Mang of the Nguyen dynasty.

My father worked as a civil servant for the French government from the 1940s through the 1950s. He spoke and wrote French fluently. In the 1960s, he entered the construction industry and became a wealthy businessman. He built a ten-story hotel, which he leased out to the United States embassy in Saigon. The Americans used it as a military headquarters for GIs on leave. He owned a six-bedroom villa, a sports car, a Mercury station wagon, and had a chauffeur and maids to look after his home and children. My mother, meanwhile, was responsible for taking care of the family, the maids, and the children's schooling. My parents made sure that all their children received a high school education. Education, whether you were a boy or a girl, was always an utmost priority in my family.

My siblings and I attended French schools. By the time I was nineteen, I spoke French fluently. I also studied English as a second language, and could speak, write, and translate English for my parents in their business dealings with Americans. Nothing in my childhood had given me the idea that boys were better, smarter, more capable, or more important than girls. However, I did know that if boys did not study, they could go into the army and die. The girls in the family were allowed to learn to sew, cook, and bake at their pleasure. No one demanded that we perfect these womanly skills; I believed this was unusual and stemmed from the fact that our privileged family had servants to help with household chores.

Our country was torn and ravaged by years of war and devastation. One thousand years under Chinese domination, a hundred years under French colonization, and then more than thirty years of war between the South and the North, with the Soviet Union and China assisting the North Army, and the United States and its allies, the South. We never knew peace. We only dreamed about it.

My most vivid memory of war was the 1967 Tet Offensive. For the Vietnamese New Year celebration, our families had gathered in Saigon. There were about sixty family members inside our home. When the Communists attacked the capital, a twenty-four-hour curfew was imposed on the entire city. From the ninth floor of my parents' hotel, we could see the city on fire, the horizon, red and orange, filled with black smoke. Fire engine sirens blared all around us. We could anticipate the next fire by following the track of smoke that the bombs left behind.

At night, from the seventh floor, we could see the jets of explosives and ammunition falling from the helicopters onto the ground. I could guess the location of the Communists' artillery from the tracts of fire that lit up the ground in retaliation. In the streets below, people who had fled the burning zones, families and kids, in despair and tears, amassed, clutching whatever belongings they had managed to save. Cars stopped in the middle of the streets to let fire engines and people pass; it was chaos. A mob sought refuge in the hotel because it was occupied by the U.S. Army, but armed guards kept them out.

That was as close as I came to witnessing the devastation of the war.

NOT UNTIL I graduated from high school did I realize there was a distinction between the treatment of boys and girls. Although I graduated magna cum laude, my parents would not permit me to enroll in a college abroad. All my male cousins, meanwhile, were sent abroad; first, to further their studies and, second, to escape being drafted into the military. My parents said they would never allow any of their daughters to be away from the family. It's a jungle out there, they said, and respectable families would never send their daughters to live without supervision. Virtue and virginity were the two most important qualities in a respectable girl. I still resent my parents for their ancient thinking. But as a good daughter, I obeyed their wishes, and attended Saigon University, where I graduated with a B.A. in English.

Before enrolling at the university, however, I was able to spend half a year in the United States. When I graduated from high school, my parents took me to Europe and the U.S. We visited France, Switzerland, Belgium, and Holland, then stopped in Fresno, California, to visit my cousin in January 1970. Realizing that this was an opportunity to brush up on my English, as well as to get an American education, I decided immediately that I wanted to take some classes at Fresno State University. It took a lot of persuasion to get my parents to agree. They had wanted to show me the world and then have me return to Vietnam and enroll in college.

At Fresno State, I signed up for some English classes and checked into a sorority. My father went home, while my mother stayed behind to watch over me. Living in a sorority was a mistake. As a female Asian, I was raised to be modest in my behavior. I was embarrassed and very uncomfortable when I saw girls walking naked down a hallway to the showers. I now understand that I went to college at the beginning of the sexual revolution. The business of male visitors was another problem. The girls could have boyfriends over any time of the day, even in their bedrooms. One night I awoke to find my roommate "talking" with her boyfriend. My mother listened in horror to my stories and decided that I would move in with her.

While attending school and making new friends, I discovered that some young Americans had been out on their own since they were sixteen or seventeen. It was very different from our customs. In Vietnam, girls usually stayed in the parents' home until they got married. Some of us never moved out because we were responsible for taking care of our parents until they died.

WHAT COULD IT be but destiny? I met my husband-to-be at Fresno State. At International Night at school, Asian students put on a fashion show from each country. The Vietnamese students presented a wedding show. I played the bridesmaid and Lac, not yet my husband, was the matchmaker who brought together the groom and bride. At that time, he had already graduated from the Saigon University of Law. He had received a U.S. scholarship and was getting an M.B.A. from Fresno State. He was eight years older than me, like an older brother I'd never had.

We continued to meet casually at school and parties. Can you imagine? Though we were both from Saigon, only by traveling across the ocean did we meet. I had lived in the "good" part of town and he grew up on "the other side." As we grew to know each other, I became attracted to qualities that I thought were absent among most of my male friends. They always talked about themselves, obsessed with their own needs and demands. I often found them selfish, egotistical, and superficial. Lac, on the other hand, always talked about his parents, his family, why he needed to make his parents proud, being responsible for his brothers and sisters, and so forth. I am a very family-oriented person, and my family always comes first.

While I was going through the difficult period of reconciling my desire for an American education with my parents' insistence that I return home, Lac was my moral support. He helped me decide to go home, both to please my parents and to be a good daughter. He received his M.B.A. and returned to Vietnam a year later in 1971. We married in 1972. I still consider the decision one of the best I have ever made.

AFTER A WEEK in the Philippines, my husband, son, and I were transported by army cargo airplane to Guam, then to Fort Chaffee, Arkansas. During our two-month stay at the fort, news from the outside world filtered in slowly. We were dying for any information. Had there been a blood bath? Did the Communists execute people in the South? How could we get in touch with our families back home? The questions and fears of what had happened to family members left behind drove nearly all of us crazy. We were also very homesick. We were like zombies standing in line for food, going through various immigration procedures, waiting for sponsorship information. We craved news from home or the sight of familiar faces.

Through an immigration service, we were eventually sponsored by an American family in Fresno. We lived with them in their home for two months until my husband found a job working at a Japanese grocery store. In February 1976, we moved to a small apartment and I found a job as a back-room clerk with Edmund Jewelers.

We decided to live in Fresno because we had lived there before. We contacted some friends and professors from college. They offered us a place to stay and helped us find work. It took about four years for us to finally turn around our lives and to begin planting roots again. Our recurring nightmares of going home, then getting arrested and jailed started to dissipate, but we were still homesick and missed our families.

As ordinary citizens, we did not have a say on how we wanted to live our lives or how our country could be served. Unfortunate political circumstances were created by the leaders of Vietnam and the United States. Having been so removed from the devastation of war in the countryside, I did not understand or grasp the full effect of lives being sacrificed for the benefit of a few. I hated being a refugee in the U.S. Though I do not wish to appear ungrateful, I resented the fact that I was uprooted from the life I loved into a country so completely different in terms of customs, habits, social, and cultural backgrounds.

Even though I had been exposed to American culture through my parents' business dealings with the U.S. Army, as well as Hollywood films and television shows, I did not anticipate my resistance to the change. I still do not know how to answer questions such as "Do you think America should be involved in the Vietnam War?" I have always felt uncomfortable expressing my opinion on the subject because I never know what is the "right" answer, or what it is that my American friends want me to say. I have pretended at times to be Chinese so people would not question me about America's involvement in the war.

AFTER WORKING AT the jewelry store for six months, I decided I wanted something more for myself. America truly is the land of opportunity. Unlike Vietnam, where education was limited to those who could afford it, in America everyone has an equal opportunity to go to school. After putting my son to bed each night, I plunged into my studies. I eventually obtained a B.S. in accounting and, many years later, an M.A. in business administration. Throughout my studies, I worked full-time and gave birth to a second son.

Because I also had to work and take care of my family, I did not have the chance to enjoy the student life. I just wanted to hurry up, graduate, and be done with it. If I had to do it all over again, I would take more time, be as free-spirited as I could be, and really experience college life to its fullest. School was a breeze; I enjoyed the term papers, the dissertations, the interaction with other classmates and professors. Unfortunately, it totally consumed any free time I had. My marriage suffered from a lack of closeness and there were threats of divorce.

My determination to succeed was informed by previous experiences, which clearly showed that Asian women will forever live in the shadow of their husbands unless they attempt to make a name for themselves. For years, I watched my mother, who had only a ninth-grade education, labor over complex blueprints of buildings that my father bid on and constructed. She spent hours, day and night, calculating how many tons of cement, sand, rock, steel, nails, wood, electric wires, etc., they had to buy and how much labor they needed to complete the job at the lowest cost. She would spread out the blueprints on the floor, manually computing the projected price of each of my father's building projects. There were no calculators back then. Once the project was awarded to him, she was the one to ask friends, banks, and relatives to raise the money necessary to finish the project. While my father basked in the glory of a job well done, my mother's hard work was never mentioned. She was always behind the scenes, raising the family, accommodating relatives, and entertaining my father's business associates. I can still vividly recall the tears, the fighting, the missed meals she endured to finish a project. Yet she had no engineering degree, not even a business degree.

I have come to realize that all Vietnamese women accept this as a natural way of life. They are born into these self-sacrificing roles, and are expected to fulfill them. At times, I wished I were a boy. Then I would not have to limit myself to being the virtuous daughter of a respectable family, I thought. I would be able to do anything I wanted, to date any girl, to boss people around, to go wherever I wished. For a long time, I considered myself smarter and brighter than any boy I knew. In high school, I refused to date a boy whose grades were lower than mine. But traditions have a hold. I got married, stayed home, and raised a family.

As a Vietnamese immigrant to the United States, I did not feel as if I was discriminated against in my lower, entry-level jobs. As long as I could speak and understand English, I was able to acquire new jobs and to receive promotions. I think it helped that I was a woman and also a minority of a different ethnic background. Sometimes, in the back of my mind I have thought that aside from my qualifications for the position, I was offered the job so the agency could meet some kind of affirmative action quota. Whatever the reason, I was glad I could find work.

However, as I moved up the career ladder, I found that it was becoming harder and harder to reach for the stars. Even though it is not apparent to the eyes, a certain form of discrimination is always lurking around the corner. In entry-level jobs, my presence did not constitute a threat to my boss. As long as I was doing a good job, and he or she could take credit for it, it was fine. But, as I said earlier, my goal was to make something of myself.

My first job after graduation from California State University at Fresno was with the Fresno Employment and Training Commission (FETC), which is now defunct. I was a supervisor of accounting with a staff of four. Some mornings, I would find ads for accounting positions with other agencies on my desk. After some investigation, my boss, who was the director of accounting, admitted that he had put the ads there. He was threatened by my potential and said he'd prefer it if I could get another job and leave. He only had a high school education, and moved up through the ranks because of his past experience and seniority. I took the hint and found myself a job. Why stay where I'm not wanted, I figured.

My second job was as a senior accountant at the Fresno Unified School District. I worked as the fringe benefits specialist in charge of the District's retirement plan. I reported directly to the assistant controller, a man of German descent. During that time, a surge of Laotian and Hmong refugees had flooded Fresno County. The district schools had difficulties accommodating such a big influx of refugee students. My boss was put in charge of finding the funds and hiring the staff to deal with the refugee students. Every day I would hear him curse and make nasty comments about refugees. One day in exasperation, he stared me straight in the eyes and said, "Why don't you just all go home and leave us alone?" I didn't think he was a racist. I just thought he was tired. How naive I was.

IN THE 1980s, federal funding for all the CETA (California Education and Training Act) programs ceased when Ronald Reagan was elected. My husband, who was a director of a CETA program, was laid off due to lack of funds. In 1984, our family relocated to Los Angeles to find work. I was accustomed to Fresno and didn't want to leave. It was a very small city, with no freeways. Practically everybody knew each other. In Los Angeles, I felt so lost and abandoned. The streets and freeways were always crowded, people were afraid to get involved in someone else's business, even Asians did not greet each other on New Year's day.

What kind of life is this, I often wonder? We go to work, come home, and lock ourselves inside, afraid of gangs, shootings, robberies, and other urban violence. We live in a sort of prison—we hardly go out at night, curfew at our house is 10 P.M. My two sons think we are paranoid. But how could you not be when there are crimes everywhere you turn?

My first job in L.A. was as an accounts payable manager at the California State University campus. In this position, I encountered sexual harassment in the workplace. My boss would call female workers into his office, then sit real close to them, trying to hold their hands, staring at their chests, and rubbing up against their hips. I watched as my coworkers would leave his office in tears. I prayed to be spared from such embarrassment. My prayers were answered when he left and was replaced with a smart, supportive African American woman who has become my mentor and good friend.

I continued my quest for more exposure in the accounting field and became controller of a small, private, liberal arts college. My employers have told me I'm very good at this job, even as they have denied me a promotion to become vice president of business and finance. I love my job and the college, but deep down in my heart, I know I was unfairly passed over. I was the only internal candidate, had been with the college for seven years, and knew the business inside and out.

IN SPITE OF believing firmly in not living in one's husband's shadow, I am quite traditional at home. I still have not attempted to be an independent woman in my family life. Because of the culture I was raised in, and the generations of Vietnamese women before me, I am living proof that old traditions are hard to break. My husband is still head of the house, and I am the gentle, docile daughter who always puts the needs of the parents ahead of her own. I will compromise my own happiness to a certain extent to get peace and happiness for the entire family. Even though I consider myself quite liberated, I still believe there are good and bad traditions in every country. It is a matter of finding a gray area where you can combine all traditions and extract the ones more applicable to your own personality.

My parents came to the United States in 1980. Though at times they appear to understand the necessity of adapting to their new environment, I know that deep down they yearn for the old Vietnam—their birthplace, their ancestors, and the way it used to be. All of my sisters and brothers immigrated to the United States in the years shortly after 1975. They married and raised families here in America. As the first wave of Vietnamese immigrants, this generation has been quite successful in preserving the old traditions. We try to instill in our children the notion that they are Vietnamese, but I am afraid and sad to say that we are not always successful. Both of my boys, as well as most of my nieces and nephews, have trouble recognizing this fact.

According to them, we are Americans.

I HAVE ALWAYS envied families who had elderly relatives to take care of their kids while they were at work. Some of my friends had their parents living at home with them. The grandparents would teach the children about their traditions. The children grew up learning old family values and the Vietnamese language. When our first son was growing up, my husband and I had to work. We placed my son in a day-care center with other American children when he was two. We were afraid he would be unable to communicate, so we taught the teachers a few common Vietnamese words. After his second day at school, he was communicating with us in English. From that day on, Vietnamese was history.

We blame ourselves for not making time to teach him Vietnamese. He was in his teens by the time my parents joined us from the East Coast. By then, he had completely forgotten Vietnamese and my parents had to learn English to talk with him. My other son also was placed in day-care at the early age of eight months, to allow me to go back to work. Therefore, again, we did not have the time to teach him the language. However, we raised both of them in the tradition of respecting their elders and being responsible for their own acts. Both of my sons grew up to be good citizens, although they do not seem to see themselves as Vietnamese. I think this may change as they grow older and experience more discrimination and disappointments. When they are denied jobs or access to better opportunities in life, perhaps then they will begin to understand that other people see them as Vietnamese.

Observing our Buddhist religion has also been difficult. Even though we have Buddhist temples, our priests and nuns do not speak or lecture in English. There are few prayer books in English and it is very hard to translate and explain what the religion is about. My sons try to follow us to the ceremonies and practice the prayers but I am fighting a losing battle.

Another disturbing fact I have to face is that both of my sons tend to be acquainted with more American girls than Asian girls. Deep down in my heart, I wish that some day one of them will go back to our roots and marry a Vietnamese girl. But I know it is a desperate wish, because we live in a region that does not have an Asian community. The chances for them to meet a Vietnamese girl is very slim. My parents have nine children, two of them have American wives, who are by far the most perfect daughters-in-law. That's 22 percent, two out of nine. I only have two sons. I doubt if there is even a 50 percent chance of either of them marrying a Vietnamese girl.

My youngest brother went back to Vietnam to find his bride. Even though he has a lot of Vietnamese girlfriends, he said "they are so Americanized" that he could not tolerate the changes. I am not against changes, but I am still learning how to adapt to new customs. I want to make our life better and to adopt new ideas that will sustain our life in the U.S. Yet I also keep hoping that one day relations between the United States and Vietnam will return to normal; that then my sons will be able to go back home, to study and adopt the traditional ways of life.

Part Seven

Coming to Terms
Forming One's Ethnic Identity

EACH OF THE fifteen essays in this book reflects the individual sensibility of its author. Though we suggested certain questions for all of the contributors to answer, each author took a different approach and developed a particular theme that was personally meaningful to him or her. The resulting essays reveal a diversity of experiences, reflecting each contributor's personality, ethnicity, gender, and family history. Yet, despite the differences, several common experiences clearly emerge.

In this final chapter, we will discuss four issues that are touched upon in many of the essays: (1) experiences with racial prejudice and discrimination; (2) growing interest in and criticisms of ethnic subculture; (3) high social assimilation; and (4) the search for an ethnic and/or racial identity. We will examine each issue separately, and then conclude with a discussion of theoretical and practical implications.

EXPERIENCES WITH PREJUDICE AND DISCRIMINATION

Nearly all of the contributors describe experiences of prejudice and racial discrimination at a relatively young age, usually in elementary and junior high schools. Often these experiences were profoundly unsettling. The majority of the essayists were school children in the 1970s and early 1980s, when Asian Americans were rare, especially in the predominantly middle- and upper-middle-class white schools that many of them attended. Outwardly different from the rest, they were easily singled out. Even well-meaning people made them feel like "strangers" or "outsiders" with uninformed remarks such as "You speak just like a real American."

David Wang, a political aide who was born and raised in a predominantly white, working-class neighborhood in Queens, New York, says that classmates at his predominantly white parochial school verbally and physically harassed him because of his race. Only after he entered the prestigious Stuyvesant High School of Science, where 40 percent of the student body was Asian American, did Wang begin to feel accepted by his classmates. He eventually ran for and won the office of student body president in his senior year. Shay Sheth, a physician raised in the Delaware Valley of southern New Jersey, also recalls racist taunts and physical assaults from his classmates. Phuong Do, a social worker in New York City, says she was verbally and physically attacked by her predominantly black and Hispanic classmates in the Sun Valley housing projects of Denver, Colorado.

Though other essayists may not have suffered such physical assaults or verbal attacks, they describe feeling alienated and excluded from white mainstream society. For example, Ruth Chung, a psychology professor in southern California, mastered English and acted like an all-American teenager; white students nonetheless subjected her to "humiliating" questions such as "Where are you from?" and "What do you eat at home?" Jean Hotta, an advisor to foreign students at the University of California at Los Angeles, also recollects feeling embarrassed by similar inquiries as a junior high school student. Alex Jeong, an assistant district attorney in Brooklyn, says that at his predominantly white junior high school in the 1970s, "[a]pproaching white girls . . . was difficult because I was not among the school's social elite."

Major American cities in general, and schools in particular, are now far more multicultural and more accommodating of Asian Americans and Asian cultures than they were in the 1970s and the early 1980s, when the essayists were school children. In the last two decades, the Asian American population has witnessed a phenomenal increase. As a result, Asian American elementary and high school students, with the exception of those in small cities, usually attend schools with a large number of Asian American students. The proportion of Asian American students in major universities has increased at an even more phenomenal level. In addition, the number of Asian American teachers and professors has increased greatly over the last two decades. Students actively interact with members of the same ethnic background, as well as other Asian Americans, and participate in ethnic and Asian American clubs. They also see many Asian American teachers, who also serve as role models.

Two other major changes since the 1970s have been an increasing emphasis on multicultural education, as discussed in Part Two, and an increasing interest in Asian countries and cultures. Many high schools and colleges in Los Angeles, San Francisco, New York, and other major cities celebrate Chinese, Japanese, Korean, Filipino, Indian, and Vietnamese festivals. Many university cafeterias with a large Asian American population serve Chinese food, which is popular with non-Asian students, too. Chinese and Korean students now proudly teach white and black students how to use chopsticks. Many universities offer Korean, Tagalog, and Hindi, as well as Chinese and Japanese, as foreign languages. They also offer a number of courses related to Asian countries and Asian American experiences. Wang says that when he was in junior high school (about fifteen years ago), he had a recurring nightmare in which he began to panic when his white classmates were given a tour of his Chinese house by his mother. Now that Chinese food and culture are more familiar to Americans, few Chinese junior high school students would probably be embarrassed to show their homes to white classmates.

Because of these positive changes, Asian American students are better accepted now in American schools than they were two decades ago. Nevertheless, Asian immigrant students, as well as other immigrant students, still have to deal with racial prejudice and even racial violence. For example, at the U.S. Commission on Civil Rights Roundtable Conference on Asian American Civil Rights Issues in 1989, Theresa Ying Hsu, the director of Asian American Communications, gave chilling examples of Asian American students who had been physically assaulted in racial incidents in New York City schools.[1] Even U.S.-born Asian American students in small cities suffer from a sense of marginality, no matter how well acculturated they are into the mainstream culture. Because of their often-exceptional academic achievements, school teachers and policymakers often fail to recognize the sense of marginality and prejudice that many Asian American children experience.

Almost all the contributors are keenly aware that people of color, including Asian Americans, are subject to discrimination in the United States. However, with the exception of Joel de la Fuente, a Filipino American actor, none of the 1.5- and second-generation essayists discuss specific experiences with discrimination in their careers. Several clearly state that they have not encountered discriminatory treatment at work because of their color or ethnic background. Their lack of experience with discrimination in the workplace may be due in part to the fact that most were in the early stages of their careers when they wrote the essays. At the start of their careers, native-born Asian Americans who are fluent in English may not encounter discrimination and may even receive preferential treatment in finding professional jobs. For example, Rose Kim benefited from an affirmative action program seeking to promote the number of ethnic journalists at daily newspapers. However, after reaching certain levels, Asian Americans are likely to encounter barriers in their career mobility—the so-called glass ceiling problem. None of the native-born contributors, however, have had careers long enough to explore this issue.

Clearly, there is a difference between the work experiences of first-generation Asian immigrants and 1.5- and second-generation Asian Americans. Two of the three immigrant essayists, Hoang Hau, a comptroller at a small, private college in southern California, and Lakshmi Malroutu, a professor of consumer studies and personal finance in New York City, discuss experiences of discrimination in the workplace. Hau and Malroutu, both of whom emigrated to America after completing high school in their native countries, feel they encountered major obstacles in their careers because of their race and ethnicity. Hau says she was "unfairly passed over" for a promotion to vice president, while Malroutu explains the disadvantages of being a non-white minority woman in white, male-oriented academia: "I still face discrimination, especially from my colleagues. Academia today is primarily a white, male-oriented arena, and women are still viewed as sideliners."

Malroutu and Hau may have encountered discrimination that others did not partly because their professional careers are longer. But, as immigrant women, they seem to have encountered more barriers to their career mobility. Interestingly, Sheth, a second-generation Indian American physician, indicates that although he "achieved professional success relatively smoothly," his parents, as immigrants, encountered anti-Asian and anti-Indian discrimination in their career trajectories. His remark clearly indicates that Asian immigrants suffer greater disadvantages than native-born Asian Americans because of their imperfect English pronunciations and lack of job information networks.

Many people—including minority members themselves—are concerned that affirmative action programs giving preferential treatment to minority members create the impression that minority members are given special favors; they worry that their real achievements will be devalued.[2] Some contributors share this sentiment. For example, Malroutu says "affirmative action has dealt an injustice to bright, young minority professionals." She says her predominantly white, male colleagues considered her race to be the main reason for her appointment to the faculty. Kim, too, initially hesitated to accept an internship with the *Los Angeles Times*'s Minority Editorial Training Program because she wondered whether being affiliated with a minority advancement program would stigmatize her. In fact, only a very small number of Asian American professionals benefit from affirmative action programs because policymakers consider Asian Americans to be successful and thus eliminate them from affirmative action programs. Nevertheless, many talented Asian American professionals who deserve their positions are in danger of being viewed by their white colleagues as merely filling racial quotas. It is therefore quite natural that Asian American professionals, whether they support affirmative action or not, have to deal with the problem of being stigmatized as "free riders."

The emphasis on multiculturalism has opened the door for a very limited number of roles for Asian American actors. Yet the relative absence of such roles and the rarity of cross-racial casting make it extremely difficult for Asian Americans to achieve popular success in the arts and entertainment fields. Those few who play the roles of Asian or Asian American characters are in danger of perpetuating damaging, stereotypical images of Asian Americans to advance their acting careers. Joel de la Fuente describes the stereotypical Asian characters portrayed by Asian American actors:

> They are of a mix and match variety, these wily, inscrutable men of the Orient. There is the bow-legged Chinese waiter; the buck-toothed Japanese soldier of World War II propaganda; the quiet, effeminate houseman; the bullying, misogynistic father; the abu-

sive, adulterous husband; the stoic businessman; the camera-laden tourist.

Women have different stereotypes: the Suzie Wong–type prostitute who served American servicemen, the obedient concubine, and the giggling Geisha girl. De la Fuente passionately believes that Asian American actors are socially obligated to humanize Asian American characters. But he suggests that it is very difficult for Asian American actors to succeed if they want to portray nonstereo-typical Asian characters.

GROWING INTEREST IN AND CRITICISMS OF ETHNIC SUBCULTURE

Lozada and de la Fuente, both second-generation Filipino Americans, stand apart from the other contributors because their parents encouraged them to assimilate into American culture. The other essayists say their parents expected them to per-petuate their native culture and sought to instill them with ethnic pride. As chil-dren, several contributors visited their parents' homelands during school breaks. Some, such as Wang, Mori-Quayle, and Bose, were enrolled in ethnic language schools by their parents, not an easy feat back in the 1970s. In fact, Bose's mother organized a Sunday morning Bengali class and recruited a dozen other children.

Despite their parents' efforts, though, most resisted learning their native language and culture, especially during adolescence. Their resistance stemmed from the pressure to be "normal" and to fit in among their predominantly white peers. Asian Americans and Asian cultures were virtually invisible in their milieu. Kim says she was ashamed of her parents' broken English and felt uncomfortable when they visited her school

Many of the essayists mention looking forward to college while still in high school. For several of the contributors, college represented an escape from always having to negotiate the differences between their parents' culture and American culture. Their families were often their strongest link to their ethnic heritage.[3] In college, they were on their own. For Kim, college provided an escape from the traditional gender roles enforced inside her parents' home. Bose, who fought with her parents about dating and other social practices in high school, describes Wesleyan University as a "sanctuary." Do writes, "I left home for college, leaving not only the physical and cultural environment of my home, but also my identification with my ethnicity and the pain associated with it."

Ironically, several contributors developed their first sense of ethnic iden-tity in college. "Growing up, I considered myself to be an 'American' and uncon-sciously avoided all things 'Asian'," de la Fuente writes. "Later in college, I explored and grew proud of my Asian American identity." Mori-Quayle resisted going to a Japanese language school as a child, but decided to go to Japan for college; she ended up staying there for seven years. As an adolescent, Mediratta clashed with her father over his efforts to teach her about her Indian cultural heritage; yet upon entering college, she developed a keen interest in Indian culture and history and later spent two years in India to learn more. Bose, too, went to India to study painting after graduating from college. Do rebelled against her ethnicity and culture in high school, but experienced a change of heart in college. Although she could not visit Laos or Vietnam for political reasons, her collegiate and post-collegiate studies in France and extensive travel to East Asian countries were closely related to her increasing interest in Vietnamese culture and history.

The essayists experienced a shift from a blind desire to blend into the white mainstream to a curiosity about their ethnic subculture in college for several reasons. First, college tended to be more diverse, cosmopolitan, and tolerant. Several contributors were able to deepen their appreciation for their cultural background by taking courses in Asian languages and Asian area studies at their colleges. The large number of Asians on campus also strengthened their sense of ethnic identity. Second, a greater acceptance of their ethnic culture in college was closely related to American society's heightened awareness of multiculturalism. Third and most importantly, the essayists' gradual appreciation of their ethnic culture had much to do with psychological dynamics of resolving their own ethnic and racial identities. This issue will be discussed at length elsewhere in this chapter.

The contributors have grown to embrace their bicultural background. They cite a strong work ethic, a reverence for scholarly achievements, and a respect for elders as some positive Asian values. Kim says that as a child she resented her parents' prohibition on television on school nights, but decided as an adult she would impose the same restriction on her own children. Jeong, an assistant district attorney, says the strong work ethic inherited from his father gave him an edge over his mostly white peers at the Brooklyn District Attorney's office. Hotta says one of the Filipino customs she taught her two children was to *mano*— to show respect to their elders by placing the palm of the elder's right hand on their foreheads.

Yet the contributors are also critical of some ethnic and Asian cultural practices and social stereotypes. The hierarchical and authoritarian Korean family structure, Jeong writes, served as a disadvantage in developing the social skills he needed to advance in the workplace. Lozada vigorously pursued athletics in high school and college to combat the stereotype of Asians as geeky science nerds. Chung writes that she needed to set aside Korean expectations of "feminine behavior" to succeed in the predominantly white, male academic environment. Although she acquired behavior that she describes as "white, masculine"—speaking out, being assertive—she said she has nonetheless been perceived as a "nice, Oriental lady," among other stereotypes.

As expected, virtually all the female essayists—immigrant and second-generation alike—are critical of the more patriarchal traditions practiced in Asian American communities in this country and in Asia. The three immigrant essayists are most critical of the sexual double standard and gender-role division associated with Asian patriarchal practices because those practices played a powerful role in restricting their careers and shaping their domestic lives. Interestingly, Margaret Kan selected "Reaching the Glass Ceiling . . . at Home" as the title of her narrative. Born and raised in an upper-class Chinese family, she was an ambitious and talented student. After getting married, however, she worked as an administrative dietician and raised two children. In her early forties, she wanted to enter law school to get a more intellectually challenging job, but her husband dismissed the idea as unrealistic. He believed that tending the home and the family was a woman's primary responsibility, and she acquiesced. Her husband's lack of support for her career ambitions strained their marriage. In a similar vein, Hau describes herself as being competitive in the workplace, but a traditional Vietnamese woman at home:

> Because of the culture I was raised in, and the generations of Vietnamese women before me, I am living proof that old traditions are hard to break. My husband is still the head of the house, and I am the gentle, docile daughter who always puts the needs of the parents ahead of her own.

In her essay, Malroutu criticizes arranged marriages, sexual double standards, and other patriarchal customs practiced in the Indian immigrant community, as well as in India.

Though the immigrant contributors say they were unaware of a sexual double standard until they grew older, it was different for the 1.5- and second-generation contributors. For Kim, "the oppression of women" was one of her earliest impressions about Korean culture. As children, she and her sister were forced to prepare food for guests, while her brothers were allowed to sit with the adults in the living room. Chung says that while dating in college she found white men more attractive than Korean men partly because of her resentment of the "oppressive Korean patriarchy." She observes that Korean American men were more likely to favor traditional gender-role orientations than Korean American women because they benefited from them.

Jeong, who became partially paralyzed in a car accident in his second year of law school, presents a biting critique of how Koreans view the handicapped. In Asia, the disabled tend to suffer more prejudice than they do in America; there are no laws enforcing equal access and protection for the disabled. Because of these cultural and structural differences, a person with disabilities is more likely to encounter uncomfortable experiences in an Asian immigrant community than in the larger American society. It is not surprising that Jeong's experiences in the Korean American community after his accident were so traumatic that he "stopped going to his church and avoided Korean social functions." Before his paralyzing accident, Jeong was treated as a highly respected member of his Korean parish; after the accident, he was treated "more like an infant than as a man." His disability is at the core of his identity, as reflected by the title of his essay, "A Handicapped Korean in America."

HIGH SOCIAL ASSIMILATION

In their pre-college years, most of the 1.5- and second-generation contributors made friends mostly with Jewish and other white students. The preponderance of white friends among the contributors was largely the function of living in predominantly white neighborhoods and attending predominantly white schools. There is also evidence, however, that they deliberately sought to associate exclusively with whites in part because of inferiority complexes about being Asian; within their social context, Asian Americans and Asian cultures were marginalized. In high school, Kim's family moved to an East Los Angeles suburb that was mostly Asian and Latino. Kim says she disdained her "minority" classmates and regarded the white students at her junior high school as "superior." She never participated in school events and avoided interacting with non-white students. Kim was later able to understand the psychological basis of her feelings:

> Many years later, I recognized these feelings as being the possible result of living in a society where Asian Americans were not regarded as members of the mainstream. When I read about the concept of "internalized racism"—the replication of racist prototypes within one's own mind—I finally was able to come to terms with my past, conflicted feelings.

In his virtually all-white parochial elementary school, Wang shunned his fellow Asian American classmates. He disliked being lumped in the same group with the Chinese girl who could not speak English well. Although Asian Americans comprised more than 40 percent of the students at his high school, he still avoided socializing exclusively with Chinese and Asian American students.

As the contributors entered college, they generally increased their contact with members of their own ethnic background, as well as with other Asian Americans. They also became more conscious of their ethnicity and of a pan-Asian identity. Chung, who had associated exclusively with white friends in high school, struggled to maintain a balance between the worlds of her Korean and white friends in college. At Harvard, Wang actively interacted with Chinese American students, editing a campus magazine specializing in Chinese American issues.

Other contributors, however, continued their preference for white friends. Kim says that in her first year of college most of her friends were white, although her closest friend was of Indian descent. She "consciously and unconsciously avoided associating with East Asians, particularly Korean Americans." Mediratta, a community organizer at New York University's Institute for Education and Social Policy, says that in the college dining hall she "moved comfortably" into the "Anglo American" social circle so familiar to her. As an Indian American woman, she "felt little connection to the handful of Asian students, who were mostly East Asian and culturally different from me." Bose, a Bengali American, says she did not feel she had much in common with the East Asians and East Asian Americans who belonged to her college's Asian American students organization.

The majority of the 1.5- and second-generation essayists discuss their dating experiences. Their comments, as well as our interviews with the contributors who chose not to discuss their dating experiences, strongly suggest that college-educated, second-generation Asian American professionals tend to prefer whites for friends, dating partners, and spouses. The contributors who openly discuss their dating experiences were either married or engaged at the time they wrote their essays; five have white spouses or partners, one has an Asian American spouse, and four have co-ethnic partners. Two of the four contributors who chose not to discuss their dating experiences in their essays are involved in serious relationships with white partners.

Although Chung married a second-generation Korean American, she was initially more attracted to white men, especially as an adolescent. Her resentment of patriarchal Korean culture played a strong role in this preference for white men. She might have married a white partner, but found it difficult to ignore the deeply ingrained script of "don't marry a non-Korean." The three female contributors who are married or engaged to white partners also seem to believe that white men are likely to maintain more egalitarian marital relations than co-ethnic partners. Bose says many Bengali men regarded her as "too aggressive" and "very Americanized." Most of the Bengali men she grew up with in Bethesda, Maryland, returned to Bangladesh or India to find a wife. (It is common for Asian American men to return to their homeland to marry,[4] and thus Asian American women historically have a higher intermarriage rate than Asian American men.[5])

Although gender-related differences offer a reason for Asian and Asian American women to marry outside their ethnic group, some male essayists also show a preference for white partners. Lozada's ex-wife and current wife are both white. Although Sheth married a co-ethnic, Indian woman, he dated mostly white women. Two other male contributors were in serious relationships with white women. As two contributors remark, the dominance of white partners was largely a function of the absence of Asians. Asian Americans today can find a large circle of co-ethnic and Asian American dating and marital partners on college campuses and in the workplace. In fact, Asian-Asian intermarriages have increased significantly from 1980 to 1990.[6]

The prevalence of white dating and marital partners among the 1.5- and second-generation contributors also indicates that college-educated, native-born Asian Americans are well accepted by white people, and that the former feel comfortable associating with the latter. It is noteworthy that some of the female contributors who married or are engaged to white partners are strongly bicultural. Mori-Quayle completed college in Japan and worked there for a few years before coming back to the United States. Mediratta and Bose both lived in India for a year or more after completing college; culturally and psychologically, they are very ethnic. Their decision to marry white partners was influenced partly by the degree to which their white partners recognized their bicultural background and binational identity.

STRUGGLE FOR ETHNIC IDENTITY

Probably the most interesting and important aspect concerning younger-generation Asian American professionals, as reflected in these essays, is the process of forming or coming to terms with their ethnic and racial identities. Often the process involved much pain and inner conflict. In fact, the title of this book, *Struggle for Ethnic Identity,* was chosen because several of the 1.5- and second-generation Asian contributors devote much of their essays to discussing their quest to define their ethnic and racial identities.

In contrast, none of the three immigrant contributors make any reference to struggling over their ethnic identity. However, as noted, two immigrant contributors discuss in detail their experiences with discrimination in the workplace, an issue not addressed by younger-generation essayists. As indicated in the introduction, Pyong Gap Min, one of the book's coeditors, has encountered the language barrier and other obstacles in his professional career because of his immigrant status. Yet he has not undergone the inner conflict over his ethnic identity that most of the 1.5- and second-generation essayists have. The struggle for an ethnic identity is a unique struggle faced by Asian Americans who are raised according to the culture of their parents, yet exposed to an entirely different culture outside the home.

As children, most 1.5- and second-generation essayists lived in homes where their parents spoke their native language, ate their native food, and practiced their native customs. Often, upon entering school the contributors realized that their ethnic group and culture were marginal and invisible in the white, mainstream culture. The essayists representing Asian countries with a more recent history of immigration to the U.S., such as the Philippines, Korea, India, and Vietnam, apparently experienced a greater sense of marginality and invisibility than those of Chinese or Japanese descent. In the 1970s, Koreans and Indians were largely unknown to most Americans, while Chinese and Japanese people were more familiar. Consequently, members of the more obscure groups developed a negative self-image and attempted to reject their ethnic culture and their non-white physical characteristics. They wanted to be white and associated mainly with white students.

As the essayists matured, however, they realized they could not hide their differences, particularly their non-white physical differences. They grew increasingly aware that they were not accepted as "American," no matter how much they sought to assimilate. Chung describes a moment in high school that triggered her decision to accept her ethnic identity. She was walking down the hallway of her high school when she suddenly caught her reflection in the mirror and realized how visibly different she was from her white friends:

> Until that point, my struggle with ethnic identity and the denial of my Koreanness had been largely unconscious, but I began to see that the cost of my denial was too high a price to pay. I accepted the reality of my biculturality, that I was inevitably both Korean and American, and that I had a unique opportunity to learn from both cultures, rather than rejecting one for the other. For the first time since that moment in the second grade when I wished I was a blond-haired girl with the last name Smith, I began to see my bicultural experience as a blessing and an opportunity rather than a curse.

Several contributors describe similar moments of accepting or recognizing their biculturality. Although the initial acceptance of their ethnic and racial backgrounds was difficult and often painful, the contributors gradually grew more comfortable with their backgrounds, more confident with the process over time.

This struggle to come to terms with their ethnic and racial identities often impacted the contributors' academic interests and career choices. Most of the 1.5- and second-generation essayists say their parents pushed them to major in pre-medicine or the sciences and to attend medical or law schools. But the struggle to define an ethnic identity often led the contributors to develop interests in the social sciences, humanities, and the arts. Mediratta says her growing awareness of her ethnic identity transformed her academic interests from the regimen of math and science courses expected of a pre-med student to Asian studies. After graduating from college, Bose spent a year studying painting in India to stay in touch with her roots. Chung observes, "My overriding motivation to pursue a career in psychology is directly related to my bicultural experiences." As a Korean American psychologist of the 1.5-generation, Chung wanted to bridge the gap between first- and second-generation Koreans. Do's decision to volunteer at a refugee service agency in Denver and to obtain a graduate degree in social work were closely related to the formation of her ethnic and racial identity as a Vietnamese and as an Asian American.

The essayists represent varying degrees of ethnic and racial identities. Whereas their ethnic identity is closely related to the ethnic subculture of their childhood homes or their parents' home country, their racial identity emerged with an awareness of their non-white status in a predominantly white society. To phrase it alternately, their racial identity was closely related to their perception that whites did not accept them fully as American citizens.

The contributors' non-white racial identity takes two different forms: pan-Asian (identifying as Asian American) and Third World (identifying as people of color, encompassing Asian, black, and Latino). Throughout his essay, de la Fuente uses the terms "Asian American identity" and "Asian Americans," never making reference to "Filipino American identity" or "Filipino Americans"; this suggests a strong Asian American identity, but a weak ethnic identity. Kim and Chung, both Korean Americans, and Wang, a Chinese American, display a moderate level of pan-Asian identity, although their ethnic identity is much stronger. These three East Asian essayists also have close friends who are East Asian American and have been affiliated with pan-Asian organizations. Kim and Wang also identify with other people of color. As a teenager, Kim participated in marches for school desegregation led by the National Association for the Advancement of Colored People, a major black civil-rights organization, and worked to gain voting rights for migrant farm workers through Cesar Chavez's United Farm Workers. Wang, meanwhile, created a conflict resolution project for African American and Latino students at a public school in Harlem.

Mediratta and Bose, both South Asians, say they felt little affinity with East Asians such as Chinese, Korean, and Japanese Americans. Bose identified with others of South Asian descent, while Mediratta describes herself as having had a Third World racial identity. She mentions African American friends, but no Chinese, Korean, or Japanese Americans friends. Her sense of kinship with African Americans is also reflected in her decision to abandon her parents' dream of her becoming a doctor, and to work as a public school teacher in a black neighborhood in urban New Jersey. Mediratta developed her identity as a person of color partly through the realization that dark-skinned South Asians were discriminated against and targeted for racial violence in ways that were similar to African Americans: "Even with their economic privilege, Indians remain dark skinned and vulnerable to the vagaries of cultural and ethnic discrimination." Keenly aware of Great Britain's history of colonizing India and African countries, Mediratta recalls that the technique of nonviolence that Mahatma Gandhi used for the Indian independence movement against the British colonial government was adopted by Martin Luther King in the Civil Rights movement.

In addition, the absence of Asian role models fostered an identification with other minorities. Mediratta was greatly influenced by the writings of Toni Morrison, the Nobel Prize—winning author who has written in rich detail about black experiences in America. Kim and Wang also mention black and Latino role models. "Growing up, I did not have any Asian American role models aside from my parents," Wang writes. "In the ridicule and prejudice that I fought in grade school, I turned instead to African Americans like Medgar Evers and Martin Luther King, Jr., and Latinos like Cesar Chavez for strength and guidance."

Mediratta, Kim, and Wang graduated from prestigious colleges and have professional occupations in the white mainstream. It is surprising that highly successful second-generation Asian American professionals feel a kinship with African Americans and Latinos, and adopt even a moderate level of the identity of a person of color because many Asian immigrants are prejudiced against African Americans and have a tendency to align with the white group in the white—black racial dichotomy.[7] Despite this trend, several 1.5- and second-generation essayists express feeling a greater kinship with African Americans and Latinos than with whites. Only a small proportion of second-generation Asian Americans may hold a Third World racial identity. Yet, the fact that many well-educated, second-generation Asian Americans find common ground with African Americans and Latinos makes real the possibility of a "rainbow coalition."

Although most younger-generation essayists do not feel fully accepted by American society, all essayists apparently agree that they feel more comfortable living in the U.S. than in their mother country or another foreign country. Although she does not feel fully accepted here, Kim writes, "I cannot imagine leaving this country, as my parents left theirs." Interestingly, many developed an awareness of their American identity while traveling abroad or visiting their mother country. Mediratta says that during her visit to India she "became more conscious for the first time of how truly American I am." Bose recollects: "In Japan, I found myself identifying as an American more than I had done before." Do, too, grew more conscious of the American side of her identity while working as an English teacher in Japan.

Finally, it is noteworthy that ethnic identity is intertwined with gender identity for many of the female contributors. Their gender identity has developed in reaction to both the patriarchal customs brought from their mother country and the gender discrimination practiced in American society. As expected, the female essayists are highly critical of patriarchal customs practiced among their parents and in the ethnic community. Two of the immigrant essayists loudly decry the way the traditional gender-role division in their marriages restricted their professional activities. As mentioned earlier, Asian American women may prefer white partners more than Asian American men partly because they expect more egalitarian marital relations from white partners. Yet, they are also keenly aware that American women suffer disadvantages as well, when compared with American men. Their gender identity is inseparably tied to their ethnic and racial identities. In their view, minority women are doubly handicapped in a white, male-dominated society. This Third World, feminist political ideology is most clearly reflected in the following paragraph from Mediratta's essay:

> With this growing awareness of my invisibility I became much more insistent on being taken on my own terms, as a woman and as an Indian. My friendships with women became much more important to me, and became a space in which to explore my sense of gender identity. This evolving political identity created a lot of conflict with [my husband]. It became increasingly difficult to understand each other across the enormous differences between how we looked at the world, as man and woman, as Anglo American and Indian American, as white and non-white.

CONCLUSION

Fifteen essays are too small a sample from which to generalize about all 1.5- and second-generation Asian Americans. Nevertheless, these narratives provide important theoretical and practical implications for understanding the modes of adaptation taken by children of post-1965 Asian immigrants in general and with regard to their ethnic and racial identities in particular.

We expected 1.5- and second-generation Asian American professionals to encounter barriers in their career mobility. But not one of them raised specific experiences with discrimination in the labor market; in contrast, two of the three immigrant essayists discussed this topic. The essays thus support the view documented by many empirical studies that compared with native-born Asian Americans, Asian immigrants suffer a great disadvantage for occupational adjustment in the United States. What is unclear from the essays is how 1.5- and second-generation Asian Americans compare to white Americans in the labor market. The younger-generation essayists' lack of experience with discrimination in the labor market seems to be due partly to the fact that they are still in the early stages of their careers. Some of them may encounter the glass ceiling problem later, after they reach a certain level.

The majority of Asian American children from professional families are generally successful in the predominantly middle- and upper-middle-class white schools they attend; these experiences are no doubt positive and rewarding. However, all 1.5- and second- generation essayists describe profoundly unsettling experiences with racial violence, prejudice, and a sense of marginality in their predominantly white elementary and high schools. Many suffered physical and verbal harassment from their classmates, while others were treated as "strangers" in a social environment generally unreceptive to non-white students. Several factors—a phenomenal increase in the Asian American population, an increasing emphasis on multiculturalism and an increasing interest in Asian countries and Asian cultures—have made Asian Americans more familiar to most Americans. Asian American students today, compared to twenty years ago, are likely to feel more accepted. At the same time, racial prejudice and anti-Asian violence still exist.

All essayists received college educations from prestigious universities and entered professional careers in the mainstream economy. According to both the classical assimilation theory and the more recently proposed segmented assimilation theory, these Asian American professionals, acculturated to the American mainstream culture, should have lost much of their ethnic subculture. However, many of the younger-generation essayists are characterized by strong bicultural experiences. The multicultural, cosmopolitan environment in American colleges, coupled with transnational ties to the mother countries, apparently have helped the 1.5- and second-generation essayists maintain strong bicultural orientations. This supports the view that post-1965 immigrants, including Asian immigrants, have advantages over earlier white immigrants in transmitting their cultural traditions to their children.

According to Gordon's theory of assimilation,[8] acculturation or cultural assimilation is a precondition for social assimilation. However, our analysis of these autobiographical essays suggests that acculturation in the sense of substituting their ethnic culture with American culture is not a precondition for social assimilation. Despite their strong bicultural experiences, the 1.5- and second-generation essayists generally feel very comfortable making friends with and dating whites. Men and, to a greater extent, women preferred white partners over co-ethnic or Asian partners. In fact, most of the younger-generation essayists who were married or engaged at the time of writing their essays had white partners. This suggests that at least highly educated, second-generation Asian Americans not only feel comfortable in company of but are well accepted by white people. However, it is especially noteworthy that Asian Americans do not have to relinquish their ethnic or Asian culture as a prerequisite for dating or marrying white partners. In fact, Mori-Quayle, Bose, and Mediratta, the three most strongly bicultural female essayists, are married to white partners.

The narratives in this collection also suggest that many younger-generation Asian Americans experience strong psychological conflicts during the process of forming their ethnic and racial identities, an experience not shared by Asian immigrants. Asian immigrants usually do not undergo severe inner conflicts over their ethnic or racial identity because they have already completed the major stages of their personality development in a culture where they were accepted. However, native-born Asian Americans struggle over their ethnic identity because they are not completely accepted as Americans. Out of their sense of marginality, several of the essayists attempted to reject their ethnic culture and their non-white characteristics during their early school years. Although the process of identity transformation was painful, it helped them grow more comfortable with their ethnic backgrounds and racial characteristics. By virtue of the phenomenal increase in the Asian American student population and the recent emphasis on multicultural education, second-generation Asian American children are likely to experience a less turbulent and smoother identity transformation. It would further facilitate the formation of ethnic identity if Asian American children were exposed to their ethnic culture through multicultural education in elementary and high schools to a greater extent than they are today; the same is true for children from other minority groups.

Our younger-generation essayists hold varying degrees of pan-Asian identity, as is expected from the bulk of literature on pan-Asian identity and solidarity reviewed in the introduction. As expected from the review of the literature in Part One, Chinese, Japanese, and Korean Americans with similar cultural and physical characteristics maintain more frequent social interactions with one another, while Indians and other South Asians with darker skin seem to feel more kinship with African Americans than with East Asians. Americans in general and policymakers in particular have treated "Asian Americans" or "Asian Pacific Americans" as one group distinguishable from other minority groups, ignoring the fact that they are composed of a number of different ethnic groups with significant physical and cultural differences. While racial lumping and the need to protect common interests may provide an impetus for a pan-Asian coalition among all Asian ethnic groups, the level of intergroup interaction and solidarity among particular Asian groups will be affected by their physical and cultural similarities.

Several of the essayists, not only those of South Asian descent, feel moderate levels of kinship with African Americans and Latinos. They do so partly because they are sensitive to the racial discrimination encountered by non-white minority groups in the United States and partly because in these minority communities they find role models who are useful in fighting white racism. As reviewed in Part One, segmented assimilation theory emphasizes that children of Asian immigrants in inner-city black ghettos are vulnerable to adopting the "adversarial subculture" that would hinder their educational advancement and occupational mobility. Yet some second-generation Asian Americans with successful professional careers adopt black role models to combat white racism. Thus the adaptation modes of second-generation Asian Americans are more complex than has been suggested by the existing theoretical generalizations.

The essays in this collection suggest that second-generation Asian Americans have multiple ethnic identities, making it difficult to limit them to any one category. A second-generation Indian American may have ethnic and racial identities that are Indian American, South Asian ethnic, and Third World, while a second-generation Chinese American may hold ethnic, pan-Asian, and Third World identities. The complex nature of their ethnic identity cannot be captured by a cross-sectional survey using multiple-choice questionnaire items. Such an approach has the danger of distorting the nature of ethnicity not only by forcing the respondents to choose a particular ethnic category, but also by measuring ethnic identity at a single point in life. The essays clearly indicate that the contributors have gone through significant changes in their ethnic identity during the course of their lives. As Kim writes, "My perception of my ethnicity and identity has undergone many permutations and it is difficult to predict how I will feel in another thirty-six years."

ENDNOTES

1. United States Commission on Civil Rights, 1992, p. 90.

2. Richard Rodriguez, *Hunger of Memory* (New York: Bantam Books, 1983); Shelby Steele, *The Content of Our Character* (New York: St Martin's Press, 1990).

3. Herbert Gans, "Toward a Reconciliation of 'Assimilation' and 'Pluralism': The Interplay of Acculturation and Ethnic Retention," *International Migration Review,* vol. 31, pp. 875–892.

4. Pyong Gap Min, "Korean Immigrants' Marital Patterns and Adjustment," in *Family Ethnicity,* edited by Harriette McAdoo (Newbury Park, CA: Sage Publications, 1993), pp. 287–299.

5. Harry Kitano, Wai-Tsang Yeung, Lynn Chai, and Herbert Hatanaka, "Asian-American Interracial Marriages," *Journal of Marriage and the Family,* vol. 46 (1984), pp. 179–190.

6. Sharon Lee and Marilyn Fernandez, "Trends in Asian American Racial/Ethnic Intermarriage: A Comparison of 1980 and 1990 Census Data," *Sociological Perspectives,* vol. 41 (1998), pp. 323–342; Larry Hajime Shinagawa and Gin Yong Pang, "Asian American Panethnicity and Intermarriage," *Amerasia Journal,* vol. 22, pp. 127–152.

7. Moon Jo, "Korean Merchants in the Black Community: Prejudice among the Victims of Prejudice," *Ethnic and Racial Studies,* vol. 15, pp. 395–411; Ronald Weitzer, "Racial Prejudice among Korean American Merchants in African American Neighborhoods," *The Sociological Quarterly,* vol. 38, pp. 587–606; In-Jin Yoon, *On My Own: Korean Businesses and Race Relations in America* (Chicago: University of Chicago Press, 1997), pp. 219–224.

8. Milton Gordon, *Assimilation in American Life: The Role of Race, Religion, and National Origin* (New York: Oxford University Press, 1964).

Selected Bibliography

Abramson, Harold. 1973. *Ethnic Diversity in Catholic America*. New York: John Wiley.

Agbayani-Siewert, Pauline, and Linda Revilla. 1995. "Filipino Americans." In *Asian Americans,* edited by Pyong Gap Min. Newbury Park, Calif.: Sage Publications.

Alba, Richard. 1990. *Ethnic Identity: The Transformation of White America*. New Haven, Conn.: Yale University Press.

Alba, Richard, and Victor Nee. 1997. "Rethinking Assimilation Theory for a New Era of Immigration." *International Migration Review* 31: 826–874.

Banton, Michael. 1983. *Racial and Ethnic Competition*. New York: Cambridge University Press.

Basch, Linda, Nina Glick Schiller, and Christina Szanton-Blanc (eds.). 1994. *Nations Unbounded: Transnational Projects, Postcolonial Predicaments, and Deterritorialized Nations*. New York: Gordon and Breach Science.

Bell, Daniel. 1975. "Ethnicity and Social Change." In *Ethnicity: Theory and Experience,* edited by Nathan Glazer and Daniel Moynihan. Cambridge, Mass.: Harvard University Press.

Bhachu, Parminder. 1985. *Twice Migrants: East African Sikh Settlers in Britain*. London: Tavistock Publications.

Bloom, Allan. 1987. *The Closing of the American Mind*. New York: Simon and Schuster.

Bonacich, Edna. 1973. "A Theory of Middleman Minorities." *American Sociological Review* 35: 583–594.

Bonacich, Edna, and John Modell. 1980. *The Economic Basis of Ethnic Solidarity: Small Business in the Japanese American Community*. Berkeley: University of California Press.

Bozorgmehr, Mehdi. 1997. "Internal Ethnicity: Iranians in Los Angeles." *Sociological Perspectives* 40: 387–408.

Butler, Jonnella, and John Walter. 1991. *Transforming the Curriculum: Ethnic Studies and Women's Studies*. Albany: SUNY Press.

Chan, Sucheng. 1991. *Asian Americans: An Interpretive History*. Boston: Twayne Publishers.

Chavez, Linda. 1991. *Out of the Barrio: Toward a New Politics of Hispanic Assimilation*. New York: Basic Books.

Chow, Esther Ngau-Ling, Doris Wilkinson, and Maxine Bach Zinn. 1997. *Race, Class, and Gender: Commond Bonds, Different Voices*. Newbury Park, Calif.: Sage Publications.

Cinel, Dino. 1982. *From Italy to San Francisco*. Stanford, Calif.: Stanford University Press.

Cohen, Steven. 1985. *American Modernity and Jewish Identity*. New York: Tavistock Publications.

Cole, S. G., and M. Cole. 1954. *Minorities and American Promise.* New York: Harper and Brothers.

Collins, Patricia Hill. 1990. *Black Feminist Thought: Knowledge, Consciousness, and the Politics of Empowerment.* New York: Routledge, Chapman & Hall.

Desbarats, J., and L. Holland. 1983. "Indochinese Settlement Patterns in Orange County." *Amerasia Journal* 10 (1): 23–46.

Despress, Leo. 1975. *Ethnicity and Resource Competition in Plural Societies.* The Hague: Mouton Publishers.

D'Souza, Dinesh. 1991. *Illiberal Education: The Politics of Race and Sex on Campus.* New York: Free Press.

Dublin, Thomas (ed.). 1997. *Becoming American, Becoming Ethnic: College Students Explore Their Roots.* Philadelphia: Temple University Press.

Endo, Russell, and William Wei. 1988. "On the Development of Asian American Studies Programs." In *Reflections on Shattered Windows: Promises and Prospects for Asian American Studies,* edited by Gary Okihiro, Shirley Hune, Arthur Hansen, and John Liu. Pullman: Washington State University.

Enloe, Cynthia. 1981. "The Growth of the State and Ethnic Mobilization." *Ethnic and Racial Studies* 4: 123–136.

Espiritu, Yen Le. 1989. "Beyond the Boat People: Ethnicization of American Life." *Amerasia Journal* 15 (2): 49–67.

———. 1992. *Asian American Panethnicity: Bridging Institutions and Identities.* Philadelphia: Temple University Press.

———. 1994. "The Intersection of Race, Ethnicity, and Class: The Multiple Identities of Second-Generation Filipinos." *Identities* 1: 234–251.

———. 1997. *Asian American Women and Men: Labor, Laws, and Love.* Newbury Park, Calif.: Sage Publications.

Farley, Raynold. 1996. *The New American Reality: Who We Are, How We Got Here, and Where We Are Going.* New York: Russell Sage Foundation.

Fernandez, Robert, and Francois Nielsen. 1986. "Bilingualism and Hispanic Scholastic Achievement: Some Baseline Results." *Social Science Research* 15: 43–70.

Fido, J. A. Antonio. 1986. *The Pilipinos in America: Macro/Micro Dimensions of Immigration and Integration.* Staten Island, N.Y.: Center for Migration Studies.

Fisher, Maxine. 1978. "Creating Ethnic Identity: Asian Indians in the New York City Area." *Urban Anthropology* 7: 271–285.

Fong, Timothy. 1994. *The First Suburban Chinatown: The Remaking of Monterey Park, California.* Philadelphia: Temple University Press.

Fordham, S. 1988. "Racelessness as a Factor in Black Students' School Success: Pragmatic Strategy or Pyrrhic Victory." *Harvard Educational Review* 58: 54–84.

Fordham, S., and John Ogbu. 1986. "Black Students' School Success: Coping with the 'Burden of Acting White'." *The Urban Review* 18: 176–206.

Friedman, Georges. 1967. *The End of the Jewish People,* translated by Eric Mosbacher. New York: Doubleday.

Gans, Herbert. 1962. *The Urban Villagers: Group and Class in the Life of Italian-Americans.* New York: The Macmillan Company.

———. 1979. "Symbolic Ethnicity: The Future of Ethnic Groups and Cultures in America." *Ethnic and Racial Studies* 2: 1–20.

———. 1997. "Toward a Reconciliation of 'Assimilation' and 'Pluralism': The Interplay of Acculturation and Ethnic Retention." *International Migration Review* 31: 875–892.

Gerson, W. 1969. "Jews at Christmas Time: Role Strain and Strain Reducing Mechanisms." In *Social Problems in a Changing World,* edited by W. Gerson. New York: Crowell.

Gibson, Margaret. 1988. *Accommodation without Assimilation: Sikh Immigrants in an American High School.* Ithaca, N.Y.: Cornell University Press.

Gibson, Margaret A., and John Ogbu (eds.). 1991. *Minority Status and Schooling: A Comparative Study of Immigrant and Involuntary Minorities.* New York: Garland.

Glazer, Nathan, and Daniel Moynihan (eds.). 1975. *Ethnicity: Theory and Experience.* Cambridge, Mass.: Harvard University Press.

Gold, Steven J. 1997. "Transnationalism and Vocabularies of Motive in International Migration: The Case of Israelis in the United States." *Sociological Perspectives* 40: 409–426.

Goldstein, Sidney, and Alice Goldstein. 1996. *Jews on the Move.* Albany: SUNY Press.

Gordon, Milton. 1964. *Assimilation in American Life: The Role of Race, Religion, and National Origin.* New York: Oxford University Press.

Goren, Arthur. 1982. *The American Jews.* Cambridge, Mass.: Harvard University Press.

Grant, Madison. 1916. *The Passing of the Great Race.* New York: Charles Scribner's Sons.

Greeley, Andrew. 1976. *Ethnicity in the United States: A Preliminary Reconnaissance.* New York: John Wiley.

Gupta, Anu. 1997. "At the Crossroads: College Activism and Its Impact on Asian American Identity Formation." In *A Part, Yet Apart: South Asians in Asian America,* edited by Lavina Dhingra and Rajimi Srikanth. Philadelphia: Temple University Press.

Gupta, Jyotirindra Das. 1975. "Ethnicity, Language Demands, and National Development in India." In *Ethnicity: Theory and Experience,* edited by Nathan Glazer and Daniel Moynihan. Cambridge, Mass.: Harvard University Press.

Hannan, Michael. 1979. "The Dynamics of Ethnic Boundaries in Modern States." In *National Development and the World System,* edited by John Meyer and Michael Hannan. Chicago: University of Chicago Press.

Hechter, Michael. 1974. "Political Economy of Ethnic Change." *American Journal of Sociology* 79: 1151–1178.

———. 1975. *Internal Colonialism: The Celtic Fringe in British National Development.* Berkeley: University of California Press.

———. 1978. "Group Formation and the Cultural Division of Labor." *American Journal of Sociology* 84: 293–318.

Hechter, Michael, D. Friedman, and M. Appelbaum. 1982. "A Theory of Ethnic Collective Action." *International Migration Review* 16: 212–234.

Horton, John. 1995. *The Politics of Diversity: Immigration, Resistance, and Change in Monterey Park, California.* Philadelphia: Temple University Press.

Hu-Dehart, Evelyn. 1994. "P.C. and the Politics of Multiculturalism in Higher Education." In *Race,* edited by Steven Gregory and Roger Sanjek. New Brunswick, N.J.: Rutgers University Press.

Hurh, Won Moo, and Kwang Chung Kim. 1984. *Korean Immigrants in North America: A Structural Analysis of Ethnic Confinement and Adhesive Adaptation.* Madison, N.J.: Fairleigh Dickinson University Press.

———. 1989. "The 'Success' Image of Asian Americans: Its Validity, and Its Practical and Theoretical Implications." *Ethnic and Racial Studies* 12: 512–537.

Isaacs, Harold. 1975. *Idols of the Tribe.* New York: Harper and Row.

Jaret, Charles. 1995. *Contemporary Racial and Ethnic Relations.* New York: Harper Collins College Publishers.

Kao, Grace, and Marta Tienda. 1995. "Optimism and Achievement: The Educational Performance of Immigrant Youth." *Social Science Quarterly* 76: 1–19.

Kasinitz, Philip. 1992. *Caribbean New York: Black Immigrants and the Politics of Race.* Ithaca, N.Y.: Cornell University Press.

Kearney, Michael. 1995. "The Local and the Global: The Anthropology of Globalization and Transnationalism." *Annual Review of Anthropology* 24: 547–565.

Kibria, Nazli. 1997. "The Construction of 'Asian American': Reflections on Intermarriage and Ethnic Identity among Second-Generation Chinese and Korean Americans." *Ethnic and Racial Studies* 20: 523–544.

Kim, Kwang Chung, Won Moo Hurh, and Marilyn Fernandez. 1989. "Intergroup Differences in Business Participation: Three Asian Immigrant Groups." *International Migration Review* 23: 73–95.

Kitano, Harry. 1976. *Japanese Americans: An Evolution of a Subculture.* Englewood Cliffs, N.J.: Prentice Hall.

Kitano, Harry, Wai-Tsang Yeung, Lynn Chai, and Herbert Hatanaka. 1984. "Asian-American Interracial Marriages." *Journal of Marriage and the Family* 46: 179–190.

Kraybill, D. B., and M. A. Olshan (eds.). 1994. *The Amish Struggle with Modernity.* Hanover, N.H.: University Press of New England.

Kwoh, Stewart, and Mindy Hui. 1993. "Empowering Our Communities: Political Policy." In *The State of Asian Pacific America: Policy Issues to the Year 2020,* edited by LEAP Asian Pacific American Public Policy Institute and UCLA Asian American Studies Center.

Kwong, Peter. 1987. *The New Chinatown.* New York: Hill and Wang.

Lee, Sharon. 1993. "Racial Classification in the U.S. Census: 1890–1990." *Ethnic and Racial Studies* 16: 75–94.

Lee, Sharon, and Marilyn Fernandez. 1998. "Trends in Asian American Racial/Ethnic Intermarriage: A Comparison of 1980 and 1990 Census Data." *Sociological Perspectives* 41: 323–342.

Lee, Stacy. 1996a. *Unravelling the Model Minority Stereotype: Listening to Asian American Youth.* New York: Teachers College Press.

————. 1996b. "Perceptions of Panethnicity among Asian American High School Students." *Amerasia Journal* 22: 109–125.

Leon, M. 1979. *The Roots of Modern Mormonism.* Cambridge, Mass.: Harvard University Press.

Lieberson, Stanley, and Mary Waters. 1988. *From Many Strands: Ethnic and Racial Groups in Contemporary America.* New York: Russell Sage Foundation.

Light, Ivan. 1972. *Ethnic Enterprise in America: Business and Welfare among Chinese, Japanese, and Blacks.* Berkeley: University of California Press.

Light, Ivan, Georges Sabagh, Mehdi Bozorgmehr, and Claudia Der-Martirosian. 1993. "Internal Ethnicity in the Ethnic Economy." *Ethnic and Racial Studies* 16: 581–591.

Lincoln, Eric. 1961. *The Black Muslims in America.* Boston: Beacon Press.

Lopez, David. 1997. "Language: Diversity and Assimilation." In *Ethnic Los Angeles,* edited by Roger Waldinger and Mehdi Bozorgmehr. New York: Russell Sage Foundation.

Lopez, David, and Yen Le Espiritu. 1990. "Panethnicity in the United States: A Theoretical Framework." *Ethnic and Racial Studies* 13: 198–224.

Madhubuti, S. L. 1977. *The Story of Kwanzaa.* Chicago: The Third World Press.

Mangiafico, Luciano. 1988. *Contemporary Asian Immigrants: Patterns of Filipino, Korean, and Chinese Settlement in the United States.* New York: Praeger.

Manning, Nash. 1989. *The Cauldron of Ethnicity in the Modern World.* Chicago: University of Chicago Press.

Manning, Robert. 1995. "Multiculturalism in the United States: Clashing Concepts, Changing Demographics, and Competing Cultures." *International Journal of Group Tensions* 25: 117–167.

McKay, James. 1982. "An Exploratory Synthesis of Primordial and Mobilizationist Approaches to Ethnic Phenomena." *Ethnic and Racial Studies* 5: 395–420.

Miller, Jack David, and Reed Coughlan. 1993. "The Poverty of Primordialism: The Demystification of Ethnic Attachments." *Ethnic and Racial Studies* 16: 183–202.

Min, Pyong Gap. 1991. "Cultural and Economic Boundaries of Korean Ethnicity: A Comparative Analysis." *Ethnic and Racial Studies* 14: 225–241.

————. 1993. "Korean Immigrants in Los Angeles." In *Immigration and Entrepreneurship: Culture, Capital, and Ethnic Networks,* edited by Ivan Light and Parminder Bhachu. New York: Transaction.

————. 1995. "An Overview of Asian Americans." In *Asian Americans: Contemporary Trends and Issues,* edited by Pyong Gap Min. Newbury Park, Calif.: Sage Publications.

————. 1996. *Caught in the Middle: Korean Merchants in America's Multiethnic Cities.* Berkeley: University of California Press.

————. 1998a. "A Comparison of Korean and Indian Immigrants in New York in Community Organization." Paper presented at the Annual Meeting of the Eastern Sociological Society.

————. 1998b. *Changes and Conflicts: Korean Immigrant Families in New York*. Boston: Allyn and Bacon.

Min, Pyong Gap, and Lucy Chen. 1997. "A Comparison of Korean, Chinese, and Indian Immigrants in Ethnic Attachment." Paper presented at the Annual Meeting of the American Sociological Association.

Min, Pyong Gap, and Youna Choi. 1993. "Ethnic Attachment among Korean-American High School Students." *Korea Journal of Population and Development* 22: 167–179.

Mirak, Robert. 1980. "Armenians." In *Harvard Encyclopedia of American Ethnic Groups,* edited by Stephen Thernstrom. Cambridge, Mass.: Harvard University Press.

Mooney, James. 1965. *The Ghost Dance Religion and the Sioux Outbreak of 1890.* Chicago: University of Chicago Press.

Moore, Joan. 1991. *Going Down to the Barrio: Homeboys and Homegirls in Change.* Philadelphia: Temple University Press.

Nagel, Joane. 1985. "The Political Mobilization of Native Americans." In *Majority and Minority: The Dynamics of Race and Ethnicity in America, Fourth Edition,* edited by Norman Yetman. Boston: Allyn and Bacon.

————. 1986. "The Political Construction of Ethnicity." In *Competitive Ethnic Relations,* edited by Susan Olzak and Joane Nagel. New York: Academic Press.

Nagel, Joane, and Susan Olzak. 1983. "Ethnic Mobilization in New and Old States: An Extension of the Competition Model." *Social Problems* 30: 355–374.

Nakanish, Don. 1993. "Surviving Democracy's 'Mistakes': Japanese Americans and the Enduring Legacy of Executive Order 9066." *Amerasia Journal* 19: 7–36.

New York City Department of Planning. 1992. *Demographic Profiles: A Portrait of New York City's Community District from the 1980 & 1990 Censuses of Population and Housing.*

Nielsen, Francois. 1980. "The Flemish Movement in Belgium after World War II: A Dynamic Analysis." *American Sociological Review* 45: 76–94.

————. 1985. "Toward a Theory of Ethnic Solidarity in Modern Societies." *American Sociological Review* 50: 133–149.

Olzak, Susan. 1983. "Contemporary Ethnic Mobilization." *Annual Review of Sociology* 9: 355–377.

Olzak, Susan, and Joane Nagel (eds.). 1986. *Competitive Ethnic Relations.* New York: Academic Press.

Omni, Michael. 1993. "Out of the Melting Pot and into the Fire: Race Relations Policy." In *State of Asian Pacific America: Policy Issues to the Year 2020,* edited by LEAP Asian American Public Policy Institute and UCLA Asian American Studies Center.

Omni, Michael, and Howard Winant. 1986. *Racial Formation in the United States from the 1960s to the 1980s.* New York: Routledge.

Padilla, Felix. 1986. "Latino Ethnicity in the City of Chicago." In *Competitive Ethnic Relations,* edited by Susan Olzak and Joane Nagel. New York: Academic Press.

Park, Kyeyoung. "Women of the 1.5 Generation: Alternative Manifestation of Korean American Identities." Paper presented at the Annual Meeting of the Association for Asian American Studies, Hawaii.

Park, Robert. 1950. *Race and Culture.* New York: Free Press.

Portes, Alejandro. 1984. "The Rise of Ethnicity: Determinants of Ethnic Perceptions among Cuban Exiles in Miami." *American Sociological Review* 49: 383–397.

———. 1995. "Segmented Assimilation among New Immigrant Youth." In *California's Immigrant Children: Theory, Research, and Implications for Educational Policy,* edited by Ruben Rumbaut and Wayne Cornelius. San Diego: Center for U.S.-Mexican Studies, University of California at San Diego.

———. 1997. *The New Second Generation.* New York: Russell Sage Foundation.

Portes, Alejandro, and Dag McLeod. 1996. "What Shall I Call Myself? Hispanic Identity Formation in the Second Generation." *Ethnic and Racial Studies* 19: 523–546.

Portes, Alejandro, and Ruben Rumbaut. 1990. *Immigrant America: A Portrait.* Berkeley: University of California Press.

———. 1996. *Immigrant America: A Portrait, Second Edition.* Berkeley: University of California Press.

Portes, Alejandro, and Richard Schauffler. 1994. "Language and the Second Generation: Bilingualism Yesterday and Today." *International Migration Review* 28: 640–661.

Portes, Alejandro, and Min Zhou. 1993. "The New Second Generation: Segmented Assimilation and Its Variants." *The Annals of the American Academy of Political and Social Science* 530 (November): 74–97.

Reitz, Jeffrey. 1980. *The Survival of Ethnic Groups.* Toronto: McGraw Hill.

Revilla, Linda. 1997. "Filipino American Identity: Transcending the Crisis." In *Filipino Americans: Transformation and Identity,* edited by Maria P. Root. Newbury Park, Calif.: Sage Publications.

Rodriguez, Nestor P. 1995. "The Real 'New World Order': The Globalization of Racial and Ethnic Relations in the Late Twentieth Century." In *The Bubbling Cauldron: Race, Ethnicity, and the Urban Crisis,* edited by Michael Peter Smith and Joe Feagin. Minneapolis: University of Minnesota Press.

Rodriguez, Richard. 1983. *Hunger of Memory.* New York: Bantam Books.

Romanucci-Ross, Lola, and George De Vos (eds.). 1995. *Ethnic Identity: Creation, Conflict, and Accommodation.* Walnut Creek, Calif.: AltaMira Press.

Roosens, Eugene. 1989. *Creating Ethnicity: The Process of Ethnogensis.* Newbury Park, Calif.: Sage Publications.

Rosenberg, S. 1985. *The New Jewish Identity in America.* New York: Hipocrene Books.

Rosenblum, Karen. 1996. *The Meaning of Difference: American Constructions of Race, Sex and Gender, Social Class, and Sexual Orientation.* New York: McGraw-Hill Companies, Inc.

Rumbaut, Ruben. 1994. "The Crucible Within: Ethnic Identity, Self-Esteem, and Segmented Assimilation among Children of Immigrants." *International Migration Review* 28: 748–794.

———. 1995a. "Origins and Destinies: Immigration to the United States since World War II." *Sociological Forum* 9: 583–612.

———. 1995b. "The New Californians: Comparative Research Findings on the Educational Progress of Immigrant Children." In *California's Immigrant Children,* edited by Ruben Rumbaut and Wayne Cornelius. San Diego: Center for U.S.-Mexican Studies, University of California at San Diego.

Rumbaut, Ruben, and Wayne Cornelius. 1995. *California's Immigrant Children: Theory, Research, and Implications for Educational Policy.* San Diego: Center for U.S.-Mexican Studies, University of California at San Diego.

Schiller, Nina Glick, Linda Basch, and Christina Szanton-Blanc (eds.). 1992. *Toward a Transnational Perspective on Migration: Race, Class, Ethnicity, and Nationalism Reconsidered.* New York: New York Academy of Science.

Schlesinger, Arthur M. 1992. *The Disuniting of America.* New York: Norton.

Shankar, Lavina Dhingra, and Rajimi Srikanth (eds.). 1997. *A Part, Yet Apart: South Asians in Asian America.* Philadelphia: Temple University Press.

———. 1997. "Closing the Gap: South Asians Challenge Asian American Studies." In *A Part, Yet Apart,* edited by Lavina Dhingra Shankar and Rajimi Srikanth. Philadelphia: Temple University Press.

Sheth, Manju. 1995. "Asian Indian Americans." In *Asian Americans: Contemporary Trends and Issues,* edited by Pyong Gap Min. Newbury Park, Calif.: Sage Publications.

Shinagawa, Larry Hajime, and Gin Yong Pang. 1996. "Asian American Panethnicity and Intermarriage." *Amerasia Journal* 22 (2): 127–152.

Smith, Graham (ed.). 1995. *Federalism: The Multiethnic Challenge.* London: Longman.

Spiro, M. E. 1960. "The Acculturation without Assimilation." *American Journal of Sociology* 66: 275–288.

Steele, Shelby. 1990. *The Content of Our Character.* New York: St. Martin's Press.

Stevens, Gillian. 1985. "Nativity, Intermarriage and Mother Tongue Shift." *American Sociological Review* 50: 74–83.

Suarez-Orozco, Carol, and Marcelo M. Suarez-Orozco. 1995. *Transformations: Migration, Family Life, and Achievement Motivation among Latino Adolescents.* Stanford, Calif.: Stanford University Press.

Sung, Betty Lee. 1988. *The Adjustment Experience of Chinese Immigrant Children in New York City.* Staten Island, N.Y.: Center for Migration Studies.

Sutton, Constance. 1987. "The Caribbeanization of New York City and the Emergence of a Transnational Socio-cultural System." In *Caribbean Life in New York City,* edited by Constance Sutton and Elsa Chaney. Staten Island, N.Y.: Center for Migration Studies.

Takagi, Dana. 1994. "Post-Civil Rights Politics and Asian American Identity: Admissions and Higher Education." In *Race,* edited by Stephen Gregory and Roger Sanjek. New Brunswick, N.J.: Rutgers University Press.

Taylor, Ronald. 1979. "Black Ethnicity and the Persistence of Ethnogenesis." *American Journal of Sociology* 84: 1401–1423.

Tomasi, S. M., and M. H. Engel. 1970. *The Italian Experience in the United States.* Staten Island, N.Y.: Center for Migration Studies.

Tuan, Mia. 1995. "Korean and Russian Students in a Los Angeles High School: Exploring the Alternative Strategies of Two High-Achieving Groups." In *California's Immigrant Children,* edited by Ruben Rumbaut and Wayne Cornelius. San Diego: Center for U.S.-Mexican Studies, University of California at San Diego.

U.S. Bureau of the Census. 1993. *1990 Census of Population, Asian and Pacific Islanders.* Washington, D.C.: U.S. Government Printing Office.

U.S. Commission on Civil Rights. 1992. *Civil Rights Issues Facing Asian Americans in the 1990s.* Washington, D.C.: U.S. Government Printing Office.

Waldinger, Roger, and Mehdi Bozorgmehr (eds.). 1997. *Ethnic Los Angeles.* New York: Russell Sage Foundation.

Warner, W. Lloyd, and Leo Srole. 1945. *The Social Systems of American Ethnic Groups.* New Haven, Conn.: Yale University Press.

Waters, Mary. 1990. *Ethnic Options: Choosing Identities in America.* Berkeley: University of California Press.

———. 1994. "Ethnic and Racial Identities of Second-Generation Black Immigrants in New York." *International Migration Review* 28: 795–820.

Wei, William. 1993. *The Asian American Movement.* Philadelphia: Temple University Press.

Wirth, Lewis. 1928. *The Ghetto.* Chicago: University of Chicago Press.

Woldemikael, T. M. 1989. *Becoming Black American: Haitians and American Institutions in Evanston, Illinois.* New York: AMS Press.

Wolfe, Diane. 1997. "Family Secrets: Transnational Struggles among Children of Filipino Immigrants." *Sociological Perspectives* 40: 457–482.

Yancy, William, Eugene Ericksen, and Richard Juliani. 1976. "Emergent Ethnicity: A Review and Reformulation." *American Sociological Review* 76: 391–403.

Yang, Pengang. 1998. "Tenacious Unity in a Contentious Community: Cultural and Religious Dynamics in a Chinese Christian Church." In *Gatherings in Diaspora: Religious Communities and the New Immigration,* edited by Stephen Warner and Judith Wittner. Philadelphia: Temple University Press.

Yinger, Milton. 1994. *Ethnicity: Source of Strength? Source of Conflict?* Albany: SUNY Press.

Yu, Elena. 1980. "Filipino Migration and Community Organizations in the United States." *California Sociologist* 3: 76–102.

Yuan, D. Y. 1963. "Voluntary Segregation: A Study of New Chinatown." *Phylon* 24: 255–265.

Zenner, Walter. 1991. *Minorities in the Middle: A Cross-Cultural Analysis.* Albany: SUNY Press.

Zhou, Min. 1997. "Segmented Assimilation: Issues, Controversies, and Recent Research on the New Second Generation." *International Migration Review* 31: 975–1008.

Zhou, Min, and Carl Bangston III. 1998. *Growing Up American: How Vietnamese Children Adapt to Life in the United States.* New York: Russell Sage Foundation.

About the Editors

PYONG GAP MIN, professor of sociology, has taught at Queens College of the City University of New York since 1987, and has been a faculty member of the Sociology Program at the Graduate School of CUNY since 1993. Min is the author of *Changes and Conflicts: Korean Immigrant Families in New York* (Allyn and Bacon, 1998), *Caught in the Middle: Korean Merchants in America's Multiethnic Cities* (University of California Press, 1996), and *Ethnic Business Enterprise: Korean Small Business in Atlanta* (Center for Migration Studies, 1988). *Caught in the Middle* was selected as the 1997 winner of the National Book Award in Social Science by the Association for Asian American Studies and was a cowinner of the 1998 Book Award by the Asian and Asian American section of the American Sociological Association. Min edited *Asian Americans: Contemporary Trends and Issues* (Sage, 1995), to which he also contributed five chapters. In addition, he has published extensively in social science journals and in anthologies on Korean and Asian Americans. He is currently at work on two book projects, one an ethnographic study of Korean victims of Japanese military sexual slavery during the Asian and Pacific War ("comfort women"), and the other a comparative study of Asian ethnic groups in New York (forthcoming from Columbia University Press).

Min was born and raised in a village in Choongchung Namdo, located in the western region of South Korea. He received a bachelor's degree in history from Seoul National University. After working as a high school English teacher and as a reporter for *Korea Herald*, an English daily, in 1972 he came to the United States to study at Georgia State University. While there, he earned a master's degree in history and two Ph.D.s, one in educational philosophy and the other in sociology.

ROSE KIM, a freelance writer in New York City, writes for various publications throughout the country. She worked for six years as a reporter for *Newsday* covering beats such as education, health care, and the court system. In 1992, she was part of the *Los Angeles Times* team awarded a Pulitzer Prize for coverage of the riots following the Rodney King verdict. She is currently enrolled in the sociology program at the Graduate Center of the City University of New York, where she is pursuing studies on the experiences of Korean and Asian Americans.

Kim was born and raised in Los Angeles, California. She is the youngest of four children, the only one born outside of South Korea. She attended the University of Chicago, graduating with bachelor's degree in art and design in 1990.

About the Contributors

MONICA JAHAN BOSE is a lawyer living in New York City. A native of Bangladesh, she moved to the U.S. at age ten, and has also lived in Pakistan, India, and Japan. She graduated from Columbia Law School in 1990 and is an associate at Arnold & Porter, where she practices environmental law and general litigation. She is also a painter and an advocate for the rights of immigrant women.

RUTH CHUNG is an assistant professor of counseling psychology at the University of Southern California. She grew up in southern California after emigrating from Korea in 1970. She received her bachelor's degree in psychology from Pacific Union College and a Ph.D. in counseling pyschology from the University of California at Santa Barbara. Her areas of research and practice are Asian American families, cultural identity and acculturation, and career development of ethnic minorities.

PHUONG DO is Vietnamese. She was born in Laos and lived there until she was eleven. At the end of the Vietnam War, her family resettled in Denver, Colorado. She received her B.A. in French from the University of Northern Colorado in 1988 and her M.S.W. from Yeshiva University in 1996. She currently works at the New York Association for New Americans, providing technical assistance and leadership training to community-based immigrant organizations. Over the past five years, she has worked as a service provider, program planner, and researcher in the field of refugee and immigrant services.

JOEL DE LA FUENTE is a professional actor. Born in upstate New York and raised in Evanston, Illinois, he is a second-generation Filipino American. He received his B.A. in theater arts from Brown University and his M.F.A. from the Graduate Acting Program at New York University's Tisch School for the Arts in 1994. His professional acting credits include *All's Well that Ends Well* and *The Two Gentlemen of Verona* in the New York Shakespeare Festival. He was also a cast member of the Fox Television series "Space: Above & Beyond."

HOANG DIEM HAU is the controller for a small, nonprofit private college in California. Born and raised in Saigon, South Vietnam, she came to the United States after Saigon fell into the hands of the Communists in 1975. She received her B.A. in English from the University of Saigon, a second B.A. in accounting from California State University at Fresno, and her M.B.A. in business administration from CSU Los Angeles in 1993. She has worked in higher education institutions for the last twenty-one years.

JEAN HOTTA is a counselor for foreign students at the University of California at Los Angeles. She was born and raised in the Philippines. At age twelve, she immigrated to the U.S. She received her bachelor's degree in linguistics from UCLA in 1988. Shortly after graduation, she married a Japanese immigrant.

ALEX JEONG is a senior assistant district attorney in New York City. He came to the U.S. from South Korea when he was nine. He received his B.A. from Colgate University in 1989 and his J.D. from George Washington University Law School in 1993. Upon graduation, he passed the New York State Bar and has since worked for the Kings County District Attorney. He specializes in trying felony cases, ranging in severity from auto thefts to murder.

MARGARET YAH-MIN KAN was born in China, raised in Hong Kong, and educated in the United States. She received her B.A. in dietetics from San Jose State University, in California. After graduation, she attended Indiana University at Indianapolis. She is a registered dietitian, in charge of the nutrition and food service department of a 380-bed hospital in Los Angeles, California.

ERIBERTO P. "FUJI" LOZADA JR. is finishing his Ph.D. in social anthropology at Harvard University. He was born in New York City to two physicians who emigrated from the Philippines. He received his bachelor's degree in chemistry and physics from Harvard in 1986. After graduating from college, he served as an infantry officer in the U.S. Marine Corps. He entered graduate school in 1990. His dissertation research examines the idea of locality in today's global world and is based on fieldwork conducted in a Chinese Catholic village in northern Guangdong.

LAKSHMI MALROUTU is an assistant professor in the Department of Family Nutrition and Exercise Sciences at Queens College in New York City. She was born and raised in Calcutta, India, and immigrated to the U.S. in 1986, after living for two years in Jamaica. She received a Ph.D. in consumer economics from Oregon State University in 1992. She is currently researching housing and financial issues of elderly Asian Indians in the U.S.

KAVITHA MEDIRATTA lives in New York City and currently codirects the Community Involvement Program at New York University's Institute for Education and Social Policy. The Institute assists New York City parent and community organizations that are working to improve the public schools. Her narrative is dedicated to the memory of Shailu Iyengar, a friend and comrade in the journey for self-definition.

SAYURI MORI-QUAYLE is a producer/writer for CNBC, a cable TV station based in New Jersey. She was born in New York City and raised in New Jersey. After graduating from high school, she moved to Tokyo. She received her bachelor's degree in linguistics from International Christian University in 1991. Upon graduation, she worked for Morgan Stanley Tokyo and N.H.K. (Japan Broadcasting Company). She moved back to the U.S. in 1993.

SHAY SHETH practices internal medicine in the Delaware Valley in southern New Jersey. He received his B.A. from Rutgers College in 1983 and an M.D. from the Robert Wood Johnson Medical School in 1987. He completed a three-year residency at Cooper Hospital in southern New Jersey. Before settling into his current practice, he worked in several medically underserved areas, including inner cities, Appalachia, and several Native American reservations.

DAVID W. WANG is currently enrolled at the Georgetown University School of Law. Before entering law school, he worked as a community liaison at the office of Manhattan Borough President Ruth W. Messinger. He also founded violence prevention programs in Boston and New York City. A native New Yorker, he graduated with a B.A. in government from Harvard University and served as a Stride-Rite Public Service Fellow at Columbia University's Community Impact.